the SECURE ONLINE BUSINESS handbook

e-commerce, IT functionality & business continuity

Third edition

consultant editor: jonathan reuvid

IoD
RECOMMENDED BY
INSTITUTE OF DIRECTORS

VeriSign®

Simmons & Simmons

KOGAN PAGE

London and Sterling, VA

This book has been endorsed by the Institute of Directors.

The endorsement is given to selected Kogan Page books which the IoD recognizes as being of specific interest to its members and providing them with up-to-date, informative and practical resources for creating business success. Kogan Page books endorsed by the IoD represent the most authoritative guidance available on a wide range of subjects including management, finance, marketing, training and HR.

The views expressed in this book are those of the authors and are not necessarily the same as those of the Institute of Directors.

Publisher's note
Every possible effort has been made to ensure that the information contained in this book is accurate at the time of going to press, and the publishers and authors cannot accept responsibility for any errors or omissions, however caused. No responsibility for loss or damage occasioned to any person acting, or refraining from action, as a result of the material in this publication can be accepted by the editor, the publisher or any of the authors.

First published in Great Britain and the United States in 2003 by Kogan Page Limited
Second edition 2004
Third edition 2005

Apart from any fair dealing for the purposes of research or private study, or criticism or review, as permitted under the Copyright, Designs and Patents Act 1988, this publication may only be reproduced, stored or transmitted, in any form or by any means, with the prior permission in writing of the publishers, or in the case of reprographic reproduction in accordance with the terms and licences issued by the CLA. Enquiries concerning reproduction outside these terms should be sent to the publishers at the undermentioned addresses:

120 Pentonville Road
London N1 9JN
United Kingdom
www.kogan-page.co.uk

22883 Quicksilver Drive
Sterling VA 20166-2012
USA

© Kogan Page and individual contributors, 2003, 2004, 2005

ISBN 0 7494 4425 8

British Library Cataloguing-in-Publication Data

A CIP record for this book is available from the British Library.

Library of Congress Cataloging-in-Publication Data

Reuvid, Jonathan.
  The secure online business handbook : e-commerce, IT functionality and business continuity / Jonathan Reuvid.
   p. cm.
  ISBN 0-7494-4425-8
  1. Computer security–Handbooks, manuals, etc. 2. Business–Data processing–Handbooks, manuals, etc. I. Title.
  QA76 9.A25S3755 2005
  005.8–dc22
                                    2005011399

Typeset by Saxon Graphics Ltd, Derby
Printed and bound in Great Britain by Cambridge University Press

excellence
is our standard

Don't risk it....
Protect your information!

BS 7799 is the widely respected management system for information security. Its adoption can carry many benefits ranging from quality improvement and competitive advantage to employee security. By selecting BSI Management Systems for BS 7799 assessment, certification and training, organisations benefit from the international reputation and recognition of a world leader in quality management system certification.

- ASSESSMENT
- COMPREHENSIVE TRAINING
- CERTIFICATION
- COMMUNICATION DAYS
- GUIDANCE LITERATURE
- ELECTRONIC TOOLS

Visit our website for more information.

www.bsi-emea.com/informationsecurity

shape the future

Tel: +44 (0)845 080 9000 Fax: +44 (0)845 080 9000 Email: informationsecurity.uk@bsi-global.com

BSI Management Systems

Start protecting your DVD revenues today

Macrovision ActiveReach
RipGuard DVD

Stop PC ripping and copying of DVDs from reducing rental & retail sales

Macrovision ActiveReach
ACP

Prevent analogue copying of DVDs and Pay-Per-View content on DVD recorders, PVRs and Media Centre PCs

Macrovision ActiveReach
Hawkeye

Use our proven Peer-to-Peer anti-piracy service to protect your content from unauthorised online distribution

Implement copy control technologies to limit illegal copying and distribution. Protect the **total** value of your content.

Tel: +44 (0) 870 871 1111
Fax: +44 (0) 870 871 1161
Email: salesinfo-europe@macrovision.com

Macrovision UK Ltd.
Malvern House, 14/18 Bell Street
Maidenhead, Berkshire, SL6 1BR

www.macrovision.com

macrovision

Contents

Foreword		xi
Miles Templeman, Director General, Institute of Directors		
Contributors' notes		xiv

Part 1: Information at risk

1.1	The information security management system	3
	Alan Calder, IT Governance Ltd	
1.2	The business case for IT security	8
	Andrew Steggles, EMEA Nokia Enterprise Solutions	
1.3	Recent attack trends	12
	The Fraud Advisory Panel's Cybercrime Working Group	
1.4	The fine art of elephant husbandry – a practical guide to patch management	18
	Chris Knowles, Computacenter	
1.5	Gone phishing	23
	Frank Coggrave, Websense	
1.6	The marketing dimension	26
	Michael Harrison, Harrison Smith Associates	

Part 2: Points of exposure

2.1	Web security	33
	Suheil Shahryar, VeriSign UK	
2.2	Broadband	48
	Paul Collins, NTL Business	
2.3	Don't indulge in unprotected wireless	54
	Ian Kilpatrick, Wick Hill Group	
2.4	No phishing: protecting employees from e-mail fraud	57
	Ed Rowley, CipherTrust Europe Ltd	
2.5	Network vulnerabilities	63
	Peter Crowcombe, NetScreen Technologies Inc	
2.6	Wireless applications	67
	Andrew Steggles, EMEA Nokia Enterprise Solutions	

Telindus SOLUTIONS > CONVERGED NETWORKS

Digital video surveillance... no strings attached

With today's move towards digital video surveillance, the convergence of video, voice and integrated applications has placed increasing demands on your network.

With over 35 years of experience, Telindus' 'No Strings' approach creates customised networked ICT solutions tailored to meet your staff productivity, capital efficiency and business continuity needs.

At Telindus we provide independent networking consultancy, integration and management services; bringing important cost savings, improving productivity, and enabling you to focus on your core business.

To find out more, call Telindus on +44 (0)1256 709200 or email sales@telindus.co.uk and let us talk about how we can use 'No Strings' to provide network integration in unison with your business strategy and goals.

TeLiNDUS®
the integrator

www.telindus.co.uk

2.7	Protecting online privacy *Alexander Brown, Simmons & Simmons*	71
2.8	Online payments: key areas of exposure *Tony Parnell, WorldPay Ltd*	78
2.9	The spy that came in from the cold *Frank Coggrave, Websense*	82

Part 3: Software protection

3.1	Firewalls *Mark Rogers, More Solutions*	87
3.2	Viruses *Mark Rogers, More Solutions*	91
3.3	Authentication and encryption *Randle Cowcher, TrustAssured*	95
3.4	Digital signatures *Johan Sys, GlobalSign*	100
3.5	Biometrics *Clive Reedman and Bill Perry, Emerging Technology Services*	105
3.6	From 'Made in Hollywood' to 'Appearing in your local car boot sale' – piracy and the business of digital entertainment *Simon Mehlman, Macrovision*	110
3.7	Keeping on the right side of the law *Frank Coggrave, Websense*	118

Part 4: Operational management

4.1	Flow clearing: financial supply chain management *Dr Markus Braun, Wire Card*	123
4.2	Developing a culture of security in the workplace *Peter Brudenall, Simmons & Simmons*	127
4.3	Security as standard *British Standards Institution*	133
4.4	Converged security – why manage three when one will do? *Mark Bouldin, Telindus*	137
4.5	Countering cybercrime: risk management *The Fraud Advisory Panel's Cybercrime Working Group*	142
4.6	Countering cybercrime *Peter Brudenall, Simmons & Simmons*	152
4.7	Centralized security management *Zuhamy Colton, Indicii Salus*	157
4.8	Electronic contracting *Peter Brudenall, Simmons & Simmons*	163
4.9	Information security training *Alan Calder, IT Governance Ltd*	169
4.10	Outsourced solutions *Martin Saunders, Easynet*	173

4.11	Securing the mobile workforce *Andy Baines, Fujitsu Services*	178

Part 5: Contingency planning

5.1	Business continuity and crisis management *Dr David Smith*	185
5.2	Dealing with the risks of peer-to-peer *Frank Coggrave, Websense*	196
5.3	Data recovery *Adrian Palmer, Ontrack Data Recovery*	199
5.4	Crisis or disaster management *Simon Langdon, Insight Consulting, part of Siemens Communications*	204
5.5	Forensics *Robert Brown, DataSec*	210
5.6	Forensic investigation *Clifford May, Integralis Ltd*	214
	Contributors' contact list	*219*
	Index	*223*
	Index of advertisers	*226*

Helping you keep control of your data

Secure Mobile Computing with SafeGuard®

Working away from the office is a fact of life for most of us today. As senior management working in a competitive and regulated world you will be dealing with issues and decisions that must remain confidential to your business. So when you're mobile you need to be certain that your confidential and sensitive information stays that way. Let us help you do that. SafeGuard® sets the standard for protection of critical data on professional mobile devices. Secure and protect all your mobile devices- laptops, PDAs, smartphones through encryption and strong authentication against unauthorised access.

For more information on how we can help you protect your mobile data visit our website at **www.utimaco.com** or email us on pauline.whitehouse@utimaco.co.uk. Or call us on +44 1784 224225

utimaco®
safeware

Payment is Communication.

PAYMENT & PROCESSING SERVICES
RISKMANAGEMENT & FRAUD PROTECTION
FINANCIAL SERVICES
MERCHANT ACCOUNT SERVICES
24/7 HELPDESK & CUSTOMER SUPPORT
RESPONSE MANAGEMENT

www.wirecard.com

WIRE CARD
GLOBAL PAYMENT & COMMUNICATION

Foreword

For many organizations their dependence on information systems, both within the company and networked up and down their supply chain, is now business critical. Any sustained loss of availability of these systems would threaten the very existence of the business.

Security is a holistic issue. Vulnerabilities in physical, personnel and electronic security all need to be addressed with equal commitment. Too many businesses still focus on physical security without sustaining even basic precautions in personnel and electronic security. For example, a recent survey of IoD members highlighted that only 90 per cent of respondents with broadband access to the internet used firewalls to protect their systems and information. Similarly only 75 per cent kept those firewalls up to date.

Simple, well designed security precautions need not place onerous burdens on the staff or operation of a business – indeed, if they do they will tend to prove useless because they will be circumvented and disregarded. Winning the hearts and minds of employees at all levels is an essential first step, complementing the technology solutions that are deployed.

This book outlines the basic steps that all businesses, of whatever size, should be taking, both to protect the operation of their information systems and to ensure that they remain compliant with their increasing legal responsibilities.

When we go home from an office or factory at night we would not dream of leaving the doors and windows open and the safe unlocked. Yet all too often, in terms of online security, organizations are doing exactly that. This book should leave no business in any doubt about the need for action on this key business issue of our times – and gives clear, practical advice on the steps they need to implement.

Miles Templeman
Director General
Institute of Directors

Think your business is secure?

Don't get caught out.

Having a secure IT system is critical to the success of any business. Our IT group has the knowledge and expertise necessary to provide you with straightforward but innovative legal advice. We can give you the assurance you need to feel confident that your IT security is watertight.

Simmons & Simmons

For further information, please contact:

David Barrett
T +44 (0)20 7825 4032
E david.barrett@simmons-simmons.com

Peter Brudenall
T +44 (0)20 7825 4346
E peter.brudenall@simmons-simmons.com

www.simmons-simmons.com
www.elexica.com

Contributors' notes

Andy Baines is a Principal Consultant in the Information Security Practice of Fujitsu Services specializing in the development of security strategies and architectures. He is a regular consultant to government departments and corporate customers.

Mark Bouldin has over 15 years' experience in the IT and electronics fields, much of which was gained at Thorn Security where he worked across a range of CCTV, intruder, access control and fire system products. Mark currently works at Telindus where he is responsible for networked digital surveillance solutions.

Dr Markus Braun brings extensive knowledge of information technology, financial risk management and payment solutions to his position as Chief Executive Officer, since he joined Wire Card in 2001. Born in Vienna in 1969, he studied commercial information technologies at the Technical University of Vienna and holds a degree in social and economy sciences. Prior to 2001, Dr Braun practised in IT research at the University of Vienna, as Senior Consultant at Contrast Management Consulting, Vienna and IT Manager for eStrategy at KPMG Munich.

British Standards Institution is a group of complementary businesses, all working to the same vision of support for business improvement and trade worldwide. BSI believes in the universal adoption of best management practices, reduction of risk throughout the trading process and the harmonization and acceptance of standards by consent as a means of achieving economic prosperity.

Alexander Brown is a Senior Associate at Simmons & Simmons.

Robert Brown is Technical Director and Forensic Analyst at DataSec.

Peter Brudenall is Technology and Outsourcing Partner at Simmons & Simmons.

The Business Continuity Institute (BCI) promotes the highest standards of professional competence and commercial ethics in the provision, maintenance and services for business continuity management (BCM). It provides an internationally recognized certification

CONTENT INSECURITY.

- Email Security
- HTTP/FTP Filtering
- Application Content Filtering
- Web Filtering
- Anti-spam
- Gateway Security

CONTENT SECURITY.

eSafe

- Multi-layered Anti-spam
- Proactive Anti-virus
- Peer-to-peer Blocking
- High-capacity HTTP/FTP Filtering
- Instant Messaging Filtering
- URL Filtering
- Spyware/Adware Blocking

Better eSafe than sorry.

A la carte content security doesn't give you a solution. It gives you a constantly shifting set of new problems. eSafe delivers one integrated, easily managed security solution that is truly content-wide. So you're ready when the next malicious code-filesharing-IM-polymorphic spam worm hits.

Get your FREE 30-day trial, white papers, success stories and more at eSafe.com/StayDry.

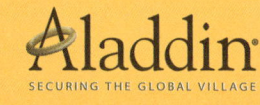

Aladdin
SECURING THE GLOBAL VILLAGE

For more information about eSafe contact 01753 622266 or www.Aladdin.com/contact

Aladdin Western Europe, Fairacres House, 2-3 Fairacres Industrial Estate, Dedworth Road, Windsor, SL4 4LE

2005 Aladdin Knowledge Systems, Ltd. Aladdin, Aladdin Knowledge Systems, Ltd., and eSafe are registered trademarks of Aladdin Knowledge Systems, Ltd.

scheme for BCM managers and practitioners. There are now over 1,850 members of the Institute working in over 45 countries across the world.

Alan Calder is founder and Chief Executive of IT Governance Ltd. He has 25 years of general manager, director and chief executive experience in medium and large organizations. He led one of the first organizations to achieve BS7799, is a member of the DNV certification committee and was involved in developing the BCS ISEB certificate for security professionals. He writes, lectures and consults on information security. He is co-author of *IT Governance: a Manager's Guide to Information Security and BS7799/ISO17799* (published by Kogan Page).

CipherTrust Europe Ltd is a leading provider of internet intrusion prevention and network security solutions for companies and their employees.

Frank Coggrave is UK Regional Director of Websense.

Paul Collins is Head of Customer Marketing at NTL Business.

Zuhamy Colton is a former Marketing Manager at Indicii Salus.

Computacenter is Europe's leading independent provider of IT infrastructure services. To help its customers maximize the value of IT to their businesses, Computacenter offers services at every stage of infrastructure investment. Corporate and government clients are served by a network of branch offices across the UK, Germany, France, Austria, Belgium and Luxembourg and, through its international partners, at locations throughout the world.

Randle Cowcher is Senior Business Development Manager at RBS TrustAssured, responsible for the assessment and implementation of leading-edge enterprise security solutions.

Peter Crowcombe is a Practice Leader at NetScreen Technologies, specializing in the analysis of network vulnerabilities and their protection.

DataSec are one of the UK's leading providers of computer forensic services and as such are registered with the Law Society as expert witnesses. The DataSec range of services includes awareness training for IT and HR managers and consultancy services for organizations considering setting up an incident response team or who already have one in place. DataSec also provides independent investigations and analysis for internal incidents, criminal cases and civil litigation and expert witness testimony.

Easynet is a leading pan-European business broadband provider and business ISP with operations in eight European countries. Established in 1994, Easynet owns and operates one of Europe's most advanced internet network and data centre infrastructures. In the UK, Easynet has a national broadband spanning 4,450 km. Easynet's unrivalled product portfolio includes a full suite of scalable broadband access and hosting solutions. In addition, Easynet offers a range of bespoke solutions, created exclusively for the education market, delivering internet access in a safe, appropriate and controlled environment. All services are complemented by quality non-stop technical support.

Unless you're the lead dog, the scenery never changes.

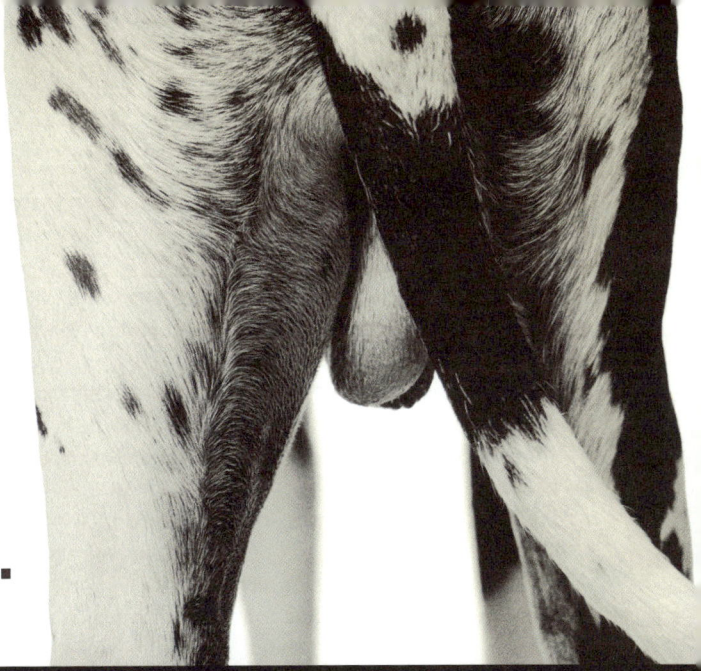

You can pick the leader in messaging security or just another follower. The choice is yours.

CipherTrust protects more of the largest enterprise messaging networks in the world. Why? Because we control spam and fraud, block viruses and zero day threats, enforce policy, and protect content, all on a platform built from the ground up to protect e-mail. Real results, real value, one solution.

Find out how CipherTrust can help your business secure its email at: www.ciphertrust.com

- No. 1 market share as rated by IDC
- Only appliance in Gartner's Leader Quadrant for enterprise spam filtering
- Highest ranked e-mail hygiene product by META Group
- SC Magazine's Best E-Mail Security Solution, GlobalAward, February 2005
- SC Magazine's Reader's Trust award for Best E-mail Security Solution, 2004
- SC Magazine "Best Buy" for both e-mail security and anti-spam
- Protects the e-mail of 30% of the Fortune 100
- 9 consecutive quarters of profitability
- History of technical innovation
    —1st secure e-mail gateway
    —1st anti-spam cocktail
    —1st e-mail anomaly detection to detect virus outbreaks
    —1st multi-vendor privacy architecture
    —1st reputation-based connection blocking

CipherTrust

The Leader in Messaging Security   +44 (0)870 990 5516

SECURE E-MAIL GATEWAY | SPAM & FRAUD PROTECTION | VIRUS & WORM PROTECTION | POLICY & CONTENT COMPLIANCE | E-MAIL PRIVACY | SECURE WEB MAIL | PROFESSIONAL SERVICES

EMEA Nokia Enterprise Solutions focuses on mobile business devices and providing IP network perimeter security (firewalls and VPN), secure content management (anti-virus scanning and SPAM filtering), and mobile connectivity (remote access VPN and content) solutions designed to help companies to mobilize their workforces and increase productivity while ensuring the security and reliability of their networks.

Emerging Technology Services is an independent technology agnostics company. Major recent initiatives include technical lead for the UK Passport Services ePassport Project, UK Home Office Biometric Pilot and many smaller but equally important projects.

The **Fraud Advisory Panel** is a registered charity comprising volunteers drawn from the public and private sector. The Panel's role is to raise awareness of the immense social and economic damage that is caused by fraud and develop effective remedies. Members of the Fraud Advisory Panel include representatives from the law and accountancy professions, industry associations, financial institutions, government agencies, law enforcement, regulatory authorities and academia.

Fujitsu Services is one of the leading IT services companies in Europe. Information security is one of the areas in which Fujitsu specializes with a full range of consultancy services and solutions, both stand-alone and managed. Typical consultancy services cover accreditation, architecture, policy development and reviews whilst the Fujitsu service group focuses on firewalls, anti-virus and intrusion detection services.

GlobalSign is Europe's leading certificate service provider offering digital certificates and co-sourced PKI solutions. GlobalSign's digital certificates allow individuals and businesses to secure e-mail communication, to conduct fully authenticated and confidential online business and to set up trusted software distribution. GlobalSign certificates are globally accepted and are not limited by any application, geographic area or business sector. GlobalSign is one of the few certification authorities in the world that has attained the WebTrust accreditation level.

Michael Harrison is Chairman of Harrison Smith Associates Ltd and Chairman, UK, of the Protecting Critical Information Infrastructures Initiative.

Indicii Salus is a London-based security services specialist offering a comprehensive suite of secure services and solutions based on Xenophon, a unique server-centric security solution. Xenophon solutions vary from the protection of e-mail to securing a variety of web content; its services are delivered via a single user identity, across a wide range of access devices, independent of location.

Insight Consulting currently employs over 50 consultants/trainers, and is one of the UK's largest specialist teams in information and communications security, risk management and business continuity management. In addition to direct support to clients, Insight provides both public and tailored training courses in risk analysis, business continuity management and crisis management.

The IT partner with something to prove – your next IT solution.

Computacenter's Solutions Centre is the largest multi-vendor proof of concept and test facility in Europe. It allows you to model your critical IT systems at no risk to your live operation, enabling you to benefit from our best practice approach to Proof of Concept, Load Testing and Datacentre Staging. De-risk your technology investment. Find out more at www.computacenter.com/solutionscentre

TECHNOLOGY SOURCING   INFRASTRUCTURE INTEGRATION   MANAGED SERVICES

computacenter
Transforming IT service delivery

telephone: 0800 617000   email: enquiries@computacenter.com

Integralis Ltd the corporate solutions division of Articon-Integralis, provides information security solutions to all industry sectors throughout the world, allowing organizations to grow and achieve their business goals securely. These solutions combine services and system integration, the deployment of 'best-of-breed' security products and managed security services, and employ some of the leading technologists and most skilled engineers in the industry. Integralis is recognized as a leading and trusted provider of Information Security Solutions in the European IT and e-commerce security market.

IT Governance Ltd is a niche consultancy business, specializing in IT governance and information security. The different needs of small, medium and large businesses are met with a range of services that all reflect the company's commitment to practical, cost-effective, long term solutions. The company can deploy vendor-neutral expertise in subjects such as compliance (Data Protection, Privacy, Sarbanes-Oxley, Turnbull, etc), standards (BS7799/ISO17799, TickIT, etc), technology (eg anti-malware, defence-in-depth), policy (processes and procedures) and training.

Ian Kilpatrick is chairman of Wick Hill Group plc, specialists in secure infrastructure solutions for e-business. Ian has been involved with the group for over 28 years and is the moving force behind its dynamic growth. He writes, consults and lectures on information security. Wick Hill is an international organization supplying most of the Times Top 1000 companies through a network of accredited resellers.

Chris Knowles is Practice Leader, Security, at Computacenter.

Simon Langdon is a recognized authority on crisis management and is a Principal Consultant at Insight Consulting, part of Siemens Communications – a division of Siemens plc, where he heads up the crisis management service line. Simon has been an operational crisis manager and has responded to acts of terrorism, chemical fires and train crashes. He has experience of crisis management in many business sectors including finance, retail, pharmaceutical, aviation, rail, oil and gas, and the media and has worked internationally in Europe and the Middle East. Simon chairs the International Disaster and Emergency Response group (IDER).

Macrovision UK develops and markets content and software value management solutions for the video, music and software industries. Macrovision's technologies are embedded in over 9.3 billion DVD, VHS and CD units representing over $130 billion of protected entertainment content. In the software market Macrovision licenses software developers the FLEXnet™ universal licensing platform and the InstallShield® suite of software installation, repackaging and update solutions, which are deployed on more than 500 million desktops worldwide. Over 50,000 software publishers and hundreds of Fortune 1000 companies use Macrovision's technologies to maximize the value of their software. Macrovision's headquarters are in Santa Clara, California and it has offices worldwide. More information about Macrovision can be found at www.macrovision.com.

Clifford May has been a Principal Consultant with Integralis since 2001. He is the primary consultant for information security, including policy development, risk analysis, security

SUBSCRIBE TO A QUICK RESPONSE

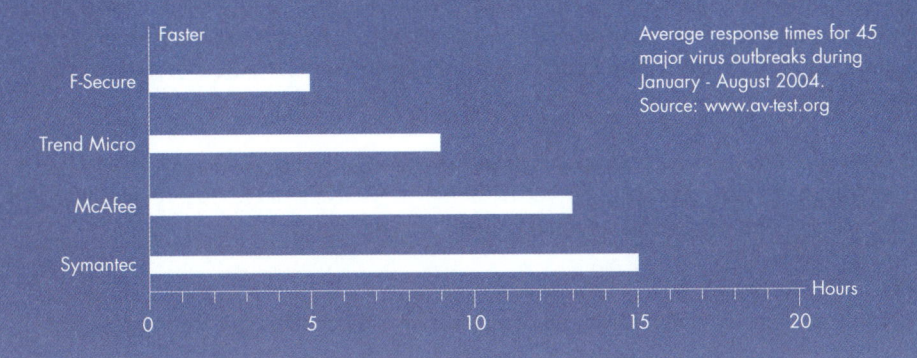

Average response times for 45 major virus outbreaks during January - August 2004.
Source: www.av-test.org

Faster

- F-Secure: ~5
- Trend Micro: ~9
- McAfee: ~13
- Symantec: ~15

Hours (0, 5, 10, 15, 20)

F-SECURE® HAS PROVEN TO BE FASTER THAN THE MAJOR COMPETITION

With F-Secure software installed on your IT network, you've got the best guarantee that unwanted intruders won't be able to get through your firewalls or virus scanners. But with seven to ten new viruses appearing in the wild every day and the ever-increasing inventiveness of virus criminals, it is not possible to predict how tomorrow's threats will look. That's why our Anti-Virus Research Lab has perfected the art of quick detection and fast response. When our specialists discover a potential risk, they will create a patch that quickly, frequently and automatically updates your system to keep you protected 24 hours a day, 7 days a week.

At F-Secure we consistently respond to threats hours earlier than our major competitors, significantly reducing the risk of infection – an essential service, as downtime equals loss of revenue. We intend to keep this pace in the future and will continue to offer fast response times, because our service comes with a subscription to a quick response.

Learn more about F-Secure; Tel: 0845 890 3300
or visit www.f-secure.co.uk/besure/

F-SECURE®
BE SURE.

audit, and BS7799 development, and heads the company computer forensic service providing confidential investigation services, incident management and forensic training.

Simon Mehlman is the European Marketing Director of Macrovision, the US-based content protection company. He has worked at Macrovision for the last four years and is responsible for their European strategic and tactical marketing, media communications and events management. Simon has worked in IT marketing management for over 15 years for technology-based and publicly listed companies.

More Solutions is a company dedicated to designing and deploying software solutions for industries that use the internet as a communications medium. With many applications involving stand-alone, unattended equipment installed miles from the nearest IT department, security and reliability are essential aspects of their business.

NetScreen Technologies Inc is a leading developer of network security and access solutions for enterprises and carriers worldwide. NetScreen's solutions offer customers multiple layers of network and application-level protection in purpose-built appliances and systems that optimize performance and reduce total operating costs. NetScreen's global HQ is located at Sunnyvale, USA.

NTL Business is a leading provider of communications solutions to businesses and public sector organizations throughout the UK. It is the business arm of NTL Incorporated, the UK's largest cable company and number one broadband internet provider.

Ontrack Data Recovery is a wholly-owned subsidiary of Kroll Inc and is a leading provider of data recovery and electronic evidence services. IT enables customers to protect, manage and recover their valuable data. Using its hundreds of proprietary tools and techniques, Ontrack Data Recovery is able to recover lost or corrupted data from all operating systems and types of storage devices through its do-it-yourself remote and in-lab capabilities. Ontrack's award-winning utility software tools help prevent critical data loss through problem-solving and file-management utilities.

Adrian Palmer is a Principal Consultant at Ontrack Data Recovery.

Tony Parnell is SME Marketing Director of WorldPay Ltd.

Bill Perry has been involved in biometrics for over 20 years and has fulfilled numerous roles in the industry ranging from developer, systems integrator, R&D for a major international bank, end-user and most recently independent consultant. He now heads up Emerging Technology Services Ltd.

Clive Reedman has been involved in biometrics for over 22 years, as a Fingerprint Expert with the Metropolitan Police, a project member of the UK's National Automated Fingerprint System and as Head of Biometric Capabilities with the Police Information Technology Organization. He is now a consultant with Emerging Technology Services Ltd and continues to work exclusively in the identification area, including the management of

PROACTIVE
INTELLIGENCE

24/7 MONITORING

TOTAL NETWORK
VISIBILITY

REAL-TIME
CORRELATION

VeriSign® Managed Security Services

Where visibility and intelligence overpower fear and doubt.

VeriSign® Managed Security Services lets you take a proactive stance on security. How? By continually monitoring and correlating data across firewall, IPS, IDS, VPN, and endpoint systems. By integrating and leveraging these unique insights with continuous vulnerability assessments and the advanced data that comes from handling billions of global email, DNS, and e-commerce interactions every day. And by processing over 250-million daily security events across some of the world's most sensitive networks. VeriSign also offers an award-winning team of hundreds of security experts, ready to monitor and protect your network 24/7. For more on how our Managed Security Services can provide you with a comprehensive view of your network's health and security, visit www.verisign.co.uk or call 0800 032 2101. **VeriSign. Where it all comes together.**™

VeriSign®

©2005 VeriSign, Inc. All rights reserved. VeriSign, the VeriSign logo, "Where it all comes together," and other trademarks, service marks, and designs are registered or unregistered trademarks of VeriSign and its subsidiaries in the United States and in foreign countries.

the UK Passport Services Facial Recognition Project. He has chaired the International Association for Biometrics for over two years.

Mark Rogers is a senior developer at More Solutions Ltd.

Ed Rowley is Senior Technical Consultant at CipherTrust Europe Ltd.

Martin Saunders is Head of Products at Easynet.

Suheil Shahryar has over 26 years' experience in IT applications, strategy and security management. He has worked for numerous FTSE100 clients across the world in financial, legal, oil and technology sectors. He is the Director of Global Security Consulting for VeriSign in the UK.

Simmons & Simmons was ranked joint second in the United Kingdom for outsourcing in a recent survey of in-house lawyers by *The Lawyer* magazine. In 2002, Global Counsel 3000 ranked Simmons & Simmons in the top 10 worldwide for performance in all major practice areas, based on the views of in-house counsel at over 5,000 companies across 74 jurisdictions. In 2003 the firm won a prestigious Queen's Award for Enterprise in the International Trade category, the only law firm to do so.

Dr David Smith is the former Editor of the BCI Good Practice Guidelines.

Andrew Steggles is a Marketing Director at EMEA Nokia Enterprise Solutions.

Johan Sys is General Manager of GlobalSign.

Telindus deliver customized voice, video and data networked ICT solutions across the UK, Europe and Asia Pacific. They provide independent consultancy, integration and management services enabling customers to concentrate on their core business. Telindus's core technologies focus on productivity and networked digital surveillance.

TrustAssured provides the services that enable companies to conduct business cost effectively and securely over the internet. With TrustAssured clients can take confidence in the knowledge that a major global bank is providing a service that enables e-commerce to operate within a secure and trusted environment. The key to this is the provision of unique digital identity credentials; these eliminate the fear of dealing with unknown counterparties over the web.

VeriSign UK operates intelligent infrastructure services that enable people and businesses to find, connect, secure and transact across today's complex, global networks. Every day, Verisign enables over 14 billion internet interactions, 3 billion telephony interactions and $100 million of e-commerce. It also provides services that help over 3,000 enterprises and 400,000 websites to operate securely, reliably and efficiently.

Websense is the world's leading provider of employee internet management (EIM) solutions. Websense Enterprise software enables organizations to manage how their employees

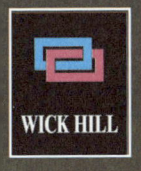

THE SCIENCE OF SECURITY

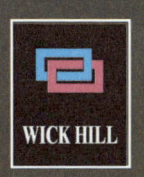

NEW — **NEW**

WICK HILL

Wireless Security Just Got Serious!
Check Point Safe@Office™ 400W
Wireless Security Appliance
802.11b/802.11g and SUPER G - up to 108mbps

Check Point SOFTWARE TECHNOLOGIES LTD.
We Secure the Internet.

Check Point SOFTWARE TECHNOLOGIES LTD.
We Secure the Internet.

Pricing starts from only £286 SRP!
- Up to double the speed and 3 x the range of competing solutions
- 4 port switch, DMZ and print server for sharing broadband connections, servers and printers
- Plug and play set-up to protect networks in seconds
- Embedded market leading NG Check Point Firewall 1 technology
- Automatic failover, traffic shaping, dial up backup, VLANS and Dynamic DNS
- Email anti-virus and web filtering services available
- Field upgradeable range

Get Serious about Wireless Security
Call Wick Hill TODAY - 0800 917 9911

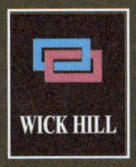

- E: info@wickhill.co.uk
- W: www.wickhill.com
- T: 0800 917 9911

WICK HILL

© 2005 Wick Hill Ltd. All rights reserved. Wick Hill and the Wick Hill logo are trademarks of Wick Hill Group Plc. Registered in the UK and other countries. Other brand and product names are trademarks of their respective owners use their computing resources, including internet access, desktop applications and network bandwidth. Implemented by more than 19,400 organizations worldwide and preferred by the FTSE100 and Fortune 500 companies, Websense Enterprise delivers a comprehensive software solution that analyses, manages and reports on employee internet access, network security and desktop application usage. Websense also helps organizations mitigate the problems caused by new emerging internet threats, such as spyware, malicious mobile code and peer-to-peer file sharing.

Wick Hill Group plc, established in 1976, specializes in secure infrastructure solutions. The company's portfolio covers security, performance, access, services and management. Wick Hill sources and delivers best-of-breed secure solutions, through its accredited partner network, for companies from SME to Times 100, backed up by customer support, implementation, training and technical services.

Wire Card AG is not only aiming at internationally oriented companies with its modular finance platform, Corporate Clearing Center, but also those of a small- or medium-sized structure. Wire Card offers payment management, worldwide payment solutions, alternative payment products such as CLICK2PAY, process optimization, financial management and risk management. The platform is based on Java and supports XML as an open standard. It also supports all major application services (Bea or IBM).

WorldPay Ltd is the UK's largest payment services provider (PSP) and is part of the Royal Bank of Scotland Group. It provides payment services for thousands of clients across the world, ranging from sole traders to multinational corporations.

Akonix

Employee [started: 13:52]
Meeting Edit Help

[employee]
Here's the document you requested.

[valued customer]
This is great! Thank you for getting it to me so quickly. By the way, I'm surprised that your company allows it to go through IM?

Type your text

[employee]
We use Akonix **Solutions for Enterprise IM** so everything is controlled... but it isn't blocked.

Send   Invite Others...   Close

IM communicating in real time . . . without violating **compliance** rules

Instant Messaging can dramatically improve the way your organization communicates, but it also creates new security, compliance and policy risks. Akonix software works with Enterprise IM solutions (such as IBM Lotus Instant Messaging and Microsoft LCS), adding powerful archiving, review and security capabilities, while enabling granular, detailed policy enforcement to meet virtually any business need. And Akonix allows you to apply the same advanced management for authorized, safe and secure external communications over public IM networks. The result – one powerful, central control point to manage multiple IM systems for compliance, corporate policy enforcement, content filtering, security, archiving and monitoring.

With Akonix you can confidently say **IM in CONTROL**.

Download a Free White Paper Today:

Managing and Securing IM in the Enterprise: Why It Should Be a Top Priority

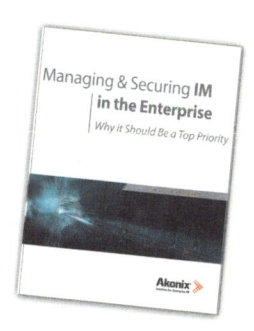

Visit www.akonix.com/iod

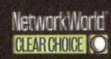

www.akonix.com/iod

Managing IM in the Enterprise

Akonix offers enterprises a simple solution to a growing problem: Controlling the use of instant messaging

Not so long ago, Instant Messaging (IM) belonged almost exclusively to the youngest generation of Internet users, who used it to communicate with friends. But the technology has quickly expanded to find an important place in the business world. In fact, the research firm Giga Information Group has predicted that workplace IM messages will exceed email use by 2006.

Today, more than 74 percent of IM use within company walls comes from employees using networks like Yahoo! Messenger, America Online's AIM and Microsoft's MSN Messenger, according to Nemertes Research. It's easy to understand why; these IM networks are free, easy to use and more than a little contagious.

Corporate IM users quickly fall in love with the ability communicate instantly, internally or externally. By contacting customers, partners and remote employees in real-time, users can improve collaboration, reduce telecom costs and eliminate the delays caused by unanswered voice mail and email.

Unfortunately, unmanaged IM use presents IT and security staff with a new problem. Since it bypasses established compliance, security and corporate policy controls, IM can introduce viruses, worms and other malicious content onto the corporate network. Recent analysis by Gartner states that if your organisation has a connection to the Internet typically some 42% of staff will be using IM. The risk exists today for corporate IM users to easily expose confidential customer data, intellectual property and proprietary company information.

In many corporations, IM may even give rise to violations of specific regulations, including Basel II, Freedom of Information Act, Sarbanes-Oxley requirements and the Health Insurance Portability and Accountability Act (HIPAA) regulations.

Given these serious issues, organisations are faced with a challenge: How to maintain employee access to IM without being left vulnerable to security threats, viruses and compliance violations.

Take Control of IM and Expand the Benefits

As with other new technologies, like email and web access in the 1990s, companies need to implement and enforce corporate security and usage policies to successfully and safely embrace IM as a strategic business communications application.

First, corporate IT must gain control of workplace IM use:

- Identify users,
- Monitor and log activity,
- Apply corporate policies, and
- Close security loopholes.

Once IM use is subject to company policy, complies with regulations and has appropriate security protections, the benefits to the business of IM expand rapidly.

Although IM use may start in small departmental pockets, once it is officially sanctioned, companies typically find that IM's advantages quickly spread throughout the organisation. On the horizon are new ways to leverage the power of IM and "presence" recognition data within corporate applications and IT infrastructure that goes well beyond person-to-person communications.

Case study: RPU Gets a Handle on IM

Rochester Public Utilities continually investigates innovative technologies to help customers realize the best value from the services they receive. As a public utility, providing electricity service to tens of thousands of customers, RPU doesn't take kindly to anything that might disrupt the reliability of its operations. So when it detected some of its 250 network users were employing public instant messaging services, RPU decided to take control of the situation before it got out of hand.

From a business perspective, RPU recognized that IM served a valuable communications function, so it didn't want to try to ban IM use. Rather, RPU took a proactive approach by defining the rules under which employees could employ IM, while adhering to required logging and security policies.

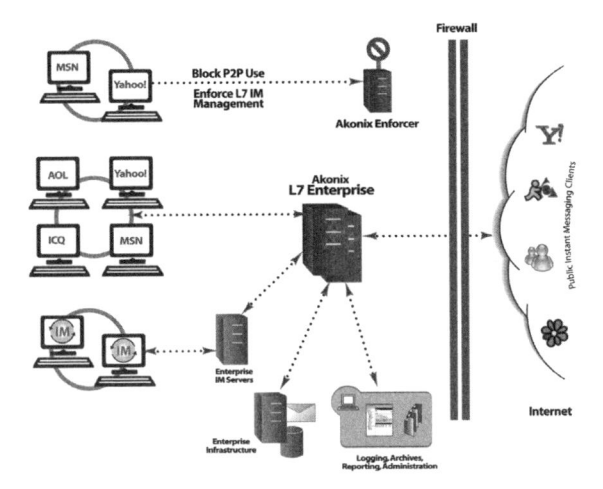

To enforce those rules, RPU opted for an IM management solution from Akonix. Specifically, the Akonix L7 Enterprise solution allowed RPU to:

- Detect and manage all the major public IM protocols
- Apply usage polices to individuals or groups of users
- Log, archive and review IM communications as required by industry regulations
- Secure internal messages within the enterprise network
- Stop conversations, messages and attachments that violate corporate policy or place the network at risk through SPIM and malware
- Block all unauthorized IM use and all peer-to-peer file sharing
- Integrate public IM services with its internal enterprise IM solution, Microsoft Live Communication Server, for unified compliance archiving & reporting

About Akonix Systems

Akonix Systems, Inc., headquartered in San Diego, Calif., with the EMEA headquarters in the Surrey Technology Centre in the UK, offers the leading enterprise IM management solution, providing the means to get control of IM with enterprise-class compliance, security and management. The company's flagship software product, Akonix L7 Enterprise, deploys within the corporate network and acts as a proxy for all IM traffic; immediately all IM use can be monitored and archived, authenticated with corporate credentials, and subjected to security, confidentiality and other corporate policies.

In the UK, Akonix works with key partners such as Pentura.

Pentura provides the latest security solutions from well established and new vendors that are focused on specific security areas. Pentura has been working with Akonix for more than two years, helping customers to secure public and enterprise IM environments to enable business to be conducted in a safe and secure manner, whilst providing full auditing and reporting capabilities.

For more information about Pentura, please visit **www.Pentura.co.uk**

Download a Free White Paper

Now is the time take action to control IM use on your network to ensure security and compliance. Visit our Web site to learn more about IM control, security & compliance, and learn more about Pentura's leading edge security solutions. You can also download a FREE white paper, Managing and Securing IM in the Enterprise: Why It Should Be a Top Priority, to understand the risks and benefits of controlling IM on your network, and how you can easily and effectively take control.

www.akonix.com/iod

WE'LL FOCUS ON SECURING YOUR BUSINESS SO YOU CAN FOCUS ON INCREASING IT.

Comprehensive Security Solutions from Trend Micro.

Protect against viruses, spam, spyware and worms with a truly comprehensive security solution. Easy to deploy, easy to manage, it's one solution you can rely on to keep costs down and productivity up while you get back to business.

Register today and receive your FREE copy of "Security Guide for the Growing Business" at http://uk.trendmicro-europe.com/iod

©2005 Trend Micro Incorporated. All rights reserved. The Trend Micro logo is a trademark or registered trademark of Trend Micro Incorporated. All other company and/or product names may be trademarks or registered trademarks of their owners.

Information at risk

1.1

The information security management system

Alan Calder, IT Governance Ltd

Information security is now too important to be left to the IT department. This is because information security is now a business-level issue:

- Information is the lifeblood of any business today. Anything that is of value inside the organization will be of value to someone outside it. The board is responsible for ensuring that critical information, and the technology that houses and processes it, are secure.
- Legislation and regulation is a governance issue. In the UK, the Turnbull Report clearly identifies the need for boards to control risk to information and information systems. Data protection, privacy, computer misuse and other regulations – different in different jurisdictions – are a boardroom issue. Banks and financial sector organizations are subject to the requirements of the Bank of International Settlements (BIS) and the Basle 2 framework, which includes information and IT risk.
- As the intellectual capital value of 'information economy' organizations increases, their commercial viability and profitability – as well as their share value – increasingly depend on the security, confidentiality and integrity of their information and information assets.

- The scale of, and speed of change in, the 'information economy' is every day creating new, global threats and vulnerabilities for all networked organizations.

Threats and consequences

The one area in which businesses of all sizes today enjoy a level playing field is in information security: *all* businesses are subject to world-class threats, all of them are potentially betrayed by world-class software vulnerabilities and all of them are subject to an increasingly complex set of (sometimes contradictory) computer- and privacy-related regulation around the world.

While most organizations believe that their information systems are secure, the brutal reality is that they are not. Individual hardware-, software- and vendor-driven solutions are not information security systems. Not only is it extremely dangerous for an organization to operate in today's world without a systematic, strategic approach to information security, such organizations have become threats to their more responsible brethren.

The extent and value of electronic data are continuing to grow exponentially. The exposure of businesses and individuals to its misappropriation (particularly in electronic format) or destruction is growing equally quickly. The growth in computer- and information-related compliance and regulatory requirements reflects the threats associated with digital data. Directors have clear compliance responsibilities that cannot be met by saying, 'The Head of IT was supposed to have dealt with that' or, 'I'm not really interested in computer security.'

Ultimately, consumer confidence in dealing across the web depends on how secure people believe their personal data to be. Data security, for this reason, matters to any business with any form of web strategy (and any business without a web strategy is unlikely to be around in the long term), from simple business to consumer (b2c) or business to business (b2b) propositions through Enterprise Resource Planning (ERP) systems to the use of extranets and e-mail. It matters, too, to any organization that depends on computers for its day-to-day existence (to produce accounts, for instance) or that may be subject (as are all organizations) to the provisions of the Data Protection Act. Even the Freedom of Information Act, which ostensibly applies only to public sector organizations, raises confidentiality issues for any business that contracts with the public sector.

Newspapers and business magazines are full of stories about hackers, viruses and online fraud. These are just the public tip of the data insecurity iceberg. Little tends to be heard about businesses that suffer profit fluctuations through computer failure, or businesses that fail to survive a major interruption to their data and operating systems. Even less is heard about organizations whose core operations are compromised by the theft or loss of key business data; usually they just disappear quietly.

Information security management today

In the vast majority of organizations, information security management is inadequate, unsystematic or, in practical terms, simply non-existent.

Small- and medium-sized businesses tend to allocate inadequate resources (manpower, management time and hard cash) to deal with the real issues, while tackling individual threats and concerns in a haphazard way. Investing in isolated solutions to individual concerns leaves so many holes that it's only slightly more useful than not bothering in the first place.

Larger organizations tend to operate their security functions in vertically segregated silos with little or no coordination. This structural weakness means that most organizations have significant vulnerabilities that can be exploited deliberately or which simply open them up to disaster. For instance, while the corporate lawyers will tackle all the legal issues (non-disclosure agreements, patents, contracts, etc) they will have little involvement with the data security issues faced on the organizational perimeter.

On the organizational perimeter, those dealing with physical security concentrate almost exclusively on physical assets, such as gates and doors, security guards and burglar alarms. They have little appreciation of, or impact upon, the 'cyber' perimeter.

The IT managers, responsible for the cyber perimeter, may be good at ensuring that everyone has a password, and that there is internet connectivity, that the organization is able to respond to virus threats, and that key partners, customers and suppliers are able to deal electronically with the organization, but almost universally they lack the training, experience or exposure to adequately address the strategic threat to the information assets of the organization as a whole.

There are even organizations where the IT managers set and implement security policy on the basis of their own risk assessment, past experiences and interests, with little regard for real needs or strategic objectives. What else could they do? They are not equipped to deal with the strategic, business issues. Of course, users within the business recognize that these sorts of rule interfere with *doing business*, so the rules tend to be ignored – leaving the board with a false sense of assurance about the level of protection they enjoy.

The board

Information security is a complex issue. It deals with the confidentiality, integrity and availability of valuable data, sitting within business critical systems, and subject to world-class threats. One has to think in terms of the whole enterprise, the entire organization, which includes all the possible combinations of physical and cyber assets, all the possible combinations of intranets, extranets and Internets, and which might include an extended network of business partners, vendors, customers and others. One has to look at the distribution and supply channels. One has to look at the information needs of the business, and the technology required to support those needs.

It's about the business model. It's about the strategic risks facing the business. And that means it's the board's responsibility. Yes, the board probably will need outside help to address the issues and, no, the board doesn't have to become expert in the technological minutiae of how information security is managed. But the board does have to face up to its information security responsibility.

The board's responsibility

There are seven areas on which the board needs to focus:

1. The information security policy – which sets out the overall policy for securing the availability, confidentiality and integrity of the company's information and which reflects senior management's commitment to it.

2. Allocation of resources and responsibilities – ensuring that adequately qualified individuals have the resources and clear objectives which, together, will enable the security policy to be implemented. This includes making decisions about the extent to which external expertise is required.
3. Risk assessment – identifying the strategic risks, and risk categories, that are likely to affect the business, and ensuring that, for each of the information assets (hardware, software, data, etc) there is a detailed risk assessment.
4. Risk treatment plan – setting the criteria by which risks are to be treated (accept, reject, transfer, or accept but control) and, for those risks that are to be controlled, setting the criteria and standards that are to guide selection and implementation of the controls. These should, in simple terms, ensure that one doesn't spend more on controlling the risk than its likely impact.
5. Project initiation, monitoring and oversight – ensuring that the development and implementation of an appropriate information security management system proceeds in line with a clearly thought-through, pragmatic plan.
6. Approval, prior to implementation, of proposed controls, irrespective of whether they are technological or procedural.
7. Ongoing, systematic monitoring of the performance of the information security management system, ensuring that it remains up-to-date, effective and meets the policy objectives laid down for it.

Information security management system

An information security management system (ISMS) is the practical outcome of the type of approach recommended above. An ISMS is, at heart, a) a set of controls that reduces those risks the organization has decided to accept but control to a level consistent with its control standard; and b) the framework within which those controls are operated.

'Controls' are a blend of technological, procedural and behavioural components which, between them, achieve the control objective.

For instance, your desktop user systems are threatened by a malicious mix of viruses, worms, Trojans, scumware and spam, whose outcome is to compromise the availability, integrity and confidentiality of the data on the desktop. The attack vectors are: e-mail, web surfing and Instant Messaging. The controls would include:

- technological – anti-virus and anti-spyware software, anti-spam filters, firewalls and automatic updating;
- procedural – configuration of the software and firewall, updating procedures, incident management procedures and acceptable use policies;
- behavioural – user awareness of and training in dealing with these threats and methods of response, including recognizing when scumware is attempting to download on to a PC.

This three-way blend is typical of all effective controls; implementation of two only leaves a significant exposure that can undo everything that has been put in place. The false sense of security that most organizations derive from only having effected a partial solution can be particularly destructive.

Best practice

In this fast-changing and complex world, it is difficult for any one individual to identify all the threats that exist and the full range of possible, workable controls that might be deployed to counter them. There is no need to. Global best practice in information security has been harnessed and expressed in two documents that are fast becoming the cornerstone of organizational information security: BS 7799 and ISO 17799.

BS 7799:2005 is a sector-neutral specification for an ISMS and it contains, in Annex A, a comprehensive list of controls. It is a business-oriented and risk-assessment driven standard that, whether or not an organization seeks external certification, is external proof of the quality of the organization's information security systems.

BS 7799 is supported by, and makes extensive reference to, the international code of practice, ISO 17799:2005. Whereas BS 7799 specifies what is required for an ISMS, ISO 17799 sets out, in substantial detail, what best practice considerations might be for each of the recommended controls. These two standards, available from the British Standards Institution, can be combined with a detailed, practical handbook (such as *IT Governance: A Manager's Guide to Information Security and BS 7799/ISO 17799,* Calder and Watkins, Kogan Page, 2005) and a range of commercially available tools (policy generator, risk assessment tool, etc) to ensure that best practice is being systematically deployed inside the business.

Conclusion

The board is responsible and accountable for managing information security in the business. A strategic, systematic and thorough approach, translated into an information security management system, is essential. With nothing less than the future of the wired economy at risk, every management team has its part to play. ISO 17799 describes best practice and an ISMS certified to BS 7799 is public proof that the board has been proactive in identifying and meeting its business and regulatory obligations to secure the availability, confidentiality and integrity of the data on which its business depends.

1.2

The business case for IT security

Andrew Steggles, EMEA Nokia Enterprise Solutions

For many years security was synonymous with having a solid firewall in place. Protecting the perimeter and thereby keeping the bad guys out was the main goal of network architects. However, recent surveys suggest that more than 70 per cent of all security breaches result from within the firewall, that is, from the people you trust – your employees, partners or consultants.

New viruses continue to employ blend threat techniques, exploiting multiple weaknesses and attacking through multiple methods (for example, e-mail, file transfers and web browsers) forcing organizations to purchase additional layers of anti-virus and content security products to deploy across the enterprise. Instant messaging has entered the corporate world and has brought with it another layer of security concerns. Instant messaging applications can provide attack points for hackers seeking to gain entry into corporate systems by presenting tunnels through firewalls.

Hacking toolkits and manuals can be found all over the internet. Today, it is possible for a 10-year-old to break into a multinational bank and steal or alter the most sensitive kinds of information: balance statements, credit card information, access rights and so on.

Understanding threats

When organizations first begin to assess network security, the tendency is to focus almost exclusively on external-facing assets to defend against unauthorized attacks. However, to establish an effective security policy, organizations must examine both external facing, publicly accessible resources, and internal facing, private networks. Recent findings by the

FBI and the Computer Security Institute indicate that internal attacks account for the majority of security breaches that organizations experience. This finding suggests that internal network security needs to be a higher priority for security and network administrators. Internal core network security is a requirement for all networks.

The threats to the security infrastructure of any network include packet sniffing, DNS spoofing (or domain name server spoofing: this is where a machine assumes the identity of a company's or service provider's web address to an IP address look-up server), IP (internet provider) address spoofing (where an unscrupulous person forges the address of the sending device to make it appear as if it has come from a different machine) and the proliferation of fake routing information. Spoofing occurs when an attacker sends network packets that falsely appear to be from a trusted host on the network. In general terms, these threats can be categorized as interception and impersonation.

Interception

The first type of attack involves interception of communication between two systems, such as a client and a server. In this scenario, an attacker exists somewhere on the network between communicating entities. The attacker observes the information passed between the client and server. The attacker might intercept and keep the information (reconnaissance), or might alter the information and send it on to the intended recipient (man-in-the-middle attack).

A man-in-the-middle, or bucket brigade, attack is one in which the attacker intercepts messages in an exchange and then retransmits them, substituting his or her own data for the requested one, such that the two original parties still appear to be communicating with each other directly. The attacker uses a program that, to the client appears to be the server, and to the server appears to be the client. The attack may be used simply to gain access to the messages, or enable the attacker to modify the messages before retransmitting them.

Impersonation

The second type of attack is impersonation of a particular host, either a client or a server. Using this strategy, an attacker pretends to be the intended recipient of a message. If the strategy works, the client remains unaware of the deception and continues to communicate with the impostor as if its traffic had successfully reached the destination.

Anticipating threats

Both of these attack techniques allow network information to be intercepted, potentially for hostile reasons. The results can be disastrous, whether that goal is achieved by listening for all packets (through a packet sniffer) on a network or by utilizing a compromised name server to redirect a certain network required to a maliciously duplicated, or compromised, host.

Over the last few years, falls in hardware prices have made it attractive and convenient for corporations and home users to go wireless, in particular using the 802.11 standard. But in the rush towards liberation from the tethers of computer cable, individuals and companies are opening the doors to a whole new type of computer intrusion. Without special software or hardware other than ordinary consumer wireless cards, hackers have found a new pastime: cruising around metropolitan areas with their laptops listening for the beacons of wireless networks and then accessing unprotected WLANs. War driving resembles the war dialling of the 1990s, with automated programs calling hundreds of phone numbers in search of poorly protected computer dial-ups.

Likewise, many hotels and airport lounges are providing free-of charge wireless LANs. Business travellers may automatically set up a WLAN and do not consider the security risks as they typically access the internet, use instant messaging, or connect to corporate accounts. The public wireless connection exposes users to direct peer-to-peer hacking from anyone else connected to the over-the-air airport lounge network. Again, downloading files and instant messaging are common ways that hackers use to install spyware and hacking tools over the internet. In the end, even safe VPN tunnels to corporate resources might be at risk since they are open to any intruder 'already on the PC'.

Protecting your corporate assets

The negative effects on a business of having insufficient security systems in place, or falling victim to security breaches and denial of service attacks, are well recorded and have made numerous media headlines. These headlines are increasing awareness of the importance of security amongst all businesses.

IT infrastructure security is clearly no longer just a concern for the IT department, but commands the attention of senior management as the face of security changes from an 'insurance policy', to a crucial business foundation. Not only is a watertight security solution mandatory, but also having the correct security systems in place can also positively impact an organization's business.

Until recently, security in the networked environment was about keeping the 'bad guys' out. Yet as organizations extend connectivity via extranets and the internet, it is no longer enough to just lock out the 'bad guys'. A company has to allow a myriad of additional and valid users (such as suppliers, customers and employees) to access its data seamlessly – to let the 'good guys' in. In fact, by allowing trusted users to access its data, it is streamlining its business functions and creating economies of scale, which will ultimately justify the initial cost of implementing security technologies.

The number of valid users is rapidly increasing. IDC forecasts an explosion in the number of individuals accessing the internet and corporate intranets over the next four years. This means that corporate infrastructures will be exposed to an unprecedented number of users, all trying to access relevant corporate resource and information that they may need to conduct business.

In the global economy, many companies are based in disparate locations and have an increasing number of mobile workers, all of whom need to communicate and share information in real time. Availability and speed of access to information on the internet, combined with the projected growth of internet usage, pose an important consideration for companies: there is a need to optimize access to information while maintaining levels of security so that the business is not endangered. A business needs to assess the risk involved in opening its networks, whilst maintaining a secure environment – this is often a headache for IT professionals.

However, once a security policy and infrastructure are in place, a company can expect increased productivity within the business process, through the creation of trust, ensured privacy of data and maintenance of integrity.

Security as a business enabler

An overall view of security, taking into consideration the risks and benefits of using the internet, will highlight the long-term benefits of a security infrastructure and policy. Here is a set of core elements that serve as a foundation to e-business:

- **Trust**: by having a security policy (and necessary security systems to back this up) in place, customers and suppliers can trust your company and be encouraged to transact with you online.
- **Privacy**: by assuring customers and suppliers that their data is secure, you are again promoting trust and encouraging more access and interactivity.
- **Integrity**: by ensuring that your e-business systems are secure, you minimize the risk of attack and the loss of trust and brand equity of your company.

Security cannot be considered in isolation from a company's business goals. Technology is ultimately a tool to enable business, and security technology is no exception. Steps to consider when implementing security technology include:

- Ensure that security is a board issue – it requires this level of governance.
- Begin with your business objectives when planning a security policy.
- Consider where your business will be in three years before implementing technology you will outgrow.
- Choose a security partner that understands your business and has the technology solutions and reputable customer service.
- Implement strong physical security.
- Make sure you revisit and update your security policy and technology as your business grows.
- Make sure that all users (staff and supply chain) are educated and trained.

To conclude, security is not an insurance policy. It is both a necessity for e-business and a positive element of infrastructure. This has been driven by the need for companies to nurture 'trusted relationships' with customers, partners, suppliers and channels. In many cases, a company's most valuable asset is its corporate data. The ability to use security technologies to enable greater access to corporate data increases the trust in these relationships. Ultimately, trusted relationships can yield significant benefits, such as higher transaction rates, lower cost per transaction and increasingly personalized services.

1.3

Recent attack trends

The Fraud Advisory Panel's Cybercrime Working Group

Introduction

A recent survey by the National High Tech Crime Unit reported that in 2003, 62 per cent of companies suffered internet fraud causing £121 million of damage.[1] Virus attacks were experienced by 77 per cent of respondents and caused £27.8 million of damage.

The losses caused to businesses and consumers by cybercrime are huge. In the year to June 2004, online banking fraud cost US financial institutions $2.4 billion in direct losses. In 2003, card-not-present fraud committed through the internet cost the UK banking industry approximately £45 million. In the 12 months to June 2004, phishing attack losses cost the industry £4.5 million[2] (source: APACS, 2004).

In addition, there appears to be a worrying increase in the number of hackers and virus writers who appear to commit cybercrimes for financial gain or as part of an organized criminal gang. In December 2004, it was reported that 90 per cent of all malicious code is developed by criminals.[3] The purpose of the code is either to steal confidential information or to develop armies of zombie computers to commit further cybercrimes.

Concerns about internet security are slowing the growth of e-commerce. It has been reported that 25 per cent of EU citizens do not shop online because they do not trust the medium.[4] Of those who do use e-commerce, 48 per cent were concerned about security in making payment.

A survey by RSM Robson Rhodes in 2004 reported that fraud costs UK businesses £40 billion a year.[5] It is estimated that companies spend £8 billion a year on fraud prevention and security measures in addition to the £32 billion a year lost to fraud.

The three main areas of fraud are embezzlement, cheque fraud and money laundering.[6] However, it is estimated that identity theft costs £1 billion per year, with many fraudsters attacking companies in an attempt to steal customer information or damage the victim's reputation. Larger companies are most vulnerable to fraud, which can cost them up to 5 per cent of their turnover.[7]

However, some of the information may be misleadingly small. Many businesses fail to report fraud and cybercrime for fear of having their reputations damaged and, therefore, the real figure may be substantially higher than £40 billion. Only a quarter of those affected by cybercrime report it to the police.[8]

Hackers

Hackers can be divided into two groups: internal and external hackers. The motivation of hackers can vary between financial gain, political or ideological beliefs and revenge, in the case of a disgruntled employee or dissatisfied customer. What hackers do once they have gained access to a computer system depends on their initial motivation. Their aim may be to steal corporate information, carry out an e-theft, plant malicious computer programs, disrupt the target's computer system, extort payments, highlight lack of security, or deface the business's website, causing damage to its corporate reputation.

It was reported in October 2003 that a teenager charged with offences under the Computer Misuse Act 1990 as a result of his alleged hacking activities, had been cleared. The teenager had been accused of effectively shutting down one of the United States's largest ports as a result of a botched denial-of-service attack he had launched. The prosecution alleged that the teenager's target had been a chatroom user who had offended him. The internet service provider was forced to divert e-mails through intermediary service providers and as a result the server that operated the US port in Houston was bombarded with electronic messages. This caused the server to shut down.

The teenager claimed that a flaw in his computer system had allowed other hackers to obtain access to his computer and plant a Trojan computer program to remotely control his computer. The computer was then used to launch an attack. The teenager claimed that the perpetrator had then edited his log files to disguise his existence. The jury cleared the teenager of the charges.[9]

In September 2003 it was reported that a 26 year-old computer expert had been convicted of masterminding the UK's largest ever credit card fraud. Over a three-year period, the fraudster, Sunil Mahtani, and his accomplices downloaded nearly 9,000 credit card details from Heathrow Express Railink. These were passed on to a gang of 11 accomplices who forged new credit cards using the details. The scam was uncovered in September 2001, at which point the gang had already stolen £2 million. Had all of the numbers been used it would have made in the region of £20 million.[10] Mr Mahtani was later sentenced to nine years imprisonment and his two associates were sentenced to four years imprisonment for their part in the fraud.[11] Despite the scale of the fraud Mr Mahtani was only ordered to pay back £1,329 as investigators were only able to locate £4.73 which he held in two building societies and a £1,000 share in a car.[12]

In December 2004 it was reported that a 21 year-old US man received nine years for hacking into the unsecured Wi-Fi network of a chain of hardware stores.[13] The hacker and an accomplice located the network by 'Wardriving'. They then placed a program on the system to capture the credit card details of the shop's customers. The program was discovered after it caused the shop's computers to crash, and the FBI was contacted. The hacker's accomplice was sentenced to 26 months.[14]

Cyber extortion

In 2004 organized gangs of criminals regularly used the threat of denial-of-service attacks to extort money from companies in the UK. The extortionists often crash a victim's website by overloading the server with data sent from zombie computers (see below). The extortionists then contact the business and threaten to cause a similar problem again unless the business pays a large sum of money.

The extortionists use armies of 'zombie' computers to launch attacks on their victims. Zombie computers are machines compromised by viruses that contain secret programs that allow them to remotely control the computer. They are often linked together in networks known as 'botnets' that can then be used to crash the victim's website by sending data to the victim's servers. This is known as a 'distributed denial-of-service' attack.

The attacks mainly focus on online businesses with no physical retail outlets, as these will suffer most from a denial-of-service attack. In addition, the extortionists target websites that make large sums of money during a short space of time. For example, US online bookmakers taking bets on the Super Bowl were threatened with having their websites attacked during the game.[15] Similar attacks have occurred in the UK during the Cheltenham Festival.

In October 2004, internet extortionists threatened a leading UK betting site with a child pornography smear campaign unless it paid £4,800.[16] Blue Square initially suffered a denial-of-service attack for five hours. This was followed by threats of a longer attack unless money was paid to an online website. The blackmailers later threatened to send child pornography e-mails from the company unless the money was paid within two days.

In November 2004, a company handling online payments for large retailers was the target of an attempted cyber-extortion.[17] The company first suffered a massive denial-of-service attack, which may have disrupted up to 4 million credit card payments to 3,500 retailers. The criminals then demanded that the victim pay $10,000 or they would continue the attack.

Netspionage and wardriving

Corporate espionage carried out via the internet continues to be an area of concern for businesses. By its very nature this form of cybercrime is under-reported. A business may not be aware that it is happening or, if it does know, may not want to publicize the problem.

In 2004 there was a significant rise in the amount of malicious software designed to steal proprietary information. For example, it was reported that there were 1,817 cases of malicious software in October 2004, a rise of 22 per cent over the previous month.[18] Of the malicious software, 47 per cent were Trojans designed to collect sensitive information.

With the advent of wireless networks a new form of snooping has become increasingly common. 'Wardriving' involves cyber snoopers driving around cities with standard wireless enabled laptops/PDAs and appropriate software which can be purchased for as little as £200. The equipment scans for open wireless networks. Information passed across the network can reportedly be stored and sold on to corporate rivals. Alternatively the snoopers can obtain free use of the target's network, the main purpose being to leach internet access.

In 2004 it was reported that a third of all companies now have wireless networks (compared with just 2 per cent in 2002).[19] However, 8 per cent of businesses with wireless networks have reported attempts to access their networks without permission. Only 20 per cent of businesses with wireless networks use additional encryption.

In 2002, it was reported that Canal Plus sued NDS for US$3 billion for deliberately sabotaging its business. It was alleged that NDS hacked the security code on the Canal Plus smart card, which gave viewers a choice of different channels. While many businesses engage in reverse engineering to examine their competitor's products, Canal Plus claimed that NDS published the security code on the internet, where international counterfeiters picked it up. In turn, it was alleged that the counterfeiters produced fake smart cards, which allowed users to watch subscription channels free. Canal Plus said this was a deliberate plan to sabotage the business in which it was a market leader.[20] Since the allegations, NDS has faced a flurry of similar lawsuits.[21]

Corporate identity theft – phishing and cybersquatting

The internet allows fraudsters to offer bogus credible banking services. It is difficult for the consumer to discern between genuine and fraudulent internet banks. Fraudsters do not need to go to great expense to dress up their sites as genuine, and will entice victims with a promise of high interest rates. A bogus internet banking site can be set up offshore, attract funds and be dismantled overnight. The two most common forms of corporate identity theft are 'phishing' and 'cybersquatting'.

Phishing involves the fraudsters sending e-mails, which appear authentic, to customers, inviting them to log on to the bank's website and verify their account information, including their personal identification details. The website to which the e-mails are linked is bogus although it also appears to be authentic. Once account details are provided at the bogus website, the phishers use the data to steal money from the victims' accounts.

In December 2004 the Anti-Phishing Working Group reported that there were 1,518 active phishing sites in November 2004, an increase of 29 per cent over the figure for October 2004. The number of active phishing websites grew by an average of 28 per cent per month from July to November 2004, and 51 brands were subject to phishing attacks. The fraudsters are often not content with simply taking their victims' deposits: they also sell the credit card details gleaned from the completed application forms.

In November 2004 NatWest was forced to suspend some of its internet banking services after it was the target of a phishing scam.[22] NatWest refused to allow its online customers to set up any new direct debits or standing orders as a measure to prevent funds being switched out of the country. In previous attacks money has been sent to countries as far apart as Romania and Nigeria.

Phishing developed considerably in 2004. In one new phishing variation, the victim is sent a spam e-mail encouraging him or her to link to a virtual postcard website where, the victim is told, a postcard is waiting. If the link is clicked, the victim is taken to a website where a 'keystroke-logger' is placed on his computer, which records data inputted on the victim's machine including passwords and PIN numbers. The recorded data is then sent to the fraudsters. In another variation, the victim is sent an e-mail. When the e-mail is opened, it runs a program that re-writes the 'hosts' file on the victim's computer. This effectively replaces a genuine website's address with the address of a bogus one. When the victim next attempts to access the legitimate website, the user is automatically redirected to the bogus website.

In addition to phishing, some fraudsters attempt to register a domain name identical or similar to a well-known brand. Disputes about domain name registrations are usually resolved through arbitration panels operated by domain name registries.

In one cybersquatting case, a company called PC World Direct Limited registered the domain name 'pcworlddirect.co.uk'.[23] However, the company was nothing to do with the Dixons Group that owns the well-known chain of computer shops. Dixons wrote a letter to PC World Direct Limited asking it to transfer the domain name. PC World Direct Limited responded with an offer to sell the name for £300,000. Dixons rejected the offer and commenced arbitration. The arbitrators forced the transfer but were very critical of Dixons' case. Specifically, the retailer was criticized for producing little evidence that it had any intellectual property rights in the name 'PC World'. However, the panel accepted that 'PC World' was well known and the offer to sell the domain name for £300,000 did constitute bad faith. The panel therefore ordered the transfer of the domain name.

In the Froogle case, a UK web hosting company registered 'Froogle.co.uk' days after Google launched a product search service under the same name.[24] Google contacted the web hosting company and offered £1,500 for the domain name but this was refused. Google then commenced arbitration. The DRS panel held that Google did have sufficient intellectual property rights in the word 'Froogle' to force the name to be transferred. The panel noted that it was not necessary for Google to have enough intellectual property rights to start an action for passing-off or breach of copyright. It was not even necessary for the intellectual property rights to be in the UK. The panel therefore ordered the transfer of the name.

In a variation known as 'cybergriping', a disgruntled Chase Manhattan customer in New York started a site to complain about errors on his bank account. As a result the bank quickly secured the rights to chasesucks, chasestinks and ihatechase.

In the Seattle protest case, a fake website was created on the basis of the official World Trade Organization website, in that it was graphically the same but with different contents. For example, the home page announced that the opening ceremony of the Third WTO Ministerial Conference had been 'suddenly cancelled'. The cybergripers even had the gall to place an alert message lower on the page about a 'fake WTO website misleading public', with a hyperlink to the original WTO website. The URL, http://www.gatt.org, was carefully chosen with obvious reference to the previous name of the WTO (the official website address is http://www.wto.org).

Notes

1. *Public Eye on Fraud and Corruption,* 6, 5, 28 March 2004.
2. Gartner IT as reported in *The Financial Times*, 15 June 2004.

3. www.zdnet.co.uk, 10 December 2004.
4. www.out-law.com, 16 March 2003.
5. 'Fraud Costs £40bn and growing', *The Times,* 18 October 2004.
6. 'Fraud Costs £40bn and growing', *The Times,* 18 October 2004.
7. 'Fraud Costs £40bn and growing', *The Times,* 18 October 2004.
8. 'Computer hackers strike at 80% of businesses' by Frederike Cave, *The Financial Times,* 25 February 2004.
9. *Daily Telegraph,* 7 October 2003, The Times Online, 17 October 2003, by PA News.
10. Times Online, 6 September 2003.
11. London Reuters, 9 September 2003.
12. Times Online, 10 September 2003.
13. www.silicon.com, 16 December 2004.
14. www.silicon.com, 17 December 2004.
15. *The Times,* 24 February 2004.
16. *The Financial Times,* 26 October 2004.
17. *The Financial Times,* 5 November 2004.
18. www.news.com, 4 November 2004.
19. www.out-law.com, 14 April 2004.
20. *Guardian,* 30 May 2002.
21. *Guardian,* 3 October 2002.
22. *The Times,* 18 November 2004.
23. www.out-law.com, 8 April 2004.
24. www.out-law.com, 21 April 2004.

The fine art of elephant husbandry – a practical guide to patch management

Chris Knowles, Computacenter

Introduction

IT infrastructures today are like elephants: big, unwieldy, expensive to look after, and they cause a lot of damage when they're down.

For many organizations the challenge of ensuring that their elephants are healthy and free from viruses is costly both in terms of time and money. New elephant vulnerabilities are being discovered on almost a daily basis and the time taken for viruses to spread has decreased rapidly. In early 2003, a particular vulnerability was discovered in SQL that could cause serious damage to a herd; it took several months before an antidote was released but another six months before the elephant hunters started to exploit the vulnerability, so the majority of organizations had immunized their herds. More recently a similar vulnerability was discovered but this time the whole timeframe between discovery, antidote and attack had been shortened to a couple of weeks.

As an example, an organization can take eight weeks to immunize just one third of its overall elephant herd for each new vulnerability that emerges. The bill for this comes to £400,000. All of this means that the window available to an organization to successfully protect its herd has become extremely constrained. This limited amount of time often means that emphasis is put on getting the immunization patches out as quickly as possible. This generates a number of issues:

- patching is done on an *ad hoc* basis;
- patches are not properly tested;
- other shortcuts in processes may occur.

Patching your herd on an ad hoc basis is very costly and time-consuming. As many of the elephants and other animals that need patching are critical parts of your infrastructure, these can only be patched out of operational hours. This means additional expense may be incurred for out-of-hours work. The unpredictability of when these new immunization patches are released means that it is a very difficult cost to budget for.

To ensure that patches are quickly deployed, important processes such as testing and validating the patch can often be skipped. Therefore, there is a risk that the patch could cause your elephant or device to become ill and lead to availability problems. Occasionally, patches have been known to make your elephants more vulnerable than they previously were. Again, testing and validation of patches will add both cost and time.

Other process shortcuts in addition to testing may also occur. For example, before patching takes place, a back-up should be done of the system, so that if the patch causes a problem it can be quickly removed. Again, due to time pressures, this is often skipped or not properly checked so that recovery of the systems can take a considerable amount of time.

What should a good solution consist of?

An effective elephant husbandry methodology is required to address the need for time to:

- research the vaccinations needed daily;
- discover what is in the paddock/enclosure and keep an up-to-date inventory;
- understand the prerequisites of vaccinations;
- know about and understand the criticality of vaccinations and priorities;
- create and maintain a report of vaccinations required;
- scan the herd and find out exactly which systems need to be patched;
- test the vaccinations and implement a rollback plan in case of further bugs;
- deploy the vaccinations on every elephant across the herd.

In an ideal world, organizations should be able to identify one particular day per month and identify this as 'Patch Day'. All vaccinations can be carried out on this occasion, thus making the cost of patching measurable and predictable. However, in order to 'buy the time' to do this, adequate protection needs to be provided to cover the herd between the monthly updates, and a process needs to be in place to allow some *ad hoc* injections for some vulnerabilities.

A good elephant husbandry or patch management solution therefore has to:

- understand the threat;
- provide an effective delivery mechanism;
- provide protection;
- provide early warning;
- adequately test;
- provide safe and effective delivery.

Choosing your elephant

When you first start to look after your elephant, there are a number of things that you need to do.

Check that it's healthy

The first is to ensure that it has had all of the latest vaccinations and inoculations and secondly, to check that it is free from any illness. Whilst these may seem like simple steps, both are full of potential pitfalls.

First, in order to ensure that your elephant has the latest protection, you will need to discover and understand what those latest cures are. The amount of time spent researching this and compiling a list of all the possible problems that you could have, and the list of available preventions/cures can prove to be very costly, and if you have more than one breed of elephant you may need to look in several different places. Even when you have built this list, it may be difficult to tell if there's a particular order in which to administer the 'shots' and whether there are any problems in combining them.

Secondly, how can you check that your elephant is free from any illness? The simple answer is to have it checked by an independent specialist. Just like acquiring domestic pets, the first thing to do is to get them checked over by a local vet.

Given the comparative value of an elephant, getting an expert to check for current problems and vulnerabilities will ensure that it is well protected and fit for purpose before bringing it home.

Doing this to your IT infrastructure means that you would have a full inventory of software assets and be able to understand the risk that each of these elements poses. You will therefore be in a position to prioritize which of these are the most critical and direct your efforts towards resolving these first.

Build infrastructure

The second element of good elephant husbandry is the creation of the infrastructure to look after your animal properly and to successfully package and deliver the immunization patches. Here, there are two key items to consider: 1) building of the infrastructure; and 2) developing and implementing processes.

There are two choices for building the infrastructure. You can either build a completely new infrastructure from scratch by implementing new software to deliver the patches, or you may already have existing software in place for other management purposes that can be adapted and reconfigured to deliver patches. There are several pieces of software available that have the sole purpose of delivering patches. These are especially useful when building an infrastructure from scratch. Alternatively, many of the framework enterprise management software solutions can be used and where an investment has already been made in this software, it may be more economical to investigate this option first.

The second item concerns processes. You will need to review how you currently take care of your elephant by examining your existing patch management process in order to make it more effective and efficient. You can then use best practice to implement a robust and reliable patch management regime.

Reduce risk

The third part of a good elephant husbandry solution is about reducing risk. Here, there are two main deliverables: 1) protection against the known; and 2) protection against the unknown.

Protection against the known is about ensuring that your elephant's anti-virus signatures are up-to-date and functioning correctly. Many organizations have purchased anti-virus licences but have no mechanism in place to ensure that their herd is properly protected. You need to review your existing anti-virus implementation and make recommendations for any necessary changes in process or configuration to reduce exposure to risk. If no anti-virus product exists, you will need to find and implement a suitable solution.

The second deliverable here is about protecting against the unknown. As mentioned earlier, the window for patching has decreased dramatically and therefore there are many periods of time in which no effective protection is available. The Computacenter service provides protection by identifying and preventing malicious behaviour before it can occur, thereby removing potential known and unknown security risks that threaten enterprise networks and applications. An agent is used which analyses behaviour rather than relying on signature matching, therefore the solution provides robust protection with reduced operational costs. For example, if one morning you visit your elephant and find it running around its pen very quickly, when normally it would be standing sedately in the corner, you would recognize that this is abnormal behaviour and something is amiss. Likewise if it's not eating its food, you may suspect something as being wrong. If you are constantly monitoring the behaviour of your animal, you can do something about it before the condition worsens or is spread to other animals.

Monitor threat

The fourth step is about providing additional intelligence on new and emerging threats and being prepared for forthcoming events.

In order to get further information on looking after your elephant, it might be a good idea to join a worldwide elephant keepers association or subscribe to an elephant-keeping magazine. This would tell you in advance if elephants on the other side of the world contract a new strain of elephant flu, which would help prepare you for a similar outbreak and enable you to take preventive action.

A good service should deliver personalized vulnerability and malicious code alerts to inform organizations of new potential threats. It should deliver notification of vulnerabilities and exploits as they are identified, providing timely, actionable information and guidance to help mitigate risks before they are exploited.

Test

The fifth step covers the testing and validation of patches. There have been instances where the deployment of a patch has either caused a system to fail, or introduced new vulnerabilities and made the elephant ill. To minimize this risk, it is important to test the patch on another animal or system that closely matches the anatomy or production environment.

Deliver

Finally, if at the end of the day, all you want to do is spend quality time with your elephant, why not let someone else take care of the feeding, grooming, medication and cleaning out of your pet? This could be done by an agent either remotely or, where there is an onsite managed service, the service can be delivered onsite. There are a number of deliverables here:

- backup of server (ensuring everything is ok before starting);
- packaging of the patch (getting it ready to feed);
- delivery of the patch (feeding);
- restoration of service;
- recovery if unsuccessful (cleaning up the mess);
- report (proving that the regime worked).

Before performing any operation on the server, a backup image would be taken. The patch will then be packaged by the appropriate delivery software and delivered to the device. The status of the device would be monitored to ensure that it is available and has been restored to active service. Should the device have not recovered, action would be taken to bring the device back to service and to restore the original configuration. A report would be produced detailing both successes and failures.

Summary

Successful elephant husbandry can only be achieved by fully understanding the vulnerabilities to which your elephant is susceptible, prioritizing these against the impact to the business, and then implementing a combination of tools and processes.

1.5

Gone phishing

Frank Coggrave, Websense

Heard about the scam where a fake e-mail is sent to your account posing as your bank or credit card provider? So have most people, but the number of phishing e-mails (as this particular scam is known) continues to rise at a shocking rate, with copycat websites opening as soon as one closes – so much so that phishing now represents the biggest form of online identity theft.

In its basic form, phishing works by persuading users to give away confidential information – such as their credit card details or online banking passwords – on replica bank or credit card provider websites. Since phishing first emerged more than a year ago, these bogus websites have become increasingly sophisticated in the way they mimic the original versions. They are also growing at a rapid rate: according to the Anti-Phishing Working Group, there were 2,625 unique phishing attacks in February 2005, representing an increase of 28 per cent on the previous month.

Phishing has become a global phenomenon, with international gangs launching attacks in multiple countries. Law authorities have begun to take phishing threats seriously, with investigations taking place both in the UK and the United States. In the UK, for example, the National Hi-Tech Crime Unit recently arrested 12 people on suspicion of laundering funds from bank accounts captured through phishing scams.

According to an article in the *New York Times*, phishing has a relatively high success rate, with between 5 and 20 per cent of e-mails resulting in a victim entering his or her private details into a bogus website. Unsurprising then, that phishing has left many victims in its wake, notably UK banks, which have paid out more than £1 million over the last 18 months.

As internet users have become more vigilant, phishing scams have had to evolve into more sophisticated security attacks. Earlier versions of phishing e-mails required the recipients to visit what appeared to be their bank or credit card provider's website and manually input their passwords. Now, a new breed of phishing e-mails simply requires the recipient to click on an embedded link in the e-mail. In the past, some phishing e-mails were poorly put together and clearly recognizable as fraudulent. By contrast, today's scams are more sophisticated and might relate to a quite plausible, but fictitious, credit card order. One click on the link activates the downloading of a Trojan worm to the user's computer. This piece of malware then monitors users' surfing activity and when they enter their bank URL, for example, transports them to a bogus website, giving criminals easy access to any confidential passwords and log-in details. To make matters worse, this is all conducted invisibly, without users realizing they have been victims of phishing until they check their financial statements and receive an unpleasant surprise.

This new form of phishing is also more likely to be successful, since there is no way a user can stop the keylogger application from downloading once they have clicked on the embedded link. It is also a lot easier to access a user's details via this method than by hacking into a bank account and could, potentially, be more lucrative.

Unlike the older generation of phishing scams, new phishing attacks carry the potential of affecting far more people than the original recipient. An employee working at home on his or her company laptop and receiving a phishing e-mail, for example, might click on a link, which could then infect other computers when his or her laptop is reconnected to the network. If a large number of employees are accessing their bank details online, this offers potentially massive spending power for hackers. It also could compromise a company's own finances and confidential information.

Seen in this light, phishing is a real security threat for businesses today. Some phishing attacks, such as Mimail-I, have combined a phishing attack and computer virus in one, launching a nasty, dual assault on businesses. Traditional hacking tools pose less of a risk since firewall technology is more advanced now and can prevent attacks from extending past the perimeter of a company's IT infrastructure.

Unfortunately, even guaranteeing that your organization is up-to-date with the latest security patches is not enough to prevent an attack. Anti-spam software fails to offer a guaranteed method of protection, since the words and phrases used in the fake web address often appear to be from a normal bank and might escape through the filter. In addition, such software places an extra burden on the shoulders of the administrative team, since they need to undertake the cumbersome tasks of checking every URL entering the firewall and creating a database of those that contain harmful malware applications or viruses.

Ultimately, these applications place the onus on employees to realize a security breach has taken place and to let the network administrator know that the rest of the network needs to be isolated from the infected system.

As attacks become more sophisticated, point security products are not enough on their own to fortify every corner of an organization's defences. Today's solution lies in a multi-layered approach to IT security. This has the dual benefits of preventing employees from accessing counterfeit websites via phishing attacks and, failing this, of protecting the corporate network from becoming infected by another machine.

As well as having a security application at the internet gateway level, researching the URLs entering the company's firewall and updating the URL database with security updates, an organization needs to ensure that, should the worst happen and an infected laptop reconnects to the network, it has in place a security application offering 'zero day' protection. This blocks unknown security threats by allowing only approved applications to run on corporate PCs and servers. In a worst case scenario, it prevents malware from running, providing a vital opportunity for network administrators to send out security updates to other PCs and servers.

With 'zero day' protection available from companies such as Websense, organizations no longer have to rely on their employees' vigilance in keeping up-to-date with new forms of phishing attacks, but can simply mind their own business.

1.6

The marketing dimension

Michael Harrison, Harrison Smith Associates

The single most important aspect of marketing is enhancement – and protection – of the **brand**. This applies equally to the company (Ltd or PLC) and to the public sector (government, local government or agency) because your clients' brand perception determines where you are in today's world. 'Client' can just as easily be a member of the public utilizing a public service, as a consumer of a product or service from a company.

But this is equally the management board's major concern – the protection and value of the brand is of prime importance. Remove trust in the brand through action or inaction and your stakeholders will very quickly seek your removal – and possibly subsequent housing by one of HM Prisons! Corporate governance applies – very, very specifically. As Turnbull made so clear, this applies just as much to the public sector as the private, and ignorance of the consequences of mistaken policies cannot ever be regarded as a valid excuse.

The most cursory review of what would happen to you if your brand's reputation fell through the floor must emphasize the importance of protecting it (and therefore yourself). But just how much time and energy do you give to this subject? Is this yet another 'must do' item that never gets to the top of the pile – unless something horrific has occurred, in which case it is too late?

Marketing also has a prime responsibility for communications – both external and internal. Therefore if you accept my arguments, not only does there have to be a complete review of your external information communications policy (and therefore everything that goes into enabling it), but there also has to be a total policy concerning the internal marketing of the need for information assurance (protection).

This is a marketing responsibility. Yes, it needs careful interrelationship with 'the IT department', but the recommendations about communication and availability of information can never be an IT decision. Why? Because how on earth can 'IT' know the relative value of every item of information that passes over the networks, and how can it possibly know when something must be kept confidential, whereas something else must be available at any time, whereas yet other items must be protected from any possibility of alteration? IT specialists cannot know – and while the owners of the information should tell them, this cannot be assumed. Therefore the area responsible for (and hopefully expert in) the whole communications issue must take overall responsibility under the guidance and policy set by the management board.

So what is different today? Why should all managers – especially senior managers – take a much closer interest in their information and how it affects their brand? What has this to do with 'online' business, and for that matter, are we all 'online' today so far as this subject is concerned?

My contention is a definitive 'yes'. No organization can pretend that it is not 'online' to some extent, and therefore it can – and probably will – be affected by cyberspace entities that had no part in our existence just a few years ago.

BI (before internet) life was simple, and marketing life especially so – not that we realized this at the time, of course. Then we had far more control of how we communicated and with whom – and what they were allowed to find out about us. Information was a commodity that we controlled, and in the instances where we lost control we were very unhappy about it, because the responsibility for what happened was normally very easy to identify. But even the loss of information control was usually very limited – leaking one snippet did not automatically lead to other exposures, certainly not to the publication of seriously important details.

The value of information was not recognized anything like as well as it should have been – but the excuse was that the threat to that information was very limited. Okay, a fire could burn the paperwork, and latterly the computer system could go AWOL – but we understood the need to have back-ups and parallel systems, so the danger was still not that bad. We were not connected to what I have described as the 'M25 Information Highway' running slap-bang through the middle of our organizations. We still had 'perimeters' that we could regard as being protected from external threats – and any attempt at breaching them involved actual physical break-in. We knew where we were, and we knew if anything had happened.

What is more, we controlled what anyone else knew about what had happened to us – more often than not including what our own staff knew about it. We had full control of our information; it was our tool to use as we wished (within reason). Now we are all in the internet age the rules have changed – or more importantly and accurately the lack of enforceable rules is the difference. But we have not made the necessary changes inside our organizations to guard against the 'new challenges'.

While this has a major marketing dimension to it, bluntly this should not be a 'marketing department decision'. Without question it is never an 'IT' decision. We are discussing a major policy change that requires full board approval, and regular and frequent board reviews.

That risk management is a fundamental board responsibility cannot be news, but in this chapter I want to emphasize the importance of the management of this (information) risk, both to the profitability and to the longer-term existence of the organization: *any* organization, of any size, in any sector.

What are the basic threats and opportunities, and why does the board need to understand them and take the overall risk policy decisions? What has this to do with marketing?

The marketing challenges

I have stated that this is neither an IT nor a marketing responsibility – but both of those departments have seriously important roles and responsibilities to bring the need for decisions to the formal attention of the board. Frequently these departments do not work together for the good of the organization as a whole. They do not recognize their joint responsibilities for the organization's most valuable asset, its information.

Marketing should – must – understand the value of every type of information, whereas IT should – must – be responsible for delivering, storing, presenting and protecting every type of information within the policies laid down. But they are not laid down by IT – they should be recommended by marketing, laid down by the board, actioned by IT.

Therefore marketing has a responsibility before the board can make those decisions – marketing has to identify and categorize different 'levels' of information, and be the catalyst to bring together all parts of the organization to agree the proposed rules, and then to obtain formal sign-off by the board.

Within our new 'e'-communicating society we have new tools that provide immense power to the user. But the word 'user' must not be confused with the word 'owner'. There are far too many ways for people to 'assume the role of user' when they have no right – in fact when they are breaking the rules, if not the law. The internal opportunities for 'information theft' today are enormous, and especially in organizations where identity theft can be relatively easy to arrange. The trouble is that this can also apply to external opportunists, sometimes just as easily.

The value and potential brand damage that this information theft provides is many times more costly than the equivalent only a few years ago. This is for two interrelated reasons: information is far more usefully available than it was before (because all users expect and demand this); plus the internet provides far greater opportunities for that information to be obtained, disseminated and used by people with 'black hats'.

There was always the challenge of the odd rogue member of staff, including the 'temp' (or the cleaner, or whoever) who was not exactly what he or she was supposed to be, but we felt secure from external attack, and an insider still had to take the information out of the premises physically, and was thus more likely to be caught.

So what had this to do with marketing? In those days, almost nothing. Security was seldom used as a differentiator. It is true that 'Safe as the Bank of England' was a saying from the past, but that was all about physical security – and more about the consumers' (or clients') property or deliverable than that of the host organization. Everyone was clear about whether or not they were a 'target'. You could identify your physical defences and contrast them with the value that an attacker might steal (such as cash, valuables and easily disposable items), or you could decide you were just not worth attacking! In retrospect, it was a nice, simple life. So marketing took security for granted, and certainly did not get directly involved, unless the organization happened to be a bank. Even then, 'security' meant one thing only: protection from actual physical loss (from being stolen, copied or destroyed).

Who thought of protecting things from being altered without anyone finding out until too late? Or from being rendered unavailable to your own key personnel for a crucial period of time? Anyway – who considered what negative affects such activities might have on the brand, and in those days would they have been particularly serious?

Today someone can do these things, and thus directly affect your reputation (and your brand) from the other side of the world, without actually meaning to do it! Certainly whether they meant to or not, they have no thought about the damage that they are doing – especially as it is at almost no cost to themselves in time, resources or risk.

The internet was originally built to allow communication amongst academic groups, known for their preference for sharing information. It was not supposed to be the world's 'trusted business backbone'. So we must take appropriate policy decisions before we continue to trust it with our 'Crown Jewels'.

And the marketing opportunities

As business-to-business, business-to-consumer, and government–public and public–government communications become more and more electronic and online, the need for information assurance becomes more absolute. We need to be re-assured! The organization that can provide that assurance will be our first – and possibly our only – choice. Those that cannot, and those that have been seen to fail, will be blacklisted. We need to know that our confidential information is genuinely protected against all three of the information assurance sub-sets:

- **Confidentiality**: that is, no one else can get at it.
- **Integrity**: that is, it will not be changed, and anything that we are sent has not been changed.
- **Availability**: that is, when it is needed it will be available, instantly if that is the requirement.

Therefore the obvious corollary is that the secure online business will obtain a differentiation that will give it very significant added value. The marketing messages will provide the stakeholders with considerable peace of mind – and therefore extra perception of corporate value. And – this is not a cynical comment – the internal marketing will be easier, especially upwards to the management board, because by creating the secure online business the board's own personal reputation and corporate governance responsibilities are protected.

However, the obvious caveat is that to promise security online, but not to be able to deliver that promise, is a serious mistake – which can be easily made through sheer ignorance of the threat and the vulnerabilities.

The expectation–experience equation

Some so-called 'hackers' carry out attacks just to be able to say that they have got through a specific organization's defences. You may claim to be secure – they may well try you out! 'They' might actually work for you – or have worked for you recently. To have an information assurance management system (IAMS) in place and working properly will provide you with the assurance that you require to make such a claim in the first place. But that is not the reason to have such a system; you must have it in order to conduct business electronically.

You must be secure online. There is no alternative if you want to continue in operation.

Enforcement; regulation; legislation; audit

This is no joke. For too long we have been attempting to operate within totally different communication conditions, opening ourselves up to immeasurable consequences, without a significant change in how we have been 'measured'.

No longer! Auditors and regulators (the FSA, NAO and so on) are becoming far more aware of the financial consequences of failure, and of the questions to ask – and the answers to question!

The government recently created a new department known as the Central Sponsor for Information Assurance (CSIA) – and it has already produced new policy guidelines for the whole of the public sector. It started with central government, moved on to the rest of the public sector – and the next target must be the private sector, for the very obvious reason that we are all interconnected and that we must be more responsible 'citizens', whether individual or corporate. For any organization's marketing function to ignore this would be a very serious mistake – and action is vital.

Become – and be seen to be – a secure online business, or face some very difficult questions from a variety of powerful sources, all under the heading of 'stakeholders'!

Summary

- A company's positive approach to security online will directly affect its marketing positioning and organizational differentiation. It will determine its very future existence.
- Security failure will destroy any organization's reputation, and thus end in total destruction. The consumer and the public will no longer forgive these errors, because they have such grave consequences.
- Information assurance is not a cost, it is a corporate investment that cannot be put off or ignored.
- Everyone is a potential target and no one can afford to ignore this subject. E-business and e-government demand the electronic exchange of ever-more important information, and the 'owner' must demand – and be given – total assurance.
- Marketing should identify and promote the internal and external advantages of having appropriate information security.
- Marketing and 'IT' must work together to achieve a perceived 'trusted status', and take responsibility for creating detailed positioning and differentiation messages for the management board to determine policy – including risk management profiles.
- Marketing must ensure that all communications are written in suitable language for each target audience – internal and external – otherwise the messages will not be understood.
- Finally, the United Kingdom has the 'Protecting Critical Information Infrastructures' initiative where senior management can be better informed about the risks and the solutions available – but in the language of the boardroom and not techno-speak. Frequently it helps the CIO and the other senior management to get these messages from the most senior government and commercial decision makers – and we will do our best to assist! Contact www.pcii-initiative.co.uk for more information.

2

Points of exposure

2.1

Web security

Suheil Shahryar, VeriSign UK

Introduction

In this chapter we take a look at the major web security threats and attacks. Our tour includes the following:

- internet security intelligence findings;
- security trends and threats;
- spotlight on phishing;
- a phishing case study;
- the correlation between web security and fraud;
- summary and conclusion.

The information comes from the VeriSign Security Intelligence Briefing reports of 2004. These are quarterly reports of current trends for internet growth, usage, security and online fraud and can be found on VeriSign's website (www.verisign.com).

Internet security intelligence findings

Growth of hybrid attacks

In 2004 there have been a growing number of hybrid attacks. By 'hybrid' we mean that they no longer simply create denial-of-service conditions and terminate, as did Code Red, SQL Slammer and many other attacks. In a series of hybrid attacks observed over the last quarter of 2004, hackers leveraged system exploits as the first stage in a larger information/identity theft attack.

Launch of social engineering attacks

Several complex attacks have also been launched during this time frame that not only exploit vulnerabilities in the Windows OS and Microsoft Internet Explorer, but also launch social-engineering attacks via AOL Instant Messenger, all as part of a larger effort to install keystroke-loggers in a victim's computer for the purpose of phishing.

Sophistication of exploit code increasing

Attackers have apparently been brushing up on their programming skills. Exploit code has become increasingly sophisticated. Sample exploits (those that can be quickly found online) used to be of very poor quality, requiring a skilled programmer to painstakingly edit the code to produce a working exploit. In contrast, recent sample exploit code has been surprisingly simple to make work. This refined skill on the part of the experts is in turn enabling junior hackers, aka 'script kiddies', to wreak havoc much more quickly.

Complexity of viruses and worms increasing

Persistence is apparent on the virus/worm front, where an almost constant stream of MyDoom, Bagle and Netsky mutations continue to appear. The complexity and sophistication of each variant has also been steadily increasing, as spammers align themselves with virus authors in an attempt to increase revenue.

Threats to PDAs and mobile computing devices

Viruses and worms also pose a threat to PDAs, mobile phones and other portable devices. In the last quarter of 2004, multiple pieces of malware began to mount a slow but steady attack on these mobile operating systems. Rapidly becoming the 'low hanging fruit' of network targets, mobile computing devices are just starting to become recognized by security managers.

New spam act in the United States

A new Federal law, the CANSPAM Act, came into force in the United States on 1 January 2004, effectively criminalizing the most profitable forms of commercial spam. Among other things, the new law provides stiff criminal penalties, prohibiting false or misleading headers and deceptive subject lines, and requiring commercial e-mailers to identify their content as an advertisement and provide a valid physical mailing address. For a more detailed description of the CANSPAM Act, see http://www.ftc.gov/bcp/conline/pubs/buspubs/canspam.htm.

Captured machines are the primary vehicle of net crime

Spam is the primary vehicle for each of the principal Net crimes, such as advance fee fraud, phishing fraud and work-at-home carding schemes. The use of networks of captured machines (botnets) to send spam is now routine. Botnets are also used to aggressively seed virus distributions and to perform distributed denial-of-service attacks.

Monetization trend of internet crime

Captured machines are traded between hacker gangs on both rental and freehold terms. Denial-of-service attacks are increasingly accompanied by extortion.

Theftware, a new phishing spyware

The problem of spyware is also gaining increased attention. Consumers are now alert to the threat posed by adware, programs that monitor the users surfing in order to deliver targeted advertising. While spam remains the primary tactic employed by phishing gangs, the use of phishing spyware known as theftware is increasing both in the number of attacks and their sophistication. Theftware allows the attackers to perform detailed surveillance of their target in order to enable a complex identity theft such as applying for a fraudulent mortgage in their name.

Rise of phishing matched by rise in carding

'Carding' is being used to convert the credentials into laundered funds or goods that can be fenced. A common tactic of carding gangs is the promotion 'work at home' schemes where gullible individuals are recruited to perform the parts of the process most likely to result in arrest. A 'Package Reshipper' recruit receives goods bought with a stolen credit card and forwards them to the carding ring via an international shipper. A 'Money Mover' recruit performs a similar function with stolen money.

Multi-vector worms becoming a serious threat

Multi-vector worms can simultaneously exploit several vulnerabilities in one attack and have a longer shelf life than single exploit worms. The most effective and potentially damaging example of this breed is called 'phatbot', 'agobot', or 'gaobot'. Its source code is public and readily available. The resource makes it relatively easy for hackers to add new exploit code to a platform.

Faster release of exploit code

Aided by toolkits, there is even more rapid development and deployment of exploit code following the public announcement of vulnerabilities. Based on these trends, users should now expect exploit code to appear shortly after the announcement of new vulnerabilities, and enterprises must move faster to test and install vendor patches to fix vulnerabilities before exploitation occurs.

Mass-mailers continue propagating worms

The first half of 2004 included many successful mass-mailers such as Novarg, MyDoom, Lovegate and Netsky, to name just a few. VeriSign noted a new, rapidly escalating arms race of worm writers versus user education. Worm writers use increasingly clever means to trick users into opening e-mails and associated attachments. Anti-virus software vendors are getting better at rapid deployment of vulnerability signatures. Unfortunately, 'zero-day' attacks are a troublesome concern for enterprises.

Backdoor codes leading to Worm Wars

There is an increasing trend for mass mailers to include a 'backdoor' code component that allows the writer or other worm writers to surreptitiously upgrade the executable. This tactic enables 'Worm Wars' wherein new worms exploit backdoors left by previous worms.

Registration of cousin address by fraudsters

Phishers use social engineering to register 'cousin' domains, which sound similar to the company they are trying to impersonate. Ninety-three per cent of all phishing advertisements were sent from forged or spoofed e-mail addresses.

Camouflaged spoofed address deceiving web users

Lately, phishers lure victims by forging an e-mail 'from' address and using browser camouflage techniques such as floating a JavaScript window over the Address Bar to fool people into thinking they are viewing a legitimate, branded site. The phisher's capture site thereby disguises its URL address with a legitimate site's address. The rogue JavaScript remains installed even after leaving the phisher's site. About 5 per cent made no attempt to hide the fraudulent 'from' address with a cousin or spoofed address.

Routines for snooping browser activity

A phisher could easily write additional JavaScript routines to record everything sent or received through your web browser until closing the application.

High false positives in automated fraud detection

In scaling risk detection operations, merchants must trade off between increased automation and greater human oversight. Data for the 2003 holiday season displayed a tendency by merchants to favour increased automation over human oversight. Merchants automated a significant amount of their risk analysis, probably due to peak transaction volumes experienced during the holiday shopping season. Of all the rejected transactions during this period, 84 per cent were automatically rejected by risk detection systems. Merchants eventually accepted about 70 per cent of the transactions that had been pulled for manual review. The bias to reject orders with automated technologies but accept orders with human oversight may have resulted in merchants turning away a significant number of legitimate sales. Integration of automated fraud detection and fraud intelligence technologies with daily e-commerce operations can limit false-positive rejections and help capture legitimate business. Bringing a greater degree of fraud intelligence to bear on each transaction is essential to managing effectively the resources applied to risk management. Fraud intelligence is a key enabler for the overall scalability of the web as a sales channel.

Simple rules being favoured for screening

Most merchants rely on a limited set of rules for risk identification. Of frequently used screening rules, Address Verification Service and Card Security Code (a credit card verification number which allows the merchant to ascertain that the shopper does have the credit card, known as CVV2 for Visa, CVC2 for MasterCard and CID for Discover and American Express, the CSC three-digit number is typically located on the back of a credit card) are most popular. About 70 per cent of merchants using VeriSign's Fraud Protection Services limit themselves to the simple rules. This practice is probably due to a lack of familiarity with more sophisticated screening logic, or the perception that more screening could increase the number of transactions merchants may erroneously reject or have to manually review. VeriSign predicts merchants will eventually need to apply greater fraud intelligence as a way to improve risk detection and overall operational efficiency.

Significance of customer errors in card information entry

Transaction data suggests that 25 per cent of e-commerce transactions flagged by a merchant's risk detection system may stem from mis-keyed or inaccurate customer information. Examples include inaccurate entry of CVV2 numbers, postcodes and credit card numbers. These inaccuracies are not always mistypes/typos. Customers may correctly type in new addresses that they have not yet updated with their bank, thereby failing AVS checks. While the risk system is correct to flag inaccurate information, the vast majority of these transactions are not fraudulent but merely indications of human error. Websites that store password protected customer profiles can reduce input error; however, the storage of financial information significantly raises the business's data security requirements.

Limitations of card screening rules

Address Verification Service (AVS) and Card Security Code (CSC) are security techniques merchants typically use to increase the trust in a customer transaction. In 83 per cent of web transactions, merchants used AVS as a form of risk intelligence. CSC was used in less than 40 per cent of transactions. Merchants receive an unambiguous match for AVS in just 54 per cent of transactions, indicating that the purchaser correctly knows the street and postcode of the billing address.

Internet security trends and threats

The data in Table 2.1.3 is a near mirror of the monthly Microsoft patch cycle. Mixed among a barrage of scanning and port-enumeration activity that serves as perpetual attack white noise, we observed the clear presence of 60-day-or-newer system vulnerabilities under attack.

Table 2.1.1 Top countries by total volume of fraudulent transactions*

Rank	Q4 2003	Q1 2004	Q2 2004	Q3 2004
1	United States	United States	United States	United States
2	UK	Canada	Israel	Vietnam
3	Nigeria	Indonesia	Canada	Indonesia
4	Canada	Israel	Ghana	UK
5	Israel	UK	Nigeria	Taiwan
6	Indonesia	India	UK	Canada
7	Germany	Turkey	Indonesia	Israel
8	Ireland	Nigeria	Germany	Switzerland
9	Ghana	Germany	India	France
10	Denmark	Malaysia	Turkey	Germany

* *Note*: The country of origin is determined by the IP address used for the transaction. It is possible that hackers use proxies or break into ISP infrastructure in other countries to hide their true origin.

Table 2.1.2 Top countries by percentage of total risky payment transactions*

Rank	Q4 2003	Q1 2004	Q2 2004	Q3 2004
1	Nigeria	Indonesia	Cameroon	Macedonia
2	Israel	Nigeria	Nigeria	Nigeria
3	Ireland	Pakistan	Indonesia	Ghana
4	Lebanon	Ghana	Slovenia	Vietnam
5	Denmark	Israel	Brunei	Egypt
6	Turkey	Egypt	Brunei	Indonesia
7	Ghana	Turkey	Israel	Taiwan
8	Egypt	Lebanon	Kenya	Jordan
9	Pakistan	Bulgaria	Lebanon	Israel
10	Russian Federation	India	Romania	Switzerland

*Note: Countries were selected based upon the number of risky transactions that originated from the identified IP addresses from that nation. Transactions are deemed risky based upon review of multiple fraud screen filters, including identification of stolen credit card numbers, comparison of shipping and mailing addresses for discrepancies, and other techniques.

Table 2.1.3 Top attacks seen during Q2 and Q3 2004

Rank	Q1 2004	Q2 2004	July 2004	August 2004	September 2004
1	POP3 Authorization overflow attempt	Telnet Server 2000 rexec password overflow attempt	Windows RPC race condition exploitation	RExec password overflow attempt	Netscape NSS SSLv2 library Client Hello with pad challenge length overflow attempt
2	Microsoft Windows ASN.1 Library buffer overflow	DDOS shaft synflood	ICMP Ping Flood	Netscape NSS SSLv2 library Client Hello with pad challenge length overflow attempt	NNTP article post without path attempt
3	RPC mounted UDP export request	ASN.1 BER Length Overflow Heap Corruption	MS-SQL version overflow attempt	MS-SQL Slammer Worm attempt	MS-SQL version overflow attempt
4	HTTP Client URL Argument Overflow Attack	ICMP Ping Flood	SYN Flood	ICMP Ping Flood	Microsoft SSLv3 library invalid Client Hello attempt
5	WEB-PHP content-disposition memchr overflow	SYN Flood	PCT Client_Hello overflow attempt	MS-SQL version overflow attempt	MS-SQL stack based overflow attempt
6	SMTP Content-Transfer-Encoding overflow attempt	RPC DCOM overflow attempt	TCP port scan detected	Microsoft SSLv3 library invalid Client Hello attempt	RPC portmap request NFS UDP
7	Mail message contains suspicious ZIP file	RPC portmap request NFS UDP	FTP Client format string attack attempt	Microsoft Windows ASN.1 library buffer overflow attempt	Netscape NSS SSLv2 library Client Hello challenge length overflow attempt
8	WWW General cgi-bin Attack	PCT Client_Hello overflow attempt	DCE RPC Locator Service overflow attempt	RPC portmap request NFS UDP	ICMP Ping Flood
9	Shell interpreters used to execute commands on Web servers	MS-SQL version overflow attempt	LSASS buffer overflow attempt	Netscape NSS SSLv2 library Client Hello challenge length overflow attempt	SMTP – suspicious attachments (PIF extension)
10	TCP port scan has been detected	RPC mounted export request	UDP RPC DCOM overflow attempt	Cisco catalyst command execution attempt	SMB remote activation request attempt

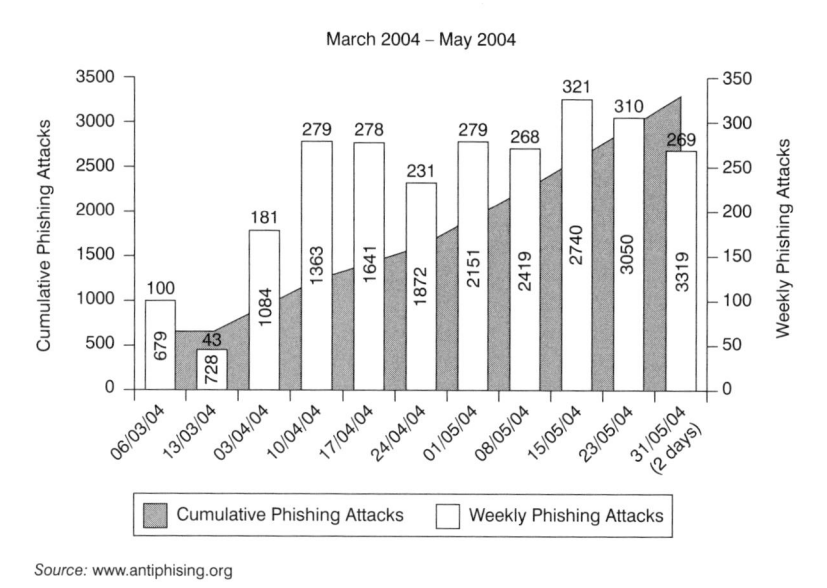

Figure 2.1.1 The incidence of phishing in 2004

Spotlight on phishing

Phishing e-mails are sent out consistently throughout the week, although VeriSign found a spike between the hours of 9.00 pm and 4.00 am – the period when IT staffers are either on call or few in numbers. VeriSign found phishing advertisements directed users to capture sites located outside the United States 37 per cent of the time, with a concentration primarily in countries such as Korea, China, Poland, Brazil, Taiwan, Singapore, Australia and Indonesia.

Phishing creates huge financial, reputation and brand equity exposures for the financial institutions, e-commerce sites and other organizations whose customers are usually the targets of such attacks. According to Gartner, phishing attacks targeted 57 million internet users during the past year. On average, 3 to 5 per cent of all individuals who received a phishing e-mail responded and became victims of the fraud. (See Figure 2.1.1.)

Model of a phishing attack

There are three basic phases in a phishing attack: preparation, attack and data recovery. (See Figure 2.1.2.)

Preparation phase

During this phase the phisher will:

- prepare the fraudulent advertisement;
- purchase or harvest victim e-mails;
- prepare the capture site (see definition below).

Attack phase

The attack begins when the phisher sends a fraudulent advertisement to the victim.

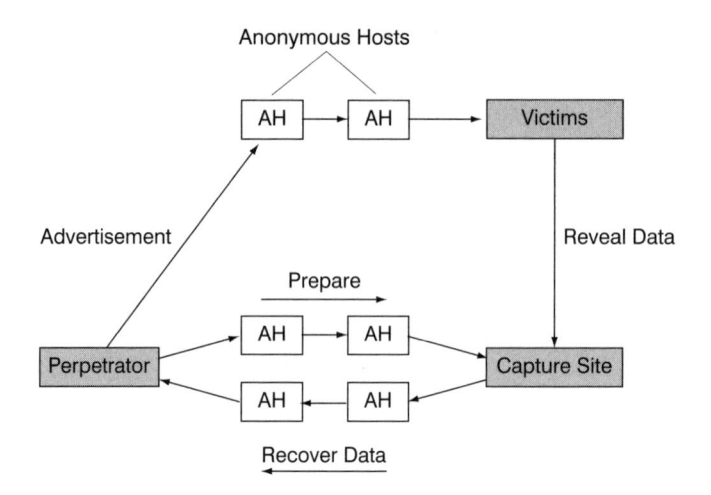

Notes
Capture site. The capture site is the machine that obtains the stolen access credentials from the victims. This is almost always a website.
Advertisement. It is unlikely that victims will discover a phishing attack site by chance, so advertising the capture site is usually required. The advertisement usually impersonates the identity of the capture site. The most common impersonation mechanisms are spam and domain name registrations.
Recovery of data. Since the capture site is typically located on some form of anonymous host, the perpetrator needs some means to recover the data obtained.

Figure 2.1.2 Model of a phishing attack

Data recovery phase

In this phase, the phisher will collect the information that the victims revealed to the capture site. For the perpetrator to realize a profit from the phishing activity he or she must make some use of the stolen credentials. In the case of stolen credit card numbers this process is known as 'carding'. The use of the stolen credentials can start immediately after a victim reveals them. In most cases a perpetrator will use a series of anonymous hosts to avoid identification. It is equally important for the perpetrator to conceal the creation of the capture site, the source of phishing spam, and the recovery of encrypted data.

What enterprises can do

A comprehensive solution for phishing should include strategies to prevent, detect and respond to attacks.

Prevention

Preventing fraud related to phishing attacks begins with policy, process and education. A communication plan for safeguarding personally identifiable information begins with assessing current policies and processes, implementing educational programmes for employees and end users, and developing a response plan to phishing attacks. An effective communication campaign should tell end users to stop, think and ask when presented with a questionable e-mail request for personal information. A scam will work only if users are tricked into revealing personal information.

Recommended phishing prevention guidelines

Stop: Users should never reveal a credit card number unless they are making a purchase.

Think: Is it likely that a bank would lose its customers' personal information? Banks never forget credit card numbers. Merchants never need a card number unless you are making a purchase.

Ask: E-mail that discourages discussion with other people is probably attempting to perpetrate fraud. Users should verify questionable e-mail from a bank with a phone call to the customer service department. Bank websites may provide other information such as an alert for a current fraud scheme.

Digital signatures on e-mails

Digital signatures provide a high degree of assurance of e-mail origination and that the contents have not been modified. The authentication provided within the SPF/Sender-ID Framework is acceptably strong for spam prevention and is the best currently available. It is available in a form that is suitable for ubiquitous deployment such that every e-mail message is authenticated. However, to meet all the requirements that are desirable in a strategic anti-phishing solution, a stronger authentication mechanism is required – one that provides greater resistance to attack and also allows for e-mail users to be provided with conspicuous proof of the authenticity of legitimate e-mail messages. Similarly, cryptographic authentication is routinely used to secure e-commerce transactions via the SSL protocol and software downloads using the Authenticode protocol.

Techniques to reduce e-mail address abuse

E-mail addresses are often gathered by using robots or spiders that crawl the web. All parties that publish e-mail addresses are strongly encouraged to help prevent harvesting. Spammers are interested in harvesting large numbers of addresses with the least effort possible. Even simple measures show a marked reduction in the number of times an address is harvested.

Prevention: If you must expose e-mail addresses, then

- spell out the special characters eg, securitybriefing AT verisign DOT com;
- display it as a graphic;
- use explicit html equivalents.

Newsgroups, standards groups and discussion boards: Anyone who has posted a message to a public newsgroup is exposed to spam. Some groups archive the discussions. Some groups are closed and place appropriate safeguards to limit exposure.

Prevention: Use an e-mail address specifically established for participation in public group discussions. This will enable better monitoring and disposal of spam.

Brute-force attacks on mail servers: Here, an attempt is made to send every conceivable combination of letters that form names. Short e-mail addresses suffer the most eg, bob@foo.com. The e-mail addresses that generated responses are marked as active.

Prevention: Spammers sometimes harvest addresses through 'dictionary' attacks on mail servers, trying a list of common usernames against the domain name of the e-mail server. Most mail servers now provide mechanisms to defeat this type of attack by limiting the number of responses to queries from a given IP address.

Directory harvesting attacks on mail servers
Prevention: Many mail server software packages have features for preventing dictionary attacks, usually by slowing down or dropping connections after a sender makes multiple attempts to send e-mail to a non-existent address. For example, Sendmail includes the BadRcptThrottle configuration option. For other mail server software, see your server's documentation or contact your software vendor.

Google searches: A simple search of '@*.com' results in over a 100 million hits. Of course, one can simply buy CDs full of e-mail addresses rather than do the work, but it is easy to write a parser to extract e-mail addresses from the results of these searches.

Prevention: Nothing can be done about this, other than limiting the exposure of your e-mail address using the above preventive suggestions.

Disclosure proof credentials

Adoption of disclosure proof credentials is a longer-term strategy for reducing or eliminating the risk of credential disclosures. Most financial transactions are currently authenticated with static identifiers such as an account number or Social Security number. The security offered by these identifiers declines with each transaction requiring disclosure. A public key credential embedded in a smartcard or other token format allows a holder to self-authenticate with a secret key without disclosing the secret. A one-time use authenticator generated by either a token device or other trustworthy means provides an attractive alternative form of disclosure proof credential. A number of European banks have already taken the first step in this process and now issue their customers sheets of passwords with a scratch-off coating. To log into the online banking site, the customer scratches off the next box on the card to reveal the password he or she should use. The bank keeps track of the passwords as they are used and sends out a new card when the customer reaches the end of the old one.

WEB SECURITY 43

> **Monitoring the internet**: With web crawlers, spam filters, and similar tools, MSSPs can monitor the internet for 'cousin' websites on a 24/7 basis.
>
> *Response – calling the ISPs to shut down the site*: The longest part of an attack time line is the interval between discovery of the phishing attack and takedown of the capture site. VeriSign believes reducing this time interval offers the best near-term opportunity for stopping fraud by phishing. Tracing the source of hacker attacks, such as phishing, is largely a manual process. Although automated tools exist for tracing attacks within a single network connected to the internet, communication between the networks requires human intervention. Attackers exploit the size of the internet to conceal their traces. The trail of an attack typically involves multiple jurisdictions, time zones and languages. Most phishing attacks are hosted at sites hosted by innocent parties. Processes improving notification between the response centre and the ISPs responsible for the machines that are the source of the attack would allow the time taken before takedown occurs to be very significantly reduced.

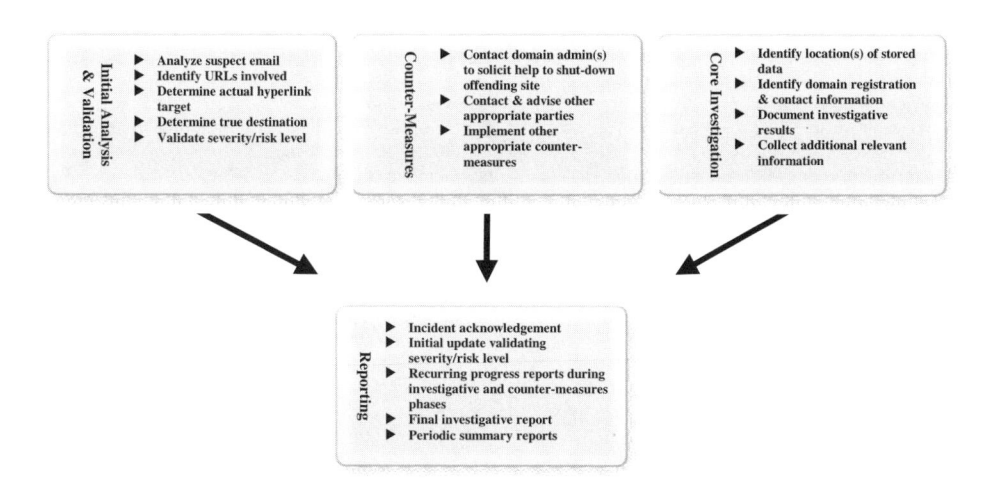

Initial Analysis & Validation
- Analyze suspect email
- Identify URLs involved
- Determine actual hyperlink target
- Determine true destination
- Validate severity/risk level

Counter-Measures
- Contact domain admin(s) to solicit help to shut-down offending site
- Contact & advise other appropriate parties
- Implement other appropriate counter-measures

Core Investigation
- Identify location(s) of stored data
- Identify domain registration & contact information
- Document investigative results
- Collect additional relevant information

Reporting
- Incident acknowledgement
- Initial update validating severity/risk level
- Recurring progress reports during investigative and counter-measures phases
- Final investigative report
- Periodic summary reports

Figure 2.1.3 Response process

The correlation between web security and fraud

VeriSign sampled two days of online transactions and recorded their origins (IP addresses). From these transactions we filtered out a number of IP addresses, including ones from the United States, Canada, Japan, Australia and parts of Europe (France and the UK). What remained were the sources of transactions from high-risk countries. One from the payment side matched the IP addresses found on ISC's suspicious list, indicating a high likelihood that the IP addresses used to launch network-based attacks are also likely to be used to commit online payment fraud, and vice versa.

Table 2.1.4 A phishing case study (March 2004)

The preparation -- approximately 4:00 am PST	Attack begins at 9:17 am PST
The phishers ■ Obtained access onto an anonymous host server at an ISP in Tacoma, WA ■ Found an unprotected FTP share ■ Uploaded a rootkit onto the server ■ Hacked into the administrative account ■ Created new logins into the terminal services for the server ■ Gained free access to all hosted websites on the hacked server ■ Set up the capture site as an unlinked page off an otherwise legitimate website, instead of using any cousin URLs ■ Spoofed the 'from' address in the e-mail ■ Sent out the fraudulent advertisements using a standard PERL mailer utility (logging from server logs and mail server activity logs show that the scam mails were initially sent out at 9:17 am) ■ Covered his tracks by deleting the mail list once the e-mails went out	The phishers sent the following fraudulent e-mail to customers: --- --- >>> "XXX" < > 03/11/04 10:19AM >>> Dear Customer, We are working hard to eliminate accounts that are no longer active. You can help us to finalize this process by confirming your account details. Thank you for choosing XXX. We look forward to providing you industry-leading service. Sincerely, XXX --- ---
Discovery – 9:42 am PST	**The take down -- 9:47 am PST**
VeriSign Fraud Team: ■ Became aware of the scam e-mail at 9:42 am (25 minutes after attack launched) ■ Analysed a copy of the e-mail ■ Clicked on the link ■ Confirmed that it was a scam ■ Determined where the capture site was hosted ■ Found that clicking on the link took the victim to a site that looked like the login page. No matter what data was entered for username and password, the phisher's site then took the victim to the page below that collected further information. ■ Investigated the mail itself, starting with the internet headers. These are easy enough for the phisher to spoof, but it still gives a good starting point for further investigation	VeriSign Fraud Team: ■ Contacted the ISP in Tacoma through their listed ARIN "abuse@" contacts ■ Got voice mail ■ Contacted them using our database of contacts ■ Got a live person ■ Let them know that they may have a server being compromised, and that they are hosting a scam page. By 9:47 am (5 minutes after VeriSign became aware of the attack) the scam page is taken down. We were able to get the site down so quickly in part because the site was domestic
Investigation – about 10:47am	
VeriSign Fraud Team: ■ Received a copy of the scam site payload in our hands ■ Started forensics investigation ■ Received the FTP logs ■ Obtained the details of where and when the phisher started this from. FTP logs show that the phishers accessed the servers from three separate IPs, two from Romania and one from Spain. This particular site was lightweight and basically just harvested data and sent it to a free e-mail account ■ Immediately initiated contact with the e-mail provider in order to get the mail account shut down	

We believe the correlation exists because this fits the hacking behaviour of serious hackers. First, hackers tend to attack a system to gain sensitive information such as credit cards or account logins that they can sell to other hackers, or they attack a system to gain privileged access (root access) to the machine, which can also be traded with other hackers or used to launch follow-on attacks. Second, hackers tend to use compromised hosts or proxies to hide their tracks – a hacker we have observed used as many as 85 different hosts for this purpose. Once hackers gain access to a machine, they tend to install a specific piece of software called 'rootkit', which gives them privileged access to the system. The rootkit ensures the anonymity of the hacker by automatically deleting the important logs on the system that can be used to trace the hacker's activities. Third, after privileged access is obtained and rootkit installed, the hacker can then use the compromised machine to attack other machines without being traced.

Our fraud study demonstrates that hackers will also use privileged access to installed automated software to launch carding attacks at a merchant's check-out page, or use the compromised machine as a way of committing payment fraud using somebody else's credit card without being traced.

Case 1: IP address registered to a Ukrainian ISP

In late November 2003, the Payments Fraud Protection team at VeriSign identified a series of fraudulent credit card transactions originating from an IP address registered to a Ukrainian ISP. The perpetrators attempted to siphon funds from stolen credit cards into a Ukrainian bank. This scheme, known as a 'credit back', is common among organized criminal groups in the region. The Payments Fraud Protection team blocked all transactions and then traced the criminal group's activity back to 48 compromised IP addresses.

This case data was shared with the VeriSign M&A team for correlation with security events data. One IP address had more than 2,200 hits with security events/MSS data collected during this same timeframe. The associated attack patterns indicated that several VeriSign customer infrastructures were being probed/scanned via established, common ports. Data showed attempts were being made to gain access to the customers' networks via the most commonly used ports. The perpetrator first attempted to discover which ports were allowing traffic through the firewall and then used that knowledge for deeper network penetration. VeriSign analysts quickly determined activity from the IP address was highly suspicious. The use of these ports (53 and 113) is not suspicious by itself, but traffic patterns became critically suspect when paired with a known fraud source that was also confirmed as a source of potentially malicious activity. VeriSign found that the source was attempting to use a DNS port to gain access and change DNS records on the customers' internal DNS server. The targeted MSS customers were contacted immediately and steps were taken to cleanse and further harden their DNS servers.

Case 2: IP address registered to the US Government

In mid-December 2003, the Payments Fraud Protection team identified a broad scale carding attack. The team isolated the attack as originating from three IP addresses, which were then reported to the M&A team for further research. These addresses were registered to a department of the US Government. VeriSign's Managed Security Services' monitoring and correlation engines recorded more than 14,000 communications to and from one of these three IP addresses during the same time period. All this traffic traversed web-related port (80), yet analysts were unable to bring up valid web traffic associated with these IP addresses. This anomaly raised the threat profile associated with these IP addresses to critically suspect. Firewall logs for the targeted customers confirmed that the firewalls had allowed inbound web traffic from these critically suspect IP addresses. VeriSign immediately alerted the targeted MSS customers to the situation. The Government agency was unaware of why any business traffic would be directed from these addresses and is currently researching the situation.

Summary and conclusion

The United States leads all countries in total volume as a source of fraud, but a handful of overseas countries continue to lead in rates of fraud (see Table 2.1.1). In terms of the top countries by percentage of total risky payment transactions, new countries are joining the group every quarter (see Table 2.1.2). The emergence of these new countries could be due to the continued rollout of high-speed internet access across the world, which allows more users to access the internet.

While the most prevalent attacks employ the most readily available tools ('script-kiddie' exploit tools), one must take a broad view of the IT-security landscape. Patching can no longer be viewed as a luxury, but a requirement that must be addressed within weeks if not days of release. Systems not connected to the internet are still at grave risk if they leave the office and become attached to home LANs. Machines infected while connected to cable or DSL networks and then returned to the office, are a prime target in the hybrid attack model. These systems now place internal networks at risk of data being siphoned outside the company.

A 47 per cent correlation between VeriSign fraud data and sources of security attacks was found from an analysis of the two data sets. However, most web merchants use a limited amount of intelligence for making risk-related transaction decisions.

It is clear that attackers are honing their craft. They are getting not only faster but more creative; they are widening their net and becoming increasingly persistent.

Another new trend is the improvement and rapid evolution of the multi-vector worm. Its ability to exploit effectively multiple attack vectors over time suggests the day of single-exploit worms is numbered. The most effective and potentially damaging example of this breed is called 'phatbot', 'agobot', or 'gaobot'. They are a serious threat to every enterprise.

Hybrid attacks are a growing threat to the enterprise and are increasingly leveraging system exploits as the first stage in a larger information/identity theft attack.

It is worth noting that quick exploitation has not followed announcements of all major vulnerabilities. For example, the complex vulnerability in Check Point Software's Firewall-1 implementation of ISAKMP has avoided public exploitation despite the high 'attraction factor' of firewalls as targets. This suggests that the cracking community cannot quickly exploit vulnerabilities that are more complex in nature. Nevertheless, when and if more complex exploits are released, distribution network and worm toolkits will ensure their fast, effective use.

Phishers no longer send crude, misspelled e-mails in plain text. Phishing advertisements are now more difficult to detect because they seem like legitimate contact by known companies.

The number of capture sites hosted internationally are and will carry on increasing because they are more difficult to shut down than domestic-hosted sites. Hurdles for closure of international capture sites include different laws; some countries do not prohibit impersonation of an organization's website. Other obstacles include language barriers and different time zones and business hours.

PDAs, mobile phones and other portable devices are increasingly coming under attack, and are now starting to become recognized by security managers.

In 2004 both spam and phishing have become more aggressive. Like the strategic solution for the problem of spam, a strategic solution to phishing will require changes to the internet infrastructure and, ultimately, changes to the financial services infrastructure. This is likely to take several years. The phishing problem is a result of the fact that the existing e-mail infrastructure allows any party to impersonate any other party at will. The customer authentication problem has traditionally been viewed in one direction only – authentication of the customer to the bank. It is now time to pay serious attention to authentication in the reverse direction – authentication of the bank to the customer.

2.2

Broadband

Paul Collins, NTL Business

When the MSBlast 'worm' attack was at its peak, a UK-based security company ran an experiment to find out just how much of a threat it posed. A PC with no anti-virus or firewall software was connected to the internet; it took just 27 seconds for the worm to infect it.

In a similar experiment, the UK internet service provider (ISP) PSINet set up an anonymous dummy server to test levels of internet hacking. It found that its server was maliciously attacked 467 times within just 24 hours of being installed.

Before I am accused of wanton scaremongering, I would stress that these are two isolated incidents and that each was set up with the express aim of proving just how vulnerable a PC connected to the internet can be to attacks from viruses, worms and hackers. That said, both incidents are pertinent to the subject matter to be discussed in this chapter. Why? Because they illustrate the pervasive and non-discriminatory nature of threats from the internet. They plainly show that it is not just big multinational corporations and government bodies that are singled out and targeted due to the sensitive and potentially valuable nature of the data they hold.

If a single PC or anonymous server can be breached so swiftly and so comprehensively, so can your business – unless you have adopted the appropriate safeguards. In fact, according to analyst firm Gartner Group, 20 per cent of enterprises will experience a serious (beyond a virus) internet security incident by 2005. Of those that do, the clean-up costs of the incident will be half as much again as the prevention costs would have been.

The statistics speak for themselves. But the remit of this chapter is not simply to expose the extent of the issue – that it is a serious problem for UK plc has surely never been up for debate. The aim of this chapter is specifically to examine how broadband relates to security, and how companies should review their security policies and safeguards as a result.

Broadband = broader threat?

The simple answer is – it doesn't have to be. With yesterday's dial-up, or 'dial on demand' services, your computer only connected to the internet when it had something to send, such as an e-mail or a request to load a web page. Once there was no more data to be sent, or after a certain amount of idle time, the computer disconnected the call. In other words, you chose when you wanted to be online and told your PC to call your ISP, log into its server and use its services – be it e-mail or web surfing.

Broadband connections, on the other hand, are by definition 'always on' because there is no call set up when your computer has something to send. The computer is always on the network, ready to send or receive data at any time. With broadband – be it via cable, DSL or leased line technology – your PC is connected to the web whenever it is switched on.

Always on, always vulnerable

While broadband is not inherently more dangerous than dial-up, the chances of an intrusion are higher simply because your computer is online and therefore accessible for longer. And since your computer acts as a gateway to the rest of your network, your entire network can be vulnerable for the length of your online session.

There is also another factor to consider. Each time one computer communicates with another via the internet, this is done via an IP (Internet Protocol) connection. Each computer connected to the web has a dedicated 'IP address' – just like a home or business has a dedicated postal address in the offline world. This IP address is unique to that computer, and identifies it from all other computers connected to the web. In most cases, corporate networks and ISPs economize on the number of IP addresses they use by sharing a pool among a large number of users. This means that your IP address is likely to be dynamically allocated by your ISP each time you log on, giving your computer a different IP address on each call. Since a broadband connection is always on, your computer's IP address will change less frequently than on dial-up, thus making it more of a fixed target for attack. If you are always connected, you are easy to find. In fact, according to a recent Yankee Group report, a broadband connection increases the likelihood of attack fivefold.

All this does not bode well for the increasing number of businesses – particularly smaller firms, typically without the resources to devote to protect systems adequately – that are adopting broadband in ever greater numbers. It serves to highlight the need for businesses of all sizes to select their broadband supplier carefully, and to ensure that the appropriate security measures are in place (more of this later).

Casting the net wider

It is not just the technical capabilities of broadband that we need to consider in this. The very nature of broadband and its ability to exchange more data with more people more quickly have opened up entirely new ways of working, all of which have their impact on a company's security.

Consider, for example, the exchange of a large, complex document such as a new business tender or contractual agreement. In the past, such documents would have been prohibitively large for an online exchange, and would simply have been printed out and sent by recorded delivery. With broadband, however, these confidential and often highly sensitive documents can be sent and received by e-mail in a matter of seconds. Are they always encrypted or password protected? The truth is, not often enough.

Broadband has also opened up the opportunity to communicate with partners, customers and suppliers like never before. The advent of intranets, extranets and private website pages means that your data – sometimes even your entire network – is available to more people, more of the time. Add to that the growing number of home-workers, tele-workers and wireless workers, even those who only access their corporate e-mail occasionally, and without the necessary security safeguards your network can start to look about as watertight as a sieve.

The nature of the beast

So we have established that your network could be vulnerable to a security breach, but what would that breach look like, and what impact would it have on your business? The topics of viruses, worms, Trojan horses and spam are covered in some depth in other chapters, so I will not dwell too long on them here. Suffice to say that an unprotected network is to a virus writer like blood to a shark – one temptation too far.

As far as hacking is concerned, thousands of companies are still turning a blind eye – despite the fact that it has firmly entered the internet mainstream. In previous times, hacking was perceived to be the preserve of hacked-off IT PhDs with an axe to grind. These days, anyone with a broadband connection and a little know-how can find their way into many companies' networks.

According to the CBI, two-thirds of its members have suffered serious cybercrime attacks. Yet only seven hackers have been charged with criminal offences over the last two years. This is due to a combination of weak e-crime laws and the fact that many attacks go unreported: it is as if there's a feeling of shame associated with admitting you have been a victim, and a concern that customers will lose faith in your business or services.

Possibly the biggest question is not 'What do I have to hide?' but 'Who is in control?' An unprotected computer is not just at risk of an incoming attack; it can also become an unwitting accessory to a crime. With access to your computer, an accomplished hacker can quickly establish it as a staging area for the exchange of illegal files, a mail relay for unsolicited commercial e-mail (spam), or a participant in a distributed denial of service attack.

The NetAction Advisory Board has identified five 'A's of security:

Awareness

Your computer is one among millions of other computers networked together. As a broadband subscriber, your computer is generally permanently and reliably connected to the internet, and your connection is quickly responsive. You have physical control over your machine, and can take informed action to protect your resources and files.

Authentication and Authorization

If you do not want to allow global access to your files, you may need to set log-ins and passwords to limit your computer's users. Authentication means verifying the user. Authorization is allowing that user access to your system. Verifying users of your machine can help you track the activity in files and resources.

Access control

To further limit access to your resources, you may wish to set permissions on individual files. For instance, you may have a text file that anyone can read. This is called global access. Another file may only be read by anyone in a special group that you design. This is group access. A third file may only be readable by you: that is, individual access.

Auditing

Your computer may generate logs that can be important diagnostic tools. For instance, your web server keeps track of machines that have requested your web pages:

- machine and domain name or IP address;
- time and date of request;
- page or file requested;
- success or error code;
- number of bytes transferred, and so on.

If you run an FTP server, you also have logs of who moved files in or out. Your security products also produce information logs that can inform you about traffic, system users, and more. In combination with active security products, logs can be a powerful tool to mitigate your security risks.

A marriage of technology and common sense

The same Yankee Group report that claimed companies running a broadband connection were five times more vulnerable to a security breach than those using dial-up also calculated that security breaches would cost UK firms almost £2 billion last year. It estimated that a significant proportion of that cost would be due to broadband, with many firms upgrading without understanding the security risks involved.

So how can firms protect themselves from attack? There are some basic guidelines that all businesses can adopt, ranging from technical solutions to simple common sense policies that will help to keep your business safe online:

- It may sound obvious, but always turn off your computers and/or modem when not in use. If you are not connected to the internet, you cannot be a target.

- Make sure you keep your operating system software up to date. This does not necessarily mean you need to keep buying the latest version. Just make sure that you have installed all available patches for your system.
- Set up passwords to shared computers on your network, and make them difficult to guess. Good passwords have mixed upper- and lower-case letters, numbers, and characters, and are not obvious. Avoid names or birth dates of family members, or common English words such as 'password' or 'guess'.
- Do not open e-mail attachments from strangers, and confirm the integrity of attachments even from known sources. Be especially wary of unexpected files ending in .vbs or .exe.
- Do not volunteer more information to websites or strangers than is absolutely necessary. You already leave plenty of information behind in the logs of sites you have visited.
- Install an anti-virus product to scan both e-mails and web traffic, and keep your virus definition profiles up to date by visiting the software manufacturer's website and downloading its virus update files on a regular basis.
- Deploy a business-grade firewall product to manage the flow of data both in and out of your network (see box below).
- Consider using intrusion detection software to monitor for potential threats from outside the organization.
- Use encrypted e-mail services and programmes whenever possible.
- In case you do suffer an attack, back up your files regularly. That way, even if your business is hit, you will not lose all your data too.

Underpinning all of this must be a comprehensive and comprehensible internal security policy. According to a National Computing Centre (NCC) survey, released earlier this year, the vast majority of employees in UK organizations do not take IT security seriously. This suggests that companies are failing to communicate the business importance of security policies to their staff. The study found that organizations' IT security culture is not keeping

How can your ISP help?

Selecting the right broadband service provider can be half the battle. If you choose carefully, your provider should be able to offer you advice and consultancy on the best solution to suit your company, and will have a range of firewall solutions for you to choose from.

The most basic firewalls are software-based, and work by setting a series of policies that accept or reject internet traffic based on IP address, ports or protocols. They have a number of limitations, for example once a particular protocol is allowed to pass, external hosts can use it to establish a direct connection to the internal network, thereby exposing that network to external threats. Software-based firewalls are, however, quick and easy to use and they do afford some level of protection.

At the other end of the scale are hardware-based solutions, which go one step further by acting as a proxy for all applications and performing the data exchange with remote systems on their behalf. They effectively make the hosts behind the firewall invisible to the outside world. Hardware-based firewalls are considered by far the most secure, but are in return more resource-hungry, harder to manage, and can result in slower response times.

Ultimately, there is no perfect solution that will suit every business; the answer will depend on the limits, strengths and weaknesses of your own company. Some solutions need more knowledge, resource and user intervention than others, while those that are the easiest to manage may not provide adequate levels of security for your needs.

Your ISP should be able to help and advise you on this, and may even be able to provide a managed service that enables you to enjoy maximum security without the potential headaches of maintenance and support.

The crucial point to remember is that any solution will be better than none. You may be best implementing a simple product to start with, thereby buying yourself a little more time to research all the options fully before committing yourself to a more advanced solution.

pace with their growing reliance on computing systems, with security breaches often leading to severe financial losses and business disruption.

The key lies in making all staff appreciate the issues, and their responsibilities in protecting the business. An awareness of security must permeate the entire organization – from the most junior member of staff to the upper echelons of senior management.

Supporting British business

The Government is committed to making Britain the G8's 'most extensive and competitive broadband market' by 2005, an achievement that is viewed as crucial in enabling British businesses effectively to compete on the international stage. For this to be achieved, it is vital that the continued roll-out of broadband goes hand in hand with an increase in security precautions, to ensure that businesses can enjoy all the benefits of high-speed internet access without worrying about the potential security risks.

Don't indulge in unprotected wireless

Ian Kilpatrick, Wick Hill Group

In the business world, smaller companies find that wireless computing frees them from the conventional restrictions of cabling. Once a wireless device has been installed, new PCs or laptops can be added without the hassle of wiring them in.

Employees can still connect to the internet, send and receive e-mails, and do all tasks they need to do. Moreover, they can do all this with greatly increased mobility. It's a very attractive proposition.

For enterprises, wireless provides laptop users with convenience and mobility. They can use their wireless laptops in the office (often without the knowledge of management), from home, and of course when they're on the move. When they're out of the office, employees can work from one of the many wireless 'hot spots' springing up in places such as Starbucks or hotel chains.

Wireless laptops let home users connect to the internet without being physically tied to a connection point. More than one user can easily connect up from different locations in the house and they can have privacy from other family members when they need it. And, of course, they can easily connect to the office.

Unprotected wireless

Unfortunately, in the enthusiasm with which people have adopted wireless, the question of security has been seriously overlooked. There is a standard for security over wireless, WEP

802.11b (Wireless Equivalent Privacy), but it is both flawed and weak, being ineffective and easily broken.

It is also rarely implemented. This is because it is easier to set up wireless with the security not enabled and, once the wireless system is working, the security tends to remain switched off. This has been confirmed by recent surveys in London, which showed that 67 per cent of sites surveyed using wireless did not have security enabled. The same problem potentially exists with the newer security standards WPA (Wi-Fi Protected Access) and 80211i: the default set-up configuration is again with the security not operating.

Some might ask what difference WEP's insecurity or the absence of any security at all makes. The answer is, 'A lot more than you might think.' The whole concept of wireless is about broadcasting, which means that the information doesn't just go to the wireless connection but is also available to anyone within broadcasting range. Sadly, while you may believe that your near neighbours or neighbouring offices may not have the will, interest or technology skills to be interested in your wireless activity, that doesn't mean you are secure.

There is a whole range of individuals and groups who have a deep and not always savoury interest in unprotected wireless users. Some groups have a very active but essentially harmless interest in unprotected wireless, being concerned mainly with finding and identifying wireless sites. You've probably heard about some of these in the press. Their activities have a name: 'war driving', which is driving around looking for locations where wireless is being used and is not secured. It has many websites devoted to it, such as www.wardriving.com.

'War chalking' is marking up street locations with special symbols to identify wireless locations. Again, many websites are devoted to it (eg, www.warchalking.org). There are even details online of where to find unprotected wireless sites in UK towns and cities.

As your wireless device broadcasts its address (SSID), it is extremely easy for anyone to locate it; it can even be done with a PDA. If you're currently indulging in unprotected wireless broadcasting, it is quite possible that you're already on one or more list.

In addition to these groups, there are those with a far from innocent interest in your wireless broadcasts. You may think, 'But there's not much at risk.' Unfortunately, this is totally wrong, even if all you ever do with your wireless PC is access harmless websites from home. It's not just what you broadcast that's at risk, but everything else on your PC or laptop. Information such as passwords, bank details and any other personal data which you wouldn't want other people to know, are all accessible, as is any information on your wireless servers.

Very worryingly, if your connection is used for illegal activity such as accessing illegal images on the internet, you or your business could be held responsible, even if you have no idea who actually did it. This is because the activity will have been carried out from your address, using your connection.

If you have staff at work to whom you have provided wireless access, or more commonly who have provided themselves with wireless access from their laptops, the odds are that they haven't enabled the weak, cursory WEP or WPA or 802.11i 'security' encryptions. As they are operating outside the normal company network and its protective measures, they are therefore not only broadcasting any information they are handling, but have opened up your network to anyone else who cares to look. This is an obviously serious security weakness, negating all the effort you have put into making your systems secure.

Unprotected wireless use exposes companies and individuals to a wide range of security problems. These range from unauthorized use of your bandwidth through to the theft of confidential personal and company information held on your laptop, illegal use of your connections and, in the worst cases, industrial espionage and fraud.

The Csi/FBI survey of 2003 shows once again that there are significant levels of hacking, system penetration, eavesdropping, sabotage, theft of proprietary information and insider abuse of company's computer systems. Wireless looks like a very easy way to carry out many of these activities, given the ease of access and the low likelihood of detection.

Protecting yourself

With all of these risks and so few people protected against them, you could easily assume that wireless protection is either desperately expensive or incredibly difficult. However, this is not the case.

For normal landline communications, most companies today use encrypted VPNs (virtual private networks), usually to the IPSec standard. These are used to protect communications between two points, primarily between a head office and branch office, suppliers or home workers. One solution to the inherent insecurity of wireless is to use IPSec encrypted VPNs for communications between the wireless user and the wireless access point (or company network).

Encrypted VPNs will create a secure connection between the wireless user and the VPN gateway of the company. This connection will hide your communications. The data on your PC is protected from prying eyes because the communication route for it is through the VPN. This method therefore not only protects and encrypts your wireless activity, but also prevents unauthorized wireless access to your PC or business servers by requiring authenticated VPNs for all wireless use. If you are communicating with a supplier, customer or indeed head office, you have not only protected confidential data, you have also prevented your connections from being used to compromise their security.

Installing and implementing VPNs is more complex than using unprotected wireless, but is not beyond the skills of PC-literate individuals who need the benefits of protection. If you're considering implementing wireless VPNs, prime features you need to look for are:

- ease of installation and use;
- compliance with standards (802.11b, 802.11g or SUPERG);
- capability to use a VPN.

Safe rather than sorry

Wireless provides many benefits to business users, including low cost, greater mobility and being able to alter desk layouts with the minimum of hassle. These benefits mean wireless is spreading rapidly. However, security breaches occurring through wireless use are also increasing, with consequent high costs.

It is both inexpensive and comparatively easy to secure yourself against broadcasting your secrets to anyone who is interested. The latest generation of wireless defence solutions means there is no longer any reason to participate in unprotected wireless.

No phishing: protecting employees from e-mail fraud

Ed Rowley, CipherTrust Europe Ltd

Phishing overview

Identity theft, or stealing a person's credentials to gain access to accounts and information, has become the number one crime in the United States. One of the fastest growing forms of identity theft is phishing, a relatively new form of online fraud that focuses on fooling the victim into providing sensitive financial or personal information. Phishing uses bogus e-mail and websites that bear a significant resemblance to a tried and true online brand. Typically, the victim provides information into a form on the impostor site, which then relays the information to the fraudster.

Although this form of fraud is relatively new, its prevalence is exploding. From November 2003 to May 2004, phishing attacks increased by 4,000 per cent. Compounding the issue of increasing volume, response rates for phishing attacks are disturbingly high, sometimes as much as 5 per cent, and are most prevalent among new internet users who are less sophisticated about spotting potential fraud in their inbox.

The dangers posed by phishing extend across the company, from employees through customers to the very backbone of the enterprise network. Among the many risks are employee exposure to phishing scams, company brand degradation, loss of customer trust, network intrusions, dissemination of trade secrets and violation of federal legislation on confidentiality. Failure to mitigate these risks can prove catastrophic to the company's ability to function.

Employee exposure

While employees are at work, the corporate network serves as a virtual ISP. This puts the onus on the company to ensure that employees are safe from all types of e-mail threats, including phishing attacks. Failure to protect employees puts the corporation at risk of being held liable for not taking steps to prevent offensive or fraudulent material from passing through the gateway. In addition, the time and effort spent dealing with each individual incident is costly, resulting in lost productivity, frustrated employees and potential missed sales.

Brand degradation

If a hacker impersonates a company, the company's reputation and brand may be tarnished or ruined because customers feel that they can no longer trust communication purporting to come from the company. Each time a phishing attack is launched, a legitimate company's brand equity is eroded. The more attacks a company suffers, the less consumers feel they can trust the company's legitimate e-mail communications or websites. This vicious circle can prove nearly impossible to break.

Loss of customer trust

The value of trust is difficult to quantify – at least until a company begins to lose customers. If a company is victimized by a phishing scam, customers no longer trust the company's ability to protect their personal information and they often defect to competitors. Companies that fail to openly communicate with customers about the dangers of phishing and how to identify legitimate messages are in grave danger of falling victim to the ever-growing threat. For those organizations that frequently process consumer credit card transactions, the risk is even greater. (See: *Electronic Safety and Soundness: A four pillar approach,* Glassner, Kellermann, McNevin, The World Bank Integrator Group, 2003.)

Network intrusions

Fraudsters use social engineering and other methods to entice employees to divulge sensitive information to people outside the organization. With even a little knowledge of an organization's business methods, hackers can easily distribute hundreds or even thousands of spoofed messages to an organization's employees. The messages may ask for network passwords and usernames, or may attempt to fool employees into providing sensitive information to competitors. Once the hackers have the information they need to access a corporate network, the damage potential is unlimited.

Dissemination of confidential information

Information gleaned by fraudsters from corporate networks can be used in a variety of nefarious ways. In the financial services industry, criminals can use credit cards to deduct money straight from accounts of unsuspecting victims. Many other organizations hold private healthcare information or personal financial information that could be used by criminals to extort payoffs from corporations wishing to avoid the bad publicity of a security breach becoming public knowledge.

Regulatory non-compliance

With the growth of legislation to enforce regulation compliance of information security policy, such as the US-based Health Insurance Portability and Accountability Act (HIPAA), Gramm-Leach-Bliley Act (GLBA) and Sarbanes-Oxley Act (SOX), enterprises are charged with protecting data residing in mail servers and on other internal systems. Security breaches violate these regulations, exposing sensitive data and opening the door to serious sanctions and costly litigation.

Preventing phishing attacks in enterprise networks

A multi-tiered approach is necessary to fully protect a company from phishing attacks. Combining employee and customer education with new technology such as the Sender ID Framework and spam filtering ensures that fraudsters will not find their victims in your enterprise.

Education

Education is a strong defence against phishing attacks in corporate environments. Employees must be well informed about phishing and how to spot fraudulent e-mails and websites. It is also important to properly train employees about what information is appropriate to share through e-mail, and specifically what steps employees should take if they are unsure about the authenticity of a request for information.

In addition, companies must make a concerted effort to educate their customers about phishing. By doing so, they make themselves much less attractive targets than companies that make no effort at all. Clearly, the goal is to convince the fraudsters that a company's customers will not fall for the scam. Having an obvious anti-phishing programme that is public for all to see can be very effective, as the fraudsters tend to follow the path of least resistance. Seeing that customers are well informed about how to avoid phishing attacks, the perpetrators simply turn their attention to other 'softer' targets.

Sender ID Framework

New technologies are available to help prevent phishing. One such technology, offered as a standard by Microsoft and supported by CipherTrust, is the Sender ID Framework (SIDF), which prevents spammers from concealing their IP address by verifying the source of each e-mail. Registering its domains with SIDF helps ensure that a company's customers will not receive phishing e-mails claiming to be from them.

■ 60 POINTS OF EXPOSURE

Of course, education and SIDF are not always enough to prevent all phishing attacks. The best protection against phishing is to keep these attacks from ever getting to the user's inbox. Since most phishing attacks proliferate through unsolicited e-mail, spam-filtering technologies can be very effective at preventing the majority of phishing attempts.

Case study: IronMail caught it – a user may not

CipherTrust, Inc is the market leader in comprehensive e-mail security including best-of-breed spam prevention. The company's powerful, award-winning IronMail appliance combines the five critical e-mail security components into a single easy to deploy and manage platform, providing rules-based protection against any form of malicious activity that can be launched against an organization's e-mail system. These components include: spam and fraud prevention, virus and worm protection, policy and content compliance, e-mail privacy and secure e-mail gateway capabilities.

Figure 2.4.1 is an e-mail recently sent to a CipherTrust employee. IronMail tagged this particular message as a threat and quarantined the message, blocking it from delivery to the employee. The following characteristics of the message are indicators that it is not, in fact, from Citibank, but a cleverly disguised phishing scam that possibly fooled enough users to make the venture quite profitable for the phisher:

1. The entire message is presented within an image, rather than as plain text, a common trick used by spammers to fool content-filtering software.

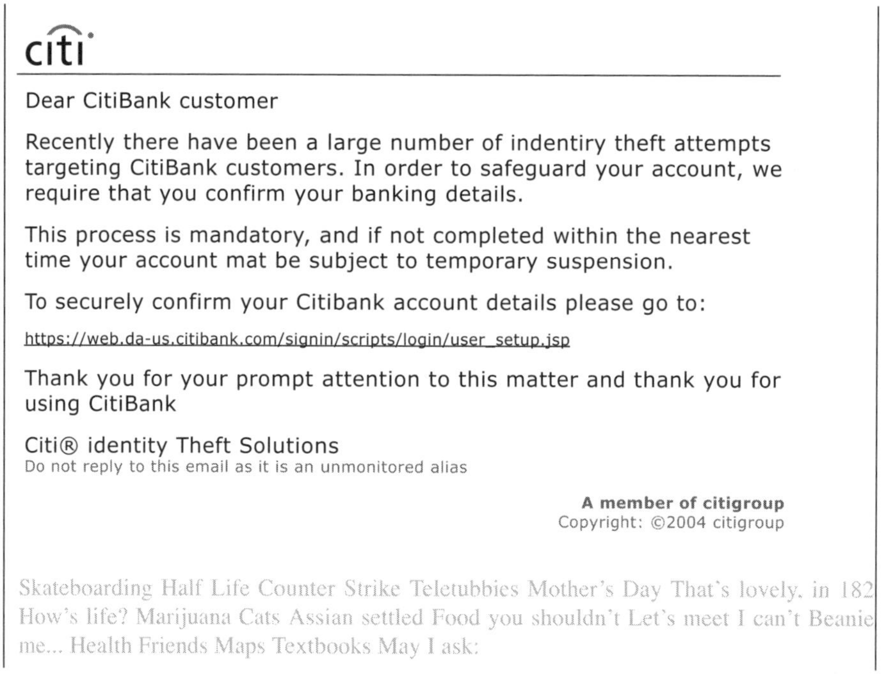

citi

Dear CitiBank customer

Recently there have been a large number of indentiry theft attempts targeting CitiBank customers. In order to safeguard your account, we require that you confirm your banking details.

This process is mandatory, and if not completed within the nearest time your account mat be subject to temporary suspension.

To securely confirm your Citibank account details please go to:

https://web.da-us.citibank.com/signin/scripts/login/user_setup.jsp

Thank you for your prompt attention to this matter and thank you for using CitiBank

Citi® identity Theft Solutions
Do not reply to this email as it is an unmonitored alias

A member of citigroup
Copyright: ©2004 citigroup

Skateboarding Half Life Counter Strike Teletubbies Mother's Day That's lovely. in 182 How's life? Marijuana Cats Assian settled Food you shouldn't Let's meet I can't Beanie me... Health Friends Maps Textbooks May I ask:

Figure 2.4.1 Clever phishing

2. The URL to which the user was asked to send their information was masked in a hex encoding to prevent realization that the destination was not actually Citibank and to prevent spam and phishing detection technology from identifying a suspicious URL.
3. The Citibank graphic and the look and feel of the message are lifted directly from Citibank's website, so it is identical to a message that might come from the company and is likely to be accepted as genuine by many victims.
4. Social engineering techniques take advantage of the victim's concerns about account security by paradoxically presenting the message as a security warning about phishing scams. By portraying the message as 'mandatory' and threatening the user with 'temporary suspension' of his or her account, the victim is coerced into a feeling of urgency and is more likely to fall for the fraud.
5. The random text at the bottom of the message is not contained within the graphic that houses the message body and is designed to fool Bayesian filters. At its most basic level, a Bayesian filter examines a set of e-mails that are known to be spam and a set of e-mails that are known to be legitimate. It compares the content in both e-mails and builds a database of words that will be used to filter messages entering the e-mail gateway and determine whether they are spam or not.
6. By using a white font on a white background, the fraudster intended to hide the random text from the user.

How did IronMail detect the scam?

IronMail detected this message with a sophisticated correlation engine called Spam Profiler, which integrates an array of technologies and evaluates more than 1,000 message characteristics to accurately differentiate legitimate messages from spam or scams. The most significant items that keyed the quarantine of this phishing scam are as follows.

Header analysis

'Spoofing' is the act of mimicking genuine e-mail addresses to give the impression of an authorized communication from a business, and is a common tactic used by spammers. In Figure 2.4.1, items such as the 'From:' address and the originating mail server were inconsistent with that of mail sent legitimately by Citibank, allowing IronMail's header analysis to detect accurately that 'spoofing' was employed. In addition, IronMail detected discrepancies in the headers that indicated that the sender was attempting to deceive the recipient server.

Bulk e-mail detection

With more than 2,000 IronMail units in the field protecting over 7 million enterprise e-mail users, CipherTrust detects new attacks quickly. While some 'mass personalization' was employed to make each version of this message unique, it was detected at multiple sites and identified as a mass e-mailing and potential spam or attack.

URL filtering

Despite the attacker's use of hex encoding to hide the URL of the fake Citibank website, IronMail was able to decode the URL and identify it as a suspected spammer URL.

Anomaly detection

IronMail's anomaly detection engine is able to scan e-mail traffic for behaviour that indicates an attack. This can include the number of messages, the origin, the delivery method or any other characteristics of the message. Anomaly detection is instrumental in detecting new and previously unknown attacks.

All of these techniques operate in real time and scrutinize the behaviour of the message rather than the weaker approach of trying only to identify content. Combining these techniques in a 'cocktail' approach enabled IronMail to discover the strategy of the scam artist and prevent this message reaching an unsuspecting end-user. If used alone, each of these techniques might contribute to stopping legitimate messages. However, IronMail's Spam Profiler enabled IronMail to consider the results of all of its detection tools simultaneously and make an accurate decision on the malicious nature of this message.

Penalty

According to CNN.com, the first federal phishing case was prosecuted by the FBI in 2004. Ironically, an FBI agent with expertise in cybercrime received an e-mail purporting to be from AOL. The agent explored the link and discovered that it was directed to a site unrelated to AOL. The agent also determined that the sender's e-mail address was invalid and that the message was sent to multiple users – telltale signs of spam or scam. The agent called for further analysis of the message in what was then called the Bureau's Special Technologies and Applications Unit of the National Infrastructure Protection Center, and the message was confirmed as a phishing scam. Upon further investigation, the FBI uncovered a trail of several stolen accounts, as well as a computer that contained account information for over 400 credit cards acquired over the course of the scam. One person has been sentenced and another is currently awaiting sentencing (see http://www.cnn.com/2003/TECH/internet/07/21/phishing.scam/).

Conclusions

Phishing is currently a tremendous e-mail security threat that can easily result in identity theft and/or corporate networks being compromised. The most effective ways to combat phishing are a combination of education, law enforcement and, most importantly, an enterprise-wide e-mail security solution that can prevent even the most clever phishing scams from reaching the desktop of unsuspecting end-users.

2.5

Network vulnerabilities

Peter Crowcombe, NetScreen Technologies Inc

Basic network security issues have changed very little over the past decade. Protecting the confidentiality of corporate information, preventing unauthorized access and defending the network against attacks remain primary concerns of network security professionals today. What have changed are the precise areas of vulnerability that challenge today's networks – the different levels of trusted users, the sophistication level and quantity of attacks, and the ease with which attacks can be launched. Security professionals and analysts agree that their troubles have only just begun. In fact, the Computer Emergency Response Team (CERT) states that an estimated 83,000 attacks occurred globally in 2002, while in the first three quarters of 2003 alone, nearly 115,000 attacks occurred (up from just above 5,000 in 1999).[1] Attacks that are increasing in number and sophistication are placing networks in an extremely vulnerable position that will continue to be a challenge made worse by several key trends:

- **Ubiquitous access to the internet**: the availability of the internet has made every home, every office and every business partner a potential entry point for attack. This ubiquitous access allows sophisticated attacks to be launched against the corporate network by deliberate attackers or unknowingly by remote users logging on to the corporate network.
- **Changing levels of trust**: the different levels of network access that are being granted (remote employees, business partners, customers) are making the network increasingly vulnerable. Remote employees, business partners, customers and suppliers may have different levels of access to corporate resources, and appropriate measures must be taken to protect the corporate network.
- **Internal attacks**: more troubling and more difficult to defend against are the attacks that are perpetrated from inside the network by employees who have access and ultimately complete control over the network's resources. Internal attacks can range from a

nosey employee trying to see how much his or her co-workers make, to a disgruntled employee destroying or stealing proprietary information.
- **Attack sophistication**: new types of attacks that target application vulnerabilities have been added to the long list of viruses, worms, denial of service (DoS) and Trojan horse attacks that IT departments need to defend their network against.
- **Wireless LANs – the unseen vulnerability**: the popularity and accepted use of wireless LANs (WLAN) is exposing many networks to security threats. Gartner Dataquest 'forecasts the penetration rate of wireless LAN into the professional mobile PC installed base will grow from 9 percent in 2000 to almost 50 percent by the end of 2003, and it is expected to surpass 90 percent by 2007'.[2] With little or no security on a WLAN, attackers can gain access to the corporate network with relative ease and as a result, may be free to roam the corporate network, inflicting damage or stealing data.

The trends outlined above exemplify how administrators must reconsider their network security architecture to address specific security threats without hindering access. Industry analysts and security experts agree that the key to striking a balance between tight network security and the network access required by employees, business partners and customers is a layered security solution.

Network vulnerabilities

- **Remote access communications**: in many cases, users who are accessing the corporate network are doing so across a public medium, possibly without the appropriate security measures, which means that all communications are being transmitted in clear text and are susceptible to hackers. The primary solution to this vulnerability is SSL (secure socket layer) Virtual Private Networking (VPN), to include strong authentication capabilities.
- **Site-to-site communications**: in this scenario, two resources (remote site and main site) that are typically connected to each other via a high-speed connection need to be protected. Potential threats include hijacked sessions, u-turn attacks, compromised PCs, malicious users and attacks originating from one site, yet targeting the other site. To counteract this vulnerability, firewalls and IPSec VPNs should be used. DoS protection is also advisable.
- **Perimeter security**: fundamentally, as the point where external communication lines enter the corporate network, this is where who and what gets in/out of the network must be controlled. Some of the vulnerabilities threatening the perimeter include hackers trying to penetrate the network, DoS, sophisticated application level and hybrid attacks. Perimeter firewall/DoS protection (preferably multi-functional to include such features as anti-virus), access control (IPSec) plus intrusion detection and prevention (IDP) layers are advised.
- **Network core security**: the network's core is the area that contains an organization's most critical data resources, so is vulnerable to unauthorized user roaming, internal attacks launched by disgruntled employees, and application-level attacks targeting specific vulnerabilities. High-performing, properly integrated firewalls, inline but independent IDPs, IPSec VPNs, should all be deployed to protect the network's core.

Layered security to help counteract network vulnerabilities

Overall, the solutions described above should be deployed as a cohesive, layered solution to optimally secure a highly distributed network. The ultimate goal of a layered security solution is to protect the critical resources that reside on the network from today's ever increasingly sophisticated attacks. A layered security solution is made up of multiple layers of complementary security technologies, all working together to provide the required level of protection – if one layer fails, the next layer will cover it. For example, administrators may deploy firewalls, VPNs, anti-virus and intrusion detection and prevention as layers of protection against attacks.

Table 2.5.1 Security layers

Security layer	Description
Firewall	Protects the network by controlling who and what can have access to the network
Denial of Service	Protects against denial of service type attacks
Virtual Private Network (VPN)	Protects communications between sites and/or users with an encrypted, authenticated communications session (tunnel)
Anti-virus	Protects against virus attacks at the desktop, gateway and server levels
Intrusion detection and prevention	Protects against sophisticated attacks such as application-level attacks
Personal firewall	Protects content on personal computers and in turn, keeps corporate networks safe

In addition to protecting network resources from attacks, the need for layered security stems from today's network extending far beyond the walls of the corporate headquarters to where remote users, regional offices, business partners and customers are accessing network resources from their location. This extension of the corporate network is forcing IT departments to treat each of these network entry points as a potential avenue for attack. A layered security solution allows an administrator to apply the appropriate levels of security to protect resources from attacks originating from any location. Layered security is an optimal solution for two reasons.

First, if a security breach occurs, the other security layers that have been deployed can stop the attack and/or limit the damages that may occur.

Second, this allows an IT department to apply the appropriate level of resource protection to the various network entry points based upon different security, performance and management requirements. For example, remote users have lower performance requirements and access to fewer technical resources but still need to protect their PC (and the corporate network) from viruses with anti-virus and from prying eyes with encryption. At the other end of the spectrum, core network security will require higher levels of performance and access to technical resources in order to support the sophisticated levels of security needed to protect the corporate network and business-critical applications.

Most organizations acknowledge that intrusions and attacks are inevitable, and a layered security strategy comprised of multiple layers of complementary security technologies, all working together, helps to minimize this risk by presenting multiple barriers to keep them from penetrating an organization's defences.

Network segmentation and user containment

In addition to various security solutions, network segmentation and user containment can further be used to protect the network against various vulnerabilities. Once thought of as only a perimeter defence security layer, firewalls are being brought into the infrastructure to protect different segments of the network such as finance, HR and engineering. Used internally, firewalls provide additional layers of access control to protect against the organization's sprawling definition of 'authorized user', as well as to provide attack containment. Adding firewalls to the infrastructure enables an organization to protect specific resources, and helps to prevent users from unauthorized roaming and contain attack damages in the event that one occurs. Rather than implementing a separate, physical firewall for every segment, a more cost-effective solution is to leverage virtual firewall functionality and VPNs that can divide the network into distinct, secure network segments.

In the network security world, one thing is certain: networks will remain the target of ever increasingly sophisticated types of attacks originating both internally and externally. Compounding the difficulty associated with protecting the network from new types of attacks is the dramatic expansion of who may or may not have access to the corporate network. These two factors are forcing IT departments to evaluate and implement layered security solutions that are designed to:

- control who and what has access to the corporate network through robust firewall functionality;
- protect against denial of service attacks through built-in intelligence and high performance;
- facilitate secure communications with a VPN so that remote users, business partners and customers can conduct business across the internet;
- detect attacks and quickly react, in a preventative manner, to minimize or eliminate any damages that may result from the attack.

Notes

1. Source: www.cert.org/stats/cert-stats.html
2. Source: Worldwide Wireless LAN shipments to grow 73 per cent in 2002, Gartner Dataquest 19 press release, September 2002.

2.6

Wireless applications

Andrew Steggles, EMEA Nokia Enterprise Solutions

Mobilizing the enterprise

In today's world, enterprises are capitalizing on mobility to gain business advantage. A large element in gaining these advantages is giving an increasing number of employees mobile access to e-mail, calendars, contacts, tasks and other corporate resources, such as the intranet. The challenge for enterprises is finding a solution that provides secure, cost-effective, usable and flexible access for employees regardless of their geographic location or preferred mobile device.

At the same time, adoption has been slowed by security concerns and less than optimal user experiences. Anyone who has remotely accessed e-mail over a broadband connection will never again be satisfied with dial up.

The rush to mobility can be explained by the growth of new technologies and businesses' desire to stay competitive – mobility offers benefits such as greater access to people and data, improved customer service and responsiveness, and improved productivity. Already, work practices are changing with the increasing decentralization of employees and the growing number of remote and home offices. Technology is making it possible to make enterprises truly mobile by providing an expanding variety and sophistication of mobile devices, connection technologies and mobile content.

Along with the devices, mobile content is also changing from being text only to include multimedia, and is being used differently by employees – evolving from information retrieval to transactions. The proliferation of wireless technologies (including Wi-Fi and 3G) and fixed broadband, combined with sophisticated PDAs and mobile telephones, has meant that the laptop is now not the only method of sharing data with the office while on the move.

The requirement for business now is quickly becoming that any device should be able to access any content.

However, as more content goes mobile, so does the threat of data crime. Devices become smaller, yet their functionality and storage capacity increase. This means the smaller things are easier to steal or misplace, while they carry more content and access information to corporate networks. Wireless networks and other wireless transmission techniques (that is, Bluetooth, Wi-Fi aka IEEE 802.11) are largely unprotected and allow interference, sniffing, easy hacking and so on.

The growing number of mobile devices accessing the internet is changing the nature of business. IDC forecasts that up to 60 per cent of internet users will be connecting to the internet via mobile devices by 2005. The ability for mobile workers to access corporate resources over the internet is great news for business productivity, but naturally raises a new set of security concerns.

The ability to offer corporate customers security and management capabilities for the mobile infrastructure is critical to the success of any mobile infrastructure initiative. Further, the ability of such software products to scale to demand and interoperate with other network components is essential. Software security and management products aimed at the mobile markets will undoubtedly speed adoption of this technology. However, other factors come into play, including more appealing carrier payment plans and the need for standards to solidify within the mobile and wireless marketing.

Mobile internet shares the same issues and risks as the fixed internet, but has additional dangers caused by the nature of its wireless transmission. The fact that users of mobile devices can move from location to location, and network to network, adds another dimension to the security discussion. Other security issues include viruses that could be a possible threat to handsets and to networks, unauthorized accessing of a network, and of course theft of devices. Companies need to consider new ways of authenticating and securing mobile devices, such as PIN codes or user biometrics.

Here is where the story starts to get convoluted for businesses. The IT department steps in and asks: how are we going to manage all these different devices, user profiles and network types? How can we ensure network integrity? And can we do it without running up huge costs?

Securing and managing the devices are the key issues in enabling mobile enterprise. IPSec VPNs have been the tried and trusted security measure used by most companies to reliably secure computers logging into the company network. However, as IPsec VPNs require a client running on the mobile device, an enterprise may be faced with the task of distributing, updating and managing many hundreds or thousands of clients. Without the right management tools, this can add to costs and increases the complexity of the solution – so if an IPSec solution is what the business needs, a tool which keeps mobile devices up to date and eases the management burden of supporting mobile devices is required. But there is another option that is getting enterprises excited – SSL (secure socket layer) VPNs.

SSL VPNs leverage the ubiquity of SSL, which is built into almost every web or WAP browser. If an appliance is used to authenticate users, restrict access and secure the connection using SSL, access can be given to the intranet and e-mail applications, eliminating the need to install a VPN client for the majority of users. This means the management cost involved with IPSec VPN is avoided, making SSL VPN much more cost-effective for businesses wanting to take their workforce mobile. SSL VPNs also allow a multitude of devices to be supported both now and in the future, and an enterprise does not have to choose a mobile device that has an IPSec client available for it.

This is not to say IPSec VPNs are now a thing of the past. SSL VPNs are perfect for accessing e-mail and web-enabled applications, which for the majority of mobile workers is all they need. However, some client server applications are not web-enabled, meaning an IPSec VPN is the best option. Enterprises will have to examine their needs and decide which solution suits the particular application being delivered, and we believe many will use a combination of the two VPN technologies to maintain remote access security.

These technologies provide the basis for secure connections, but simplifying the management of many user profiles, devices, and network types – and doing it cost effectively – requires businesses to select their supplier carefully.

Management software for provisioning IPSec VPN client software to mobile devices on a large scale is key for companies wishing to take this route. Vendor and application independence is also important, as is the expandability of the network product – businesses should not lock themselves into proprietary technology. They need to ensure their investments can cope with future requirements.

Similarly with SSL VPNs, businesses should look for vendor offerings that support many authentication methods and device types, as well as legacy applications. In-built tools that can automatically recognize device type and security settings are vital to simplifying management and ensuring adequate levels of security. For example, logging into the office from a laptop with up-to-date virus definitions and a personal firewall is very different from accessing the network from a hand-held device that has no firewall and outdated virus protection. The access levels for each device can and should be altered accordingly.

With Gartner predicting that by 2007 more than 40 per cent of corporate applications will have some mobility element built-in, planning how to secure, support and integrate mobile devices will be key to enabling a truly mobile workforce. As public Wi-Fi hotspots and broadband access points multiply daily, and new powerful phones and PDAs become affordable and easy to use, it will not just be the travelling business person logging into e-mail from the hotel any more.

Many companies are rushing to embrace wireless networking and install access points without first understanding the security implications. One of the most common reasons for WLAN security breaches is the failure by companies to take any security precautions at all. Wireless networking is great technology and allows great freedom for business, but while pushing a WLAN as a solution, often the security issues are not taken into account, either because companies do not understand the risks or because they think they are nothing to worry about.

This leads to another common security concern, when the corporation attaches the WLAN access points to the network backbone rather than the firewall, meaning everything is broadcast from the backbone – including file transfers, financial information and so on – and it is easy for anyone with the right Wi-Fi equipment and tools to listen in and either read company information, or corrupt data on servers.

Companies need to understand not only how a WLAN can help their business but also what security risks come along with those benefits. The main thing is, the risks are manageable – hardened security technology is available now to deliver strong encryption and flexibility so businesses can take advantage of the great benefits of a WLAN without putting their organization in harm's way. These same solutions can also be used to provide secure remote access over solutions like ADSL, dial-up, hotel broadband solutions and remote WLAN hotspots.

To conclude, a company must understand the importance of technology as a tool to enable business, just as decisions about technology should be made with the overall business objectives in mind – details such as planned expansion, increased numbers of remote workers and the growing number of suppliers needing to access a corporate network should be considered with a long-term view. Security cannot be viewed within a vacuum, and security is no longer just an insurance policy.

Companies are beginning to realize that at one level security is a necessity, and at another it is a very positive infrastructure element. This has been driven by the need for companies to expand 'trusted relationships' with customers, partners, suppliers and channels. In many cases a company's greatest asset is information. The ability to use security technologies to enable greater access to corporate content deepens and stabilizes relationships. These 'trusted relationships' can yield numerous benefits, such as higher transaction rates with greater scalability, lower cost per transaction, and transference of personnel from low-value interactions to a high-value personalized service.

Protecting online privacy

Alexander Brown, Simmons & Simmons

As part of the UK implementation of a suite of EU legislation designed to regulate electronic communications networks and services across the EU, the Privacy and Electronic Communications (EC Directive) Regulations 2003 (the '2003 Regulations') were implemented in the United Kingdom on 11 December 2003. The Regulations are designed to be more 'technology neutral' than the Telecommunication (Data Protection and Privacy) Regulations 1999 (the '1999 Regulations') which they replace. As a result, the 2003 Regulations broaden the data protection legislation framework from one focused on telecommunications services to one relevant to both telecommunications and new technologies (such as e-mail and SMS). The technology neutral nature of the 2003 Regulations also means that they will be applicable to future technologies that involve the processing of personal data.

Background

The 2003 Regulations implement the Directive on Privacy and Electronic Communications (formerly known as the Communications Data Protection Directive) (the 'Directive').[1] Both the 2003 Regulations and the Directive are derived from the suite of European legislation designed to harmonize Member States' laws in the electronic communications sector. The Communications Act 2003 implements the bulk of this suite of legislation. The Directive, however, is implemented through the 2003 Regulations.

The old regime

The 1999 Regulations focused on the processing of personal data in the telecommunications field. One of their principal features was the rules governing the use of unsolicited calls and faxes for marketing purposes, but the rules, on a literal interpretation, were restricted to voice telephony and fax. Indeed the advent of the 2003 Regulations, which deal with other forms of communication, may suggest that there was previously no regulation on the processing of personal data in connection with the sending of marketing via electronic communications. This is, of course, not the case. Data protection laws in the United Kingdom regulated (and continue to regulate) the processing of personal data in connection with the sending of electronic communications to individuals. The over-arching rules relating to the processing of personal data are contained in the Data Protection Act 1998 (the DPA) which will apply where the marketing concerned involves the processing of 'personal data'. 'Personal data' means information relating to a living individual who can be identified either from the data concerned, or from the data plus additional information in the possession of, or likely to come into the possession of, the body controlling the data (the 'data controller').

Compliance with the DPA is monitored and enforced by the Information Commissioner's Office (ICO), an independent supervisory authority reporting to Parliament, which was set up to develop respect for the private lives of citizens and to encourage the accountability of public authorities. The ICO produces guidelines on new legislation when the legislation has an affect on the privacy of individuals.

Marketing via electronic communications was therefore previously regulated by the DPA and the ICO guidance on the DPA (and continues to be so regulated). In addition, in guidelines published in relation to the 1999 Regulations, the ICO indicated that those contacting individuals via e-mail should apply the principles of the 1999 Regulations to unsolicited e-mails. This is despite the fact that e-mail was not expressly referred to in the 1999 Regulations.

In practice, then, the narrow drafting of the 1999 Regulations was broadened by the ICO's guidelines. This resulted in a degree of uncertainty as to the rules relating to marketing via electronic communications. The 2003 Regulations remove a lot of the uncertainty, even if they may be viewed by some as restrictive.

The new regime under the 2003 Regulations

Before we deal with the specific rules set out in the 2003 Regulations it is worth noting that under the new regime, the DPA is still relevant. As a result, those making use of electronic means to contact individuals must continue to ensure that the processing of the individual's personal data complies with the eight data protection principles set out in the DPA.

For example, if a company wishes to send a text message to an individual it must ensure that its use of the individual's personal data (such as the mobile number) is fair and lawful (the first data protection principle), and as part of that it must ensure that it has told the individual how the data will be processed. In other words, the company should tell the individual it might send him/her SMS messages, and the purposes for which those SMS messages will be sent.

Within the DPA, section 11 is particularly relevant as it gives the individual a right to prevent processing of his or her personal data for direct marketing. To exercise this right, the individual must give a reasonable period of written notice to the data controller following which the data controller must cease processing the individual's personal data for marketing purposes. If it does not cease, the court can order it to take such steps to comply with the notice as the court thinks fit.[2]

The 2003 Regulations are an extra layer of legislation on top of the DPA. They broaden out the scope of the 1999 Regulations by using fairly broad technology-neutral definitions reflecting those used under the Communications Act. Instead of using terms relevant to traditional telecommunications and voice telephony, the 2003 Regulations refer to 'electronic communications networks and services'. 'Telecommunications' is replaced by 'communications', and the latter is defined as 'any information exchanged or conveyed between a finite number of parties by means of a public electronic communications service'.

Specific changes introduced by the 2003 Regulations

Electronic mail (Regulations 22 and 23)

The problem of spam

According to the European Commission, spam now accounts for more than 50 per cent of all e-mails sent. This results in annoyance for the users whose inboxes it clogs, and reduces productivity in the workplace (according to the European Commission an estimated 2.5 billion euros loss was suffered by EU businesses in 2002) and significantly increases costs of transmission and storage for Internet service providers and network operators. The 2003 Regulations take steps to counter spam e-mailing but at the same time take account of the fact that in business-to-business relationships, marketing by all means (including electronic means) is necessary in order for businesses to promote their goods and services effectively.

The 2003 Regulations apply to 'electronic mail'

The 2003 Regulations include new provisions that specifically regulate how businesses may use 'electronic mail' to market to individuals. However, the 2003 Regulations regulate more than the use of just *e-mail* since the definition of 'electronic mail' is very broad. It encompasses 'any text, voice, sound or image message sent over public electronic communications network which can be stored in the network or in the recipient's terminal equipment until it is collected by the recipient and includes ... short message service'.[3]

In other words, and as the Guidelines state, e-mail, SMS text, mobile picture and video marketing messages are all considered to be 'electronic mail'. In addition, the rules also apply to voice-mail or answerphone messages left by marketers. Therefore, there are stricter obligations placed upon those marketers who make live calls but who wish to leave messages on a person's voice-mail or answerphone, than on those marketers who avoid leaving messages.

The subscriber must 'opt in'

Under the 2003 Regulations, the subscriber recipient of a marketing e-mail must have 'opted in' to the communication being sent by the sender. In the words of the 2003 Regulations the recipient must have previously notified the sender that he/she consents to the communication being sent.[4] This differs slightly from the text of the Directive that states 'prior consent' is all that is required to authorize marketing e-mail. This might have given rise to the argument that those who are already receiving e-mails and have not 'opted out' have implied consent to continued receipt of marketing e-mails.

However, there are two problems with this argument since it is clear that, for the purposes of the DPA, consent requires active communication, and in any event the matter is put beyond doubt by the 2003 Regulations' requirement for 'previous notification', which makes it clear that some active notification on the part of the subscriber is required.

That said, the ICO seems unwilling to take a rigid line on this point. The Guidelines recognize the fact that the new legislation imposes upon marketers a higher standard for data collection than they were obliged to follow before 11 December 2003. Accordingly, for the time being the ICO is taking the view that if mailing lists were compiled in accordance with privacy legislation in force before 11 December 2003 and were used recently, marketers can continue to use them unless the intended recipient has already opted out. (The Guidelines take the view, however, that privacy legislation in force before 11 December 2003 did not permit the sending of unsolicited text/video messages without prior consent.)

The 'soft' opt-in exception

There is an exception to the requirement of consent. The so-called 'soft' opt-in applies to suppliers who obtain e-mail details in the context of a sale of goods or services or negotiation in respect of a sale (suggesting that a concluded sale is not necessary for the soft opt-in to apply). In these limited circumstances, suppliers can send direct marketing of their own 'similar products or services only' to existing customers providing that the addressee is able to opt out of future e-mail marketing easily and free of charge.[5] However, no definition of 'similar' is provided and so this may be problematic, as may be the use of the word 'only' which suggests that a company could not market similar products as well as other products that it might also sell.

The Guidelines, however, adopt a purposive approach to the phrase 'similar products and services only'. They state that the intention of this section is to ensure that an individual does not receive promotional material about products and services that he or she would not reasonably expect to receive. An example given is someone who has shopped online at a supermarket's website (and has not objected to receiving further e-mail marketing from that supermarket) who would expect at some point in the future to receive further e-mails promoting the diverse range of goods available at that supermarket.

Ultimately, as the ICO also points out, if an individual feels that a company has gone beyond the boundaries of their reasonable expectation, that individual can opt out. Accordingly, the ICO's focus will be on failures to comply with opt-out requests rather than suppliers' interpretation of the term 'similar'.

The sender must be identified, and the electronic communication must be identified as marketing material

Spam is further stamped on by Regulation 23 of the 2003 Regulations that prohibits the sending of communications by electronic mail that disguise the identity of the sender and do not include a valid opt-out address.

This builds on the requirements of the Electronic Commerce (EC Directive) Regulations 2002[6] (the 'E-Commerce Regulations'). The E-Commerce Regulations require commercial communications connected with an information society service to be clearly identifiable as such, and for an unsolicited commercial communication also to be clearly and unambiguously identifiable as such as soon as it is received.[7]

In a similar vein, the 2003 Regulations state that, assuming the subscriber has clearly consented to the receipt of messages, each message will have to identify the sender and provide a valid suppression address. This is easy to achieve in the case of e-mail, but not so easy in the case of SMS messages. Nevertheless the requirements must be met and the Guidelines suggest that the following sort of formulation may be appropriate in an SMS message: PHLtdPobox97SK95AF.

Clearly, attaching an appropriate heading to an e-mail is relatively easy but applying a heading to an SMS message is more difficult. None the less, the Guidelines state that 'the practical limitations of standard mobile screens do not mean that marketers can avoid the rules' despite the fact that a standard mobile phone screen can only hold 160 characters.

The Guidelines suggest that a company can give information about the marketing it intends to do before a marketing message is sent or even before the mobile number is collected. For example the information could be given in an advert, or on a Web site where the recipient signs up for the service.

In addition to the E-Commerce Regulations and the 2003 Regulations, marketers must be aware of other regulation and other statutory bodies that restrict methods of marketing. The Code of Practice (CAP Code) of the Advertising Standards Authority (ASA) is particularly relevant to marketing, as is the Code of Practice of the Direct Marketing Association (DMA Code). Marketers should also be aware of regulation specific to their particular industry. For example, law firms must take account of Law Society Rules when reviewing their marketing policies.

When the 2003 Regulations do not apply: business e-mail

During consultation on the drafting of the 2003 Regulations a large number of respondents felt that corporate subscribers should not have the same rights as individuals in relation to electronic mail. Many highlighted concerns that a universal opt-in would be harmful for business-to-business selling.

Consequently, the 2003 Regulations' restrictions on sending marketing e-mails only apply to e-mails sent to individuals, sole traders and non-limited liability partnerships. They do not apply to marketing e-mails sent to employees of companies or limited liability partnerships, since such persons are not 'subscribers' and the rules only apply to electronic mail sent to subscribers.[8]

However, corporate subscribers and individual corporate users whose e-mail addresses include or constitute personal data continue to enjoy protection under section 11 of the DPA as above.

Other new elements of the 2003 Regulations

Clearly, the rules relating to marketing messages sent by electronic means will make a significant impact on marketers using electronic mail in the United Kingdom. However, the Regulations also impact on the use of cookies and location data.

Cookies (Regulation 6)

Cookies are small data files that many internet sites automatically upload to a user's hard drive. They are primarily used in helping websites recognize previous visitors and in recording users' preferences. Originally, it appeared that the proposed 'opt-in' rule would apply to the use of cookies as well as to unsolicited e-mail marketing messages. However, as a result of pressure from groups such as the Federation of European Direct Marketing (FEDMA), the legislation was drafted in a manner that means that it is sufficient to make the end-user aware that there is a cookie, and what the function of the cookie is.

Regulation 6 requires that a person wishing to use cookies need only tell the individual that cookies are going to be used and how the cookies can be rejected or removed. It also requires that a user or subscriber be provided with clear and comprehensive information about the purposes of the storage of, or access to, the cookie.

The 2003 Regulations do not prescribe the way in which a user or subscriber should be able to refuse the use of a cookie – according to the Guidelines the method is seen as less important than the fact that the mechanism must be 'uncomplicated, easy to understand and accessible to all'.

Regulation 6 is drafted very broadly, referring to the use of an electronic communications network to store information to gain access to information stored in the terminal equipment of a subscriber or user. As with electronic communications above, this is a very wide definition, which is deliberately technology-neutral to allow other future forms of information gathering technology to be collected. Accordingly, although the use of 'cookies' is the principal application of the rule, the definition and future application of Regulation 6 may extend beyond that.

Location data (Regulation 14)

The 2003 Regulations also deal with the processing of location data, or 'data processed by an electronic communications network indicating the geographical position of the terminal equipment of a user of a public electronic communications service' and this includes information relating to:

- the latitude, longitude or altitude of the terminal equipment;
- the direction of travel of the user;
- the time the location information was recorded.[9]

The processing of location data will enable the provision of helpful location-based services such as directory enquiries services that are able to use customers' locations to send text or even map details of local amenities. The processing of location data is regulated and can only be processed if the subscriber cannot be identified from the data, or if processing is necessary for the provision of a value added service and the individual's consent has been received.[10]

In this context, a value-added service means any service which requires the processing of location data beyond that which is necessary for the transmission of a communication or the billing of that data.[11] Before consent can be obtained, the communications provider must provide the subscriber with the following information:

- the types of location data that will be processed;
- the purposes and duration of the processing of those data; and
- whether the data will be transmitted to a third party for the purposes of providing a value-added service.[12]

The Regulations do not prescribe how consent should be obtained. However, the Guidelines state that to receive valid informed consent the service provider must give 'sufficient, clear information' to the subscriber. In the light of this, the service provider will not be able to rely on a blanket 'catch all' statement on a bill or website. Instead, it should obtain specific informed consent for each value-added service requested and for the marketing of its own electronic communications services.

Subscribers should be able to withdraw consent at any time, and the communications provider should make them aware of this.

Conclusion

It is clear that the 2003 Regulations have had a massive impact on companies in the communications industry. Companies providing communication services will have to ensure that they follow the 2003 Regulations carefully. They influence their use of – and the way their customers can make use of – electronic mail and cookies. All companies in the EU will have to ensure that their marketing policies comply with the 2003 Regulations, paying particular attention to the rules regarding electronic mail (including SMS and picture messaging) and cookies.

The law is more restrictive following the implementation of the 2003 Regulations. However, while the 2003 Regulations are restrictive, they also clarify grey areas of the law and provide a framework for the future of the communications industry, which represents a step forward from the old telecommunications regime.

Notes

1. Directive 2002/58/EC of the European Parliament and of the Council of 12 July 2002.
2. Section 11(1) of the DPA.
3. Regulation 1.
4. Regulation 22(2).
5. Regulation 22(3).
6. Directive 2000/31/EC.
7. Regulation 7 of the E-Commerce Regulations.
8. A 'subscriber' is defined in Regulation 1 as any person party to a contract with a provider of publicly available electronic communication services for the supply of such services.
9. Regulation 1.
10. Regulation 14(2).
11. Regulation 1.
12. Regulation 14(3).

2.8

Online payments: key areas of exposure

Tony Parnell, WorldPay Ltd

Securing internet payment

Retailers are experts in the business of retailing – rarely are they experts in the security of online financial transactions. Rather than build their own online payment systems, therefore, they often outsource these to a payment services provider (PSP) or a bank. A number of specialist processes can be offered by the PSP or bank to ensure that the payments made to the business are secure and that the business is protected from unnecessary exposure to risk. These are described below:

- **Encryption – keeping card details safe**: this is the process by which the PSP or bank 'scrambles' card data submitted to the company's online shop, to ensure that it cannot be intercepted en route. Encryption is usually achieved through a technology called Secure Sockets Layer (SSL for short), which is now built into most web browsers as standard (Microsoft Internet Explorer version 3.02 or higher and Netscape Navigator version 3.03 or higher).

    When shoppers shop on a site protected by SSL, an unbroken padlock icon or a key symbol appears at the bottom of their screen and the beginning of the site's web address changes from 'http' to 'https.'

    Encryption is the absolute minimum requirement of any transactional website and it has been proven to be very effective in preventing data being intercepted en route.

According to the Association of Payment and Clearing Services (APACS), fraudulent internet transactions are almost exclusively the result of the card details being illegally 'skimmed' (copied using an electronic card reader) in a physical environment – the restaurant, the bar, the petrol station – and then used on the internet thereafter.

- **Card data invisibility**: some PSPs and banks can accept and process online payments on your business's behalf without at any time communicating the card details to that business; the only thing passed on to your business is the funds. The benefit of this approach is that your business does not need to expose itself to any risk of losing, incorrectly managing or compromising card data – the entire process is managed externally.
- **Automated fraud detection**: some PSPs and banks can now offer automated fraud detection services as an integral part of their online payment platforms. These services use a number of methods to identify quickly fraudulent buying behaviours, alert the retailer, and prevent the transaction being processed.
- **AVS and CVV**: your bank or PSP may also offer address verification (AVS) and cardholder verification (CVV, known in its latest form as CVV2) as integral elements of their payment services. AVS checks the card holder's name against the billing address to ensure that there is no mismatch. CVV2 is a three or four-digit number printed on the strip on the back of the card (it is sometimes also referred to as the security code) and cannot be copied by skimming. A card holder who is able to enter the correct CVV2 code is more likely to be in physical possession of the card and therefore less likely to have obtained the card data by skimming.
- **Authentication**: the card holder's online 'signature': MasterCard and Visa, the world's biggest card companies, have both developed services (MasterCard SecureCode and Verified by Visa respectively) that use passwords to protect ('authenticate') card holders and their online transactions. Card holders are invited to type in their password, via a secure pop-up or similar, when they are buying online. This serves to prove that card holders are who they say they are, and prevents fraudulent use of the card.

In many ways, authentication is the online version of the high street 'Chip and PIN' scheme rolled out in the United Kingdom during 2004/2005 – and it offers a similar degree of protection for both shopper and retailer.

Authentication means that:

- Cardholders will benefit from the same level of security as when they use a cashpoint – eventually, there will be fewer and fewer online shops where card purchases can be made without the input of the password. Those that do not request the input of the password will lose credibility.
- Retailers will suffer lower volumes of charge-backs. A charge-back is where a card holder's bank claims the cost of the transaction back from the retailer. This can be because of fraud (someone using someone else's card or card data to purchase goods without the card holder's authority – a problem that authentication, with its password system, addresses very effectively), or because the consumer has challenged the quality of the goods or services in some way. Charge-backs expose your business to significant financial risk, so any way of reducing their occurrence should be welcomed.

Data from MasterCard indicates that 'card holder non-authorization' charge-backs (the category into which fraudulent charge-backs fall) represent an increasingly large percentage of all e-commerce charge-back expenses – over 80 per cent in recent years. Visa believes that the use of online authentication will reduce the level of online fraud by as much as 50 per cent – or, in other words, online shopping is about to become twice as safe.[1]

Some PSPs and banks will offer authentication as a standard part of their service, although it will be some time before all card holders' banks support the scheme and all card holders are fully enrolled.

Other risk of fraud

The increasing level of security surrounding online payment has meant that fraudsters have now evolved other means of attempting to obtain sensitive financial information. Currently, a highly fashionable variant of this is the 'phishing expedition'. Here, a fraudster sets up a spoof website to look very much like yours and then tricks customers into entering their confidential card details and other confidential information (password, PIN) under a false pretext (such as implying that a recent order that the shopper has placed may not have been processed correctly). The fraudulently obtained data is then used to purchase goods on the internet or to perpetrate identity theft.

The nature of this fraud is such that ordinarily only the largest retailers (or, more likely, banks) are targeted. Card holders are becoming far more aware of the dangers and are exercising greater protection of their confidential details, but phishing remains a risk nonetheless. It is good practice to reiterate to online customers that they should never divulge confidential card data in the circumstances described above (and, more importantly, that your business would never ask them to submit confidential information in this way).

Phishing activity does not cause the same liability to the retailer as conventional online card fraud does (see Authentication above) – the liability lies entirely with the card holder, who has failed to protect confidential card data. None the less, the spoof sites can be extremely convincing – often using graphics and logos copied from the genuine sites – and so it is easy to see how card holders can be duped.

Proving trustworthiness

Whilst online payment itself is relatively low-cost, creating an end-to-end e-commerce operation (including supply chain and logistics) can be a major investment. This leaves the business exposed to a considerable risk if the perceived trustworthiness of the site is not sufficient to attract the business necessary to amortize the investment.

Major brands have less of a problem in this respect, as their offline brand reputation tends to 'rub off' on their online brand. Smaller and less well-known businesses, however, often need an extra reputational 'shot in the arm'. Online shoppers are not always instinctively trusting; 30 million adults in the United Kingdom have accessed the internet, but only 14 million of those – less than half – have actually shopped online.

Businesses should consider investing in a 'trustmark' to help address shopper trust issues. There are several schemes in existence but one of the most manageable and sensibly-priced is Internet Shopping is Safe (ISIS), which is run by IMRG Ltd, one of the e-commerce industry's most respected bodies. For the modest sum involved – at the time of writing, £125 + VAT for a year's listing – it is an accessible and affordable scheme that enables small businesses as well as large to create a collective commitment to honesty and trustworthiness to which online shoppers will attach considerable importance. More information is available at www.imrg.org/isis

In addition, businesses should also clearly display key information on their website in order to inspire trust, including:

- a complete description of the goods and services offered and details of any guarantee, membership or subscription period offered in the price;
- details of the returns/refund policy;
- details of the privacy policy – which data is collected, who this information is shared with and how shoppers can opt out;
- customer service contact, including e-mail address, phone number and address – so that shoppers can contact the firm directly when they have a query;
- delivery policy and prices.

Conclusion

- The internet is a fantastic medium for delivering your company's products/services. Inevitably, there are risks, but if these are properly managed then taking payments online can be a real boost to your business's chances of success.
- Be aware that your customers' card details in particular, as well as their names, addresses and other contact details, are highly sensitive and confidential. By outsourcing the management of this data to a bank or PSP, you remove a potentially major technical and legislative headache.
- Anti-fraud technologies are constantly evolving in order progressively to reduce the risks to both card holder and merchant. These include Verified by Visa and MasterCard SecureCode, as well as other fraud screening services. All these services reduce the likelihood of the retailer losing significant sums of money by inadvertently sending goods to fraudsters and then suffering a charge-back. The best source of these services is the bank or PSP that handles the payment technology.
- Taking payments online is key to successful online trading, but so is trust. Make consumers feel confident that their online shopping experience is safe, and word of your reliability will spread.

Note

1. www.e-visa.com/security/main.asp

2.9

The spy that came in from the cold

Frank Coggrave, Websense

In the face of recent viruses, such as Sasser and Netsky, spyware might not seem an important risk to business, but malicious spyware is a serious threat that cannot be ignored. Traditionally, spyware surreptitiously and invisibly gathers information on a user and transmits the information back to website operators, who then use the data to present users with targeted adverts or sell their database of internet usage statistics to other organizations. But to play down the real threat of spyware, and the risk for misuse, would be to vastly underestimate the potential harm it can cause.

Take the example of a big investment house that was recently a victim of hacking and fraud that resulted from a malicious form of spyware. A day trader at the stockbrokers was shocked to discover that he had lost more than $40,000 (£26,000) after installing what he thought was a market analysis program. This later turned out to be a keylogger application that transmitted his account login details and passwords back to a hacker. Thankfully, the hacker has since been tracked down, but the incident can't have done much good for the company's reputation.

Unfortunately, this example is not an isolated case. Perhaps more troubling is the reality that hackers using spyware can commit not just fraud, but industrial espionage. After all, if spyware can be installed covertly on anyone's PC, determined hackers could target those with access to financial reports, confidential business information or client reports and send these surreptitiously through the firewall without the user even knowing.

The problem for businesses is that spyware is prolific. It is estimated that 90 per cent of PCs with internet access are infected with spyware. Add to this the fact that the average spyware program transmits copious amounts of data – typically 300 items of personal information totalling 1MB of data from each infected machine every day – and it is easy to see why spyware is a growing problem for businesses today.

One major insurance company recently ran reports and found out that it had sent 800,000 outbound spyware messages in just four days. Likewise, a large consultancy that installed anti-spyware software discovered that it had blocked 1.6 million outbound spyware messages in less than two months.

Until the widespread emergence of the internet, spyware was not even a problem. Since the internet was first adopted as a useful tool for working and communicating, it has enabled viruses, worms and spyware programs to spread rapidly. Unlike other pieces of malicious code, however, a user might not realize that their IT systems have been infected by spyware.

According to Websense's 2004 Web@Work survey, there is a huge discrepancy between employees' knowledge and understanding of spyware and the reality IT managers discover on corporate workstations. For example, only 6 per cent of employees who access the internet at work claim to have ever visited any websites that contain spyware while at work. Compare this to the statistic mentioned above, that 90 per cent of PCs are affected by spyware. And what's more, IT managers say that spyware is on the rise, with 40 per cent of managers believing that the number of spyware-infected workstations in their organization has increased.

The trouble with spyware is that it often appears after users download software through seemingly legitimate products. These include anything from file sharing and instant messaging applications, to e-mail customization (such as hot bars) and click-throughs on online advertisements. Without realizing it, users are inadvertently opening the door to spyware – unless they stop to read the small print in the online licence agreement.

One of the most popular examples of spyware infecting computers is via downloading files from websites such as Kazaa or Grokster. More covert forms of spyware exploit vulnerabilities in internet browsers or can be found in seemingly innocuous software programs, such as parental and employee monitoring tools.

Spyware is also becoming more intelligent. For example, spyware can download on to a user's sound card, or if there is a microphone on the PC, potentially enable the intruder to listen in on confidential conversations. These surveillance forms of spyware are markedly more dangerous than basic adware that spawns multiple windows featuring advertising information.

From this perspective, spyware represents a breach of company privacy that could open the door for rival businesses to gain access to secret company documents. More pertinently for law firms, it could jeopardize the confidentiality of classified client information. In a worst case scenario, this could result in time-consuming lawsuits costing hundreds of thousands of pounds for organizations, if left unmanaged. For IT managers, spyware is seen at best as a nuisance eating up bandwidth capacity on the network or, at worst, as an expensive threat destroying entire hard drives, in cases where spyware is so embedded it is impossible to free the machine.

The trouble with spyware is that it is very difficult to find where it is hidden, especially as spyware applications are continually finding new ways of evading detection. Spyware is not obvious, unlike viruses that intend to damage machines, and therefore make their presence felt. However, there are some simple steps that can mitigate a company's risk.

To manage the control of spyware across every aspect of the business, it is paramount to have a company internet use policy in place so that every user is aware of the dangers. If employees are allowed to download software to their PCs, reading the online licence agreement, however small the print, should be enforced throughout the organization.

Until recently, spyware was not included in most company's security policies, simply because conventional security products do not protect machines from this type of attack. Spyware programs are not viruses, so anti-virus software fails to protect a company's IT infrastructure from this threat. Likewise, installing a firewall is also almost useless in the face of spyware, given that many spyware programs communicate through the same internet port as general web traffic.

To make matters worse, some of the anti-spyware software that claims to delete existing spyware files from IT systems and protect the infrastructure from future threats, is alleged to install its own spyware programs when downloaded. This is a serious problem and one that legal authorities in the United States and Europe are looking at addressing fast.

The only solution for IT managers in a corporate environment is to install anti-spyware products that automatically prevent users from downloading and installing programs that contain spyware. It will also ensure that any spyware application already installed on a user's PC is unable to run, and thus stop it from transmitting confidential information. Given the dangers of spyware, IT managers who have no such solutions in place already should seriously consider investing in these tools as a key part of their IT security portfolio.

3

Software protection

WARNING! Copying software can degrade your experience

Macrovision technologies are fundamentally transparent to the honest user. However when someone tries to make an illegal copy of protected content they can encounter several layers of protection designed to deter, inconvenience and ultimately, frustrate them.

For all your content management requirements, for video (DVD, cable & satellite Pay TV etc), for music (CDs and downloads) and software (product activation, anti-hack solutions and electronic licensing), call Macrovision today.

macrovision®

www.macrovision.com

Macrovision Europe Limited
Malvern House, 14/18 Bell Street, Maidenhead, Berkshire, SL6 1BR
Tel: +44 (0) 870 871 1111   Fax: +44 (0) 870 871 1161
Email: salesinfo-europe@macrovision.com

3.1

Firewalls

Mark Rogers, More Solutions

The analogy

I live in a modest house in a normal street. My home has a front door, secured with a Yale lock, and back doors and several windows, all of which can also be locked. It also has a fenced garden with a locked gate. While at home I can see more or less unimpeded through my windows, although passers-by cannot easily see in through the net curtains. My girlfriend and a few family members have keys to the house, and know the code to my alarm. Other than that I have few visitors, including the postal worker who leaves me a never-ending stream of bills and junk mail, and the newspaper deliverer who drops a free local paper through my door once a week. I also have a gardener who visits once a week, and my windows are cleaned every month or so.

I am reasonably happy about this level of security, although I am well aware that there are shortcomings and should anyone have a deep desire to get into my house they will do so.

If I were a computer then I could achieve most of this in virtual terms with a *firewall*.

What is a firewall?

You probably do not care about the security of my house, but if your office network is connected to the internet you certainly *do* worry that you do not really know who can get in or what they could do if they did. You have probably heard of firewalls, but you do not have time to take a technology degree to work out whether you need one, so let us look again at the analogy.

Your office is your house and garden, and your firewall is what controls the boundary between this and the rest of the world. Striking a balance between security and convenience has many similarities between the two, but worryingly many organizations provide access to their network in ways that would seem cavalier in home security.

Some basics

In theory, at least, my house is secure to anyone who does not have a key. In practice, complete security could not even be guaranteed in a house with no windows or doors (the equivalent of an office network not connected to the internet). However, while I know that every door or window makes intrusion much simpler, I live in a real world where the benefits in having access to the outside world from my house outweigh the risks, provided that I take reasonable steps to manage those risks.

My front door Yale lock is good at stopping people getting in, and at the same time allows anyone inside to get out without a key. This is similar to many basic network configurations, where access to everything on the internet is allowed to those on the network, with nobody on the internet allowed access to the office. This may or may not actually be desirable; if I had small children I would be keen to ensure they could not just leave the house when they felt like it, and similarly there may be certain people who you wish to prevent accessing certain services on the internet (maybe a blanket ban for some people, or web browsing but no downloading of movies and games by others). This is a decision based more on personnel management than security, though, and we will return to this later.

In firewall terms, it is common to allow access to the outside world for specific purposes. This is done by applying criteria which must be met in order for access to be allowed, and at a basic level relates to IP addresses and TCP ports. Using a different analogy for a moment, IP addresses are like telephone numbers and TCP ports are like extension numbers; to ring me you need to know both my telephone number and my extension, as without the former you cannot make the call and without the latter our receptionist will not put you through. IP addresses are simply the addressing system used on the internet, and allowing access to specific addresses is a bit like giving access to certain people.

Returning to the original analogy, appropriately enough the comparison here is between my postal mail and business e-mail. The standard TCP port for incoming e-mail is port 25, and 'opening port 25' on the firewall is the equivalent of having a letterbox on my front door. Unfortunately, it does nothing at this level to ensure that what comes through the port is genuine and wanted e-mail, and this is why firewalls are almost useless at preventing e-mail-borne viruses unless they prevent e-mail altogether. Some firewalls are 'stateful' – that is they do more than just open the letterbox but also check that what comes in them is mail (preventing newspapers or less savoury items passing through), but even then this does nothing to ensure that the mail you receive is mail you want.

Outward bound

Even basic firewalls are able to decide what to do based on the direction data is flowing, and more importantly, which side of the firewall initiated the connection. For example, browsing the web is clearly bi-directional; your browser 'uploads' the address of the page you want to view, and the graphics and text of the web page are then 'downloaded' back to the browser for display. Since the connection was initiated by your browser, inside your protected network, it is often safe to assume that data coming in through a connection initiated within the network can be allowed in, unchecked.

On the other hand, if an external device tries to access your computer without a request from you, then the firewall can inhibit the attempted access as being unwanted (most office networks do not usually need to allow any incoming connections at all). This results in a very simple configuration where all un-initiated incoming access is inhibited. However, in practice, this is over-simplistic for all but the smallest networks.

The data transfer capacity ('bandwidth') of the connection between your network and the internet is finite, and some users can consume disproportionate amounts of this capacity. For example, 'peer-to-peer' (or P2P) protocols allow users to share files with others elsewhere on the internet with little control or accountability. As well as consuming resources these protocols also allow – even encourage – sharing of copyrighted materials such as film and music files. A firewall, blocking outbound access to the ports used by these protocols, can be an invaluable (if not foolproof) weapon to prevent such abuse. Additionally, many e-mail-borne viruses contain software that, when triggered, makes outgoing connections to pass on passwords or allow external control of the infected PC, so leaving most outbound ports closed brings a degree of protection.

In summary, by acting at the boundary between your network and the internet a basic firewall can restrict access to certain types of internally initiated connection (such as e-mail and the web).

What a firewall looks like

Conceptually all firewalls can be seen as a black box with two network ports. One is connected to your local network, the other to the internet, and their sole job is to monitor and limit the data flowing from one to the other.

There are many firewall vendors such as Cisco, Watchguard and Nokia, each with a range of hardware options to suit a range of medium to large budgets, although comparing the options is beyond the scope of this article.

Also worth considering are the increasing number of PC-based firewalls, often based around the free Linux operating system. All worthwhile firewalls of this type require a dedicated PC (that is they do not run alongside other applications on the same hardware) since any additional software is a potential weak point. These packages (for instance, IPCop and Smoothwall) are ideal for lower budgets since they typically cost little if anything above the cost of a basic PC and provide more than adequate protection for many enterprises.

Some enterprises have areas of their network that need to provide services to the outside world, and therefore need different firewall rules from the network core. Recalling our analogy, this is akin to my garden – an area where security is reduced to allow access to the gardener and window cleaner, but with additional security maintained between the garden and the house. In firewall terminology this is often called a 'demilitarized zone' (DMZ), and it is achieved by having two firewalls, one between the outside world and the DMZ, and another with tighter controls between the DMZ and the core. Some firewall hardware combines these two (or more firewalls) in one box with separate network ports for separate zones.

The weakest link

Securing a network almost always makes life a little more difficult because it restricts the things you can do or the ease with which you can do them. We accept this with home security of course; many a time I have returned home in the rain and wished I did not have to stand out in the cold, fumbling for my keys, but however frustrating it is I would not just leave the house unlocked instead.

If firewalls have weak spots it is usually because humans, who create holes to make life easier without proper regard for their consequences, manage them. They are often a temporary measure 'just to get this working', and temporary fixes frequently become permanent. For example, it is possible to set up secure 'tunnels' into and between networks (for instance, to allow network access to home workers or travelling salespeople). These Virtual Private Networks (VPNs) are efficient and secure methods of allowing external access in a controlled fashion, but they can be complicated to set up compared with just opening a few ports for remote access using remote control software, so the simpler (and less secure) approach gets chosen, offering a relatively easy approach for hackers.

Therefore, an essential part of any security configuration is a routine audit of holes in your firewall. It is a minor task to run a basic scan across the ports of your firewall (from outside your network) to see if any are open, and this should be done regularly (and weaknesses corrected), as it will almost certainly be scanned (and weaknesses exploited) by someone else if you do not. Companies such as ESoft provide subscription services (www.securityspace.com) that can run these scans automatically.

Summary

Conceptually, a firewall is a very simple product that does a very simple job. In practice, the job it does is difficult to achieve, and as attacks get more sophisticated so too must the firewalls; however this is a job for the people who build firewalls, not for those who deploy them.

It is the nature of the job that firewalls do, that results in them being surrounded by jargon and acronyms. If they seemed complicated as a result, hopefully they seem less daunting now.

Now, where did I put my keys?

3.2

Viruses

Mark Rogers, More Solutions

You could be forgiven for thinking that computers are getting more like their owners every year. Few could doubt that they seem to be getting cleverer, and unfortunately, most people are aware that they can also catch the computer equivalent of the common cold. However, while we all know that computer viruses exist, many of us lack knowledge of what they actually are, how they spread, and how to prevent or (if necessary) cure them.

Of course a computer virus is just a piece of software. Gardeners define weeds simply as plants growing in the wrong place, and computer viruses are similar, working like the applications you use every day, but doing things you did not want done. Usually it is simply their presence that is the problem, and the fact that they spread almost uncontrollably using resources not meant for them. Less often, but usually more worryingly, their impact can be more destructive.

Computer viruses are not a new phenomenon, although their methods of propagation have evolved dramatically since internet use has become widespread. For a virus to jump from one computer to another has always required a transport mechanism, and while the floppy disk was effective a few years ago, the availability of direct connections between computers (with local networks, or LANs), and between those networks (the internet) has simplified that transport dramatically. Furthermore, the increased power and functionality of computers has made it possible for viruses to do things they could never have done before.

Anti-virus software

Ironically, the increased power of computers and the connections between them is also the biggest weapon in our defence against viruses. We can run anti-virus programs that transparently check every e-mail we receive and every program we run for viruses, without the computing overhead being noticeable. Furthermore, we can keep ahead of virus outbreaks (or, more accurately, no more than one step behind them) by keeping our anti-virus software up to date, again transparently, using the internet to download updates every few days. Updating your anti-virus software regularly is almost as important as installing the software in the first place.

Anti-virus software is therefore one of the most effective steps every business can (indeed must) take to protect itself from damage. The computer equivalent of immunization will keep most viruses at bay. It is remarkable that many of the viruses still being encountered today were first released months if not years ago, suggesting that many businesses still do not run up-to-date anti-viral software on their networks. However, just as in humans, viruses mutate and new ones are developed (thus being unrecognizable to the software sent to catch them, at least until their updates have arrived). Unfortunately a reliance on software protection alone is at best insufficient, and at worst brings a dangerous false sense of security.

Other measures

Viruses, and their cousins 'Trojans' and 'worms', rely for their spread on certain behaviours of their computer host, its operator, or both. Keeping the computer's operating system and its applications updated ('patched') with security updates can go a long way to limiting the ability of the computer to be an unwitting party to the viral spread.[1]

The operators are a much bigger challenge. Trust is the biggest problem – most people trust (or even fear) their computer in situations they should not. Here are some common approaches designed to trick the unwary operator, all primarily delivered by e-mail:

- Looking like a joke, funny movie clip, screen saver, or similar.
- Appearing to have come from someone you know. (Very often viruses do actually come from people you know, as they often spread by working through address books, so trusting the source cannot be confused with trusting what he or she appears to have sent you.)
- Appearing to have come from some other trusted source, such as Microsoft. A recent trend has been to send fake security patches, cleverly using Microsoft's corporate images and style of presentation in the e-mail to make it look official. Sometimes the sender's e-mail address will give this away, but often this too is 'spoofed' to look like it came from Microsoft.

Most of these approaches are properly called Trojans, as they are not infectious unless the attached program is run by the recipient, but this is encouraged by their pretending to be something they are not, as with the legendary wooden 'gift' horse of Troy. When activated they deliver some kind of payload, which increasingly includes 'spyware' which monitors your activity on the PC and attempts to collect passwords and credit card details to forward to someone else for their gain (and, inevitably, your loss). They then attempt to send copies of themselves to every e-mail address they can find on your system, by searching your address books and other sources on your PC.

Since it is important to the success of the Trojan that it is not recognized by its recipient, several increasingly ingenious methods of disguise are used. As well as collecting e-mail addresses from your PC, other details such as typical e-mail subjects can be collected and used to make the recipients of the resulting e-mail look more like it really did come from you. At least one even took the step of forwarding a random document from the PC with the e-mail, which could result in sensitive information being leaked to competitors or customers alike.

Potential damage

The biggest concern that many people have is that a virus could damage their PC in some way. In truth, physical damage is pretty much impossible, although formatting the computer's hard disk and deleting all the important data can be pretty devastating to both the individual and the organization he or she works for. As well as taking steps to avoid virus infection and thus avoid this potential damage, it is important that important data be backed up regularly so that its loss is much less significant.

The damage to a reputation that can be caused by sending confidential documents to the wrong people, or the damage to trust and respectability from just propagating a benign virus, are more serious threats to a computer literate business. This, combined with the costs of downtime assessing damage and restoring back-ups, are the real reasons why prevention is much better than cure.

Virus hoaxes

No introduction to computer viruses would be complete without mentioning hoax viruses. Since we have established that the biggest potential threat from a real virus can be to an organization's reputation, it can be true that hoax viruses have the potential to cause real damage to a business despite their false basis.

Hoax viruses usually take the form of an e-mail warning about something that is not a real threat. If they are believed, as they often are, they get forwarded by well-meaning recipients to all their colleagues and friends, often spreading as far if not further than a real virus might.

Some example hoaxes include:

- Simple lies, detailing serious but non-existent (and often technically implausible) threats. Probably the best known is the 'Good Times' virus hoax, which has been doing the rounds for many years now.
- Hoax warnings about legitimate programs. A good example is slfnbk.exe, a benign program on most Windows PCs that most people do not use and would not be aware of. The hoax warns of a serious and potentially damaging virus, and describes how this file is a sign of an infection. People follow the instructions to find that the file is indeed there, and delete it, glad that they caught it in time (and then forwarding the hoax on). If the hoax refers to a program that is genuinely important to the system operation the hoax can cause as much damage as a real virus.

Since these are not real viruses, they are not 'detected' by anti-virus programs. The hoaxes often play on this, describing how the threat is so new that most anti-virus programs will not detect it, thus adding to the urgency with which the hoax gets forwarded.

The 'cure' for hoaxes is remarkably simple, but few people think to use it. Typing a few key words from the hoax (such as 'slfnbk' in the example above) into an internet search engine such as Google will quickly show plenty of references to the hoax. In any case, anti-virus software writers do not send random warnings around by e-mail, any more than organizations like Microsoft send security update patches out by e-mail. A cool head and a quick check can be the best antidote to many threats.

Many non-virus hoaxes also exist, which can be just as damaging to reputations if forwarded without at least basic checks of their validity. Many claim something to the effect that 'for every person you send this e-mail to, <insert large corporation here> will donate <sum of money> to <very worthwhile cause>'.

Summary

- Computer viruses can be pervasive and damaging, but most serious problems are easily avoided with preventative action. Up to date anti-virus software and common sense are essential in equal parts.
- Many viruses do so little that a first scan for viruses can throw up several (even hundreds) which have lain dormant and unnoticed for years, and a panic response will usually do far more harm than the virus itself.
- However, the most important lesson to learn is that while actual damage to data is a tangible but relatively small risk, the real danger from viruses is the damage they cause to reputations, and this more than anything else is why they cannot be ignored.

Note

1. It is unfortunate that updates offered by software publishers could themselves contain weaknesses that are worse than those they seek to fix, particularly when the update is not security-related and perhaps fixes a bug that your organization has not been affected by. Our view is that for a small organization, installing all 'critical updates' is both essential and sufficient; however larger organizations with competent IT departments should assess the individual updates more thoroughly.

3.3

Authentication and encryption

Randle Cowcher, TrustAssured

As business processes become increasingly computerized and companies use the internet to work more closely with trading partners, they face new threats to their operations. Authentication and encryption can help your company deal with some of these issues:

- **Theft of proprietary data**: which gives your business competitive advantage – encrypting critical data when stored and in transit, so that only certain users can access it easily, prevents casual theft of proprietary data and makes it much more likely professional attempts to steal proprietary information will fail.
- **Identity theft**: robust authentication processes based on encryption make it harder for malicious individuals to fake identities that fool systems into giving them access, or to borrow the identities of real users.
- **Non-repudiation of transactions**: even if someone has legitimate access to your systems, you want to exercise control over their actions from a business perspective. For your own staff, that means ensuring they do not enter into contracts your company cannot (or should not) fulfil, while you want to be sure that trading partners cannot subsequently deny they placed orders or agreed specific terms. Encryption-based identities can be used to sign electronic documents and transactions, with the same legal status as a signature on a paper document, and to create an audit trail that provides evidence in the event of a dispute.

However, encryption and authentication-based services can be more than a defensive response to new threats. They enable you to change the way your business operates to deliver significant bottom-line benefits. For instance, you can:

- **Use low-cost but untrusted infrastructure** such as the internet to streamline business processes, but be sure your systems are protected from accidental or malicious damage.
- **Develop online collaboration solutions** that allow your employees to work more closely with business partners or overseas colleagues as easily and securely as if they were all in the same office.
- **Broaden your trade networks**: finding new customers or suppliers on a global basis – by finding partners online, but still be able to create the same level of trust you would look for in a traditional real-world relationship.

Encryption: how it works

All encryption uses an algorithm or mathematical procedure to 'scramble' or encode a message in a particular way. Anyone receiving the message needs to understand how to 'unscramble' or decode the message. A very simple form of transcription is simply to replace each letter in a message by the next letter in the alphabet. Modern encryption solutions are rather more complex, and rely on a key to specify how the message should be encoded. This allows the same algorithm to be used by many different users, but generate encoded messages that are unique to each user.

Encryption can be based on a single secret key that both sender and receiver need to know. However, the process of sharing that key represents a security risk. Most encryption solutions today use a method called public key encryption that allows users to decrypt the messages of others without having to exchange secret keys securely. It works by using algorithms that encrypt and decrypt data using different, yet mathematically linked, keys. One key is 'public' and can be sent out to the people you want to communicate with over an insecure network. The other 'private' key is kept secret and cannot be discovered through knowledge of the public key or its underlying algorithm, except by applying 'brute force' computing power.

If a computer receives a message encrypted with someone's private key, it can decrypt it using that person's public key – and being able to decrypt it successfully also verifies that it was sent by that particular person, since only their private key could have been used to encrypt the message initially. This allows public key encryption to be used for authentication when connecting to systems or services and for legally binding digital signatures. In addition, public key encryption includes a 'checking' mechanism which confirms that messages have not been altered in transit.

In practice, if you want to exchange messages between more than a few users or between users in many different locations, you need some form of public key infrastructure (PKI) to allow you to manage the process of issuing keys to users and sharing public keys.

Authentication: how it works

While public key encryption can provide a technical basis for authenticating a user, authentication itself is achieved in one of three ways, through:

- something only the user knows;
- a physical item only the user has;
- a physical trait unique to that user.

The simplest form of identity verification, which relies on *something only the user knows*, is a user ID and password. The user ID/password combination is extremely cheap and easy to implement, but also relatively straightforward to break or steal. The ease with which user IDs and passwords can be stolen has been shown recently by a number of scams to harvest the IDs of customers of several online banking services. In addition, a simple user ID/password combination only verifies users when they log in or on other occasions when they are asked to re-enter their password. It does not allow users to provide legally binding digital signatures confirming that it was they (and not someone else) who were the originators of a message, approved a document or authorized a transaction.

A more complex form of user ID and password that can support legally binding authentication is a PKI certificate. Certificates are encryption keys and, as described previously, can be used to both secure and authenticate a message.

As with the simple user ID/password combination, the certificate can be simply something that the user knows, although since these keys are typically long, complex alphanumeric strings, it is not practical for a user to remember them. Certificates are therefore typically held on some form of token, requiring users to authenticate themselves through a physical item only they have. Certificates can be implemented purely through software, but there is a risk that a user could be impersonated if someone were to gain access to that user's account on the system in some way.

There are several different forms of token, but the most common is a smart card, since it generally provides the best combination of:

- **flexibility**: a single card has the capacity to support several different applications;
- **security**: since the processing capabilities of the smartcard chip allow it to take an active part in the authentication process;
- **cost**.

The final kind of authentication solution centres on biometrics or checking a physical trait unique to the user, such as a fingerprint or iris print. Biometric systems are expensive to implement, can raise concerns amongst users that they are a threat to their civil liberties, and fingerprint-based biometric systems have already been outwitted by a number of methods for duplicating fingerprints, with or without the knowledge of the user.

Biometric systems are therefore only truly effective when combined with a token or smartcard-based certificate. In these circumstances, the biometrics element usually adds little to the overall strength of the security solution.

The business case for encryption and authentication

Failing to secure data and authenticate users creates risks in many different ways for businesses, such as:

- **operational risks** if transactions are corrupted or changed while in transit or being stored;
- **financial risk** in the event of identity fraud, so that bills are unpaid;

- **reputation risk and damage** to your brand if customer data is misused as a result of a security breach;
- **strategic risk** if critical proprietary data such as formulae or designs falls into the hands of your competitors.

Any business case for introducing authentication and encryption solutions will weigh these risks against the costs of implementing the solution. The main factors affecting those costs include:

- **Key strength and processing overhead**: the longer the key, the more difficult it is for a hacker to use brute force to break the code and get access to your information, but the more processing power required to perform the encryption. You should also look at whether you need to encrypt all data or just the most sensitive information. For example, do all e-mails need to be encrypted in transmission or held in encrypted form on the server, or just some of them? A final consideration is that encryption is classified as a military technology by the US and UK governments, which place restrictions on the export of the strongest forms of encryption technologies to certain countries.
- **How the key is held**: as noted above, users' encryption keys can be held in a number of ways. In the typical commercial scenario, balancing risks and costs almost always leads to the conclusion that a smart-card-based PKI solution is the most cost-effective approach.
- **Key management and distribution**: considerable effort is required to issue, distribute and manage encryption keys.

In practical terms, companies such as Entrust, VeriSign and RSA provide the technical elements needed to implement encryption and create a PKI. However, the strength of the solution depends as much, if not more, on having robust processes for issuing and revoking encryption keys or certificates and verifying them each time they are used.

The process can be broken down into steps managed by three different kinds of organizations:

- **Registration authorities**: provide background checks on individuals to confirm their identity before they are issued with a certificate.
- **Certification authorities**: handle the mechanics of issuing and revoking certificates.
- **Verification authorities**: provide confirmation of the certificate owner's identity as transactions are processed.

It is possible to build your own PKI and deliver all registration, certification and verification services yourself, but it is expensive to create, requires specific and scarce skills to implement and maintain, and a programme of continuous development to update it in line with the latest technical developments and threats.

You could work with some of the managed services suppliers who have sprung up to offer one or two of the three steps outlined above. However, a robust process and PKI which will allow you to reap the full benefits of authentication and encryption depends on three factors which a single organization will struggle to implement by itself, even with this support:

- Someone to act as the guarantor of that certificate. The kind of self-certification offered by many PKI-based products and by most certification authorities (who cannot offer

registration authority services) is about as valuable as someone offering you a membership card for a local gym as proof of identity, whereas a guarantor-backed certificate is equivalent to a credit card or passport.
- A set of rules for issuing and revoking certificates and for checking them each time they are used – and a standards-based process and infrastructure for applying those rules.
- Support for global operations with any partner, current or potential. The real returns of encryption and authentication come not from deploying locally with existing trading partners but from using PKI to facilitate low-risk trade with people you have never dealt with before.

There are few organizations that can provide all these aspects of the certificate management process. A lead in this area is being taken by the banks, which have traditionally provided trust services to businesses. The availability of end-to-end managed PKI services from providers such as RBS TrustAssured allows companies to provide smart-card-based certificates for their employees and trading partners in an extremely cost effective fashion.

Conclusion

Large and small businesses alike will increasingly find their trading partners looking to introduce encryption and authentication solutions to secure online transactions and allow trust to be created between online trading partners. The benefits will be great, and the costs and management challenge of meeting these requirements do not need to be painful.

The Ministry of Defence, with the assistance of Cap Gemini Ernst & Young, has implemented the Defence Electronic Commerce Service, a secure portal that allows suppliers to bid for contracts and make use of a collaborative environment that supports joint working on specific programmes.

The MoD deals with thousands of suppliers, who provide everything from toilet rolls to tanks, in transactions worth in total several billion pounds each year. DECS will allow the MoD to cut its procurement costs by 20 per cent, as well as deliver improvements in design time, risk reduction and lifecycle costs.

Suppliers authenticate themselves when connecting to the DECS service by using ChamberCard, which provides them with a digital identity held on a smartcard. ChamberCard is being provided by TrustAssured from the Royal Bank of Scotland (RBS) and the British Chambers of Commerce. The British Chambers of Commerce provides the branch network where suppliers can present their credentials to obtain a ChamberCard, while TrustAssured's fully managed service provides the processes and technical infrastructure to issue and revoke ChamberCards and validate them each time they are used.

3.4

Digital signatures

Johan Sys, GlobalSign

As e-mail increasingly is substituted for the use of letters and faxes, and as commercial transactions on the web become increasingly important to organizations, the need for secure communications grows to the same extent, especially with spoof attacks, interception of transmissions and other hacking methods becoming more widespread and getting more 'intelligent' every day. So, if the web is to achieve its true commercial potential, it is important that the right technological infrastructure is in place. Public key infrastructure (PKI) enabled by cryptography provides a secure basis. PKI is the technology behind digital certificates and digital signatures.

What digital signatures are

Like the signature you use on written documents today, digital signatures are now being used to identify authors/co-signers of e-mail or electronic data. Digital signatures are created and verified using digital certificates. To understand what digital certificates are, we need to take a closer look at *cryptography*. Cryptography is the science of transforming information anyone can read (in plain text) into information not everyone can read. In this process, information is coded (encryption) to stop information from being read or altered by anyone but the intended recipient. It may be intercepted, but it will not be intelligible to someone without the ability to decode (decrypt) the message. Encryption and decryption require a mathematical formula or 'algorithm' to convert data between readable and encoded formats, and a key.

There are two types of cryptography: symmetric (or secret key) and asymmetric (public key). Symmetric key cryptography is characterized by the fact that the same key used to encrypt the data is used to decrypt the data. Clearly, this key must be kept secret among the communicating parties; otherwise the communication can be intercepted and decrypted by others. Until the mid-1970s, symmetric cryptography was the only form of cryptography available, so the same secret key had to be known by all individuals participating in any application that provided a security service. However, this all changed when Whitfield Diffie and Martin Hellman introduced the notion of *public key cryptography* in 1976.

In such a system, in order for two parties to exchange information in a secure fashion, each participant requires two keys: a public key and a private key. If one key is used to encrypt a message, then only the other key in the pair can be used to decrypt it. Although the keys of the public and private key pair are mathematically related, it is computationally infeasible to derive one key from the other, so the private key is protected from duplication or forgery even when someone knows the public key. Therefore, it is safe to openly distribute your public key for everyone to use, but it is essential that your private key remains closely guarded and secret. The public key can be used to verify a message signed with the private key, or encrypt messages that can only be decrypted using the private key. If someone wants to send you an encrypted message, they encrypt the message with your public key and you, being the sole possessor of the corresponding private key of the pair, are the only one who can decrypt it.

How are digital signatures created and verified?

To create a digital signature, the signer creates a 'hash', an algorithm that creates a unique shortened version of the message, and then uses his or her private key to encrypt the hash. The encrypted hash is the digital signature. If the message were changed in any way, the hash result of the changed message would be different. The digital signature is unique to both the message and the private key used to create it, so it cannot be forged. The digital signature is then appended to the message, and both are sent to the message recipient. The recipient recreates the hash from the received message, and then uses the public key of the original sender to decrypt the hash included in the received message. If the two hash results are identical, two things have been verified. The first is that the digital signature was created using the signer's private key (assurance that the public key corresponds to the signer's private key) – no one is pretending to be or masquerading as the signer. This verifies the *authenticity* of the signer, and the signer cannot claim to have not signed the message. The second is that the message has not been changed: this verifies the *integrity* of the message.

The role of a certificate authority (CA)

A digital signature is created using a digital certificate, which binds a public key to an individual or organization. The binding of a public key to an individual or organization is certified by a trusted source, typically a certification authority (CA). A CA is a trusted authority that issues and manages digital certificates. A CA uses a PKI to perform the life-cycle management of digital certificates. These certificates typically include the owner's public key, the expiration date of the certificate, the owner's name, and other information about the public key owner. CAs may also be involved in a number of administrative tasks such as end-user registration, but these are often delegated to the registration authority

(RA). The role of the RA is to verify the identity of the person or organization that attempts to register.

Legal framework

Digital signatures can be compared to the traditional hand-written signature that has been used for centuries to do business. The only difference is that the transactions take place via a new medium, the internet. Therefore, new laws have to be implemented to reflect this new reality.

The use of digital signatures is supported by recent legislative actions that provide credibility to the concept of electronic signatures and recognition to the need for such a capability. Both the US E-Sign Law, (passed in 2000) and the EU Digital Signature Law (passed in 2001) are examples of this trend.

Using digital signatures in your business

One of the most crucial questions in any business transaction is the identity of the entity with which the transaction is being conducted. Historically, personal relationships, face-to-face contract signings, notaries, and third-party counsel are used to help establish trust in this most important aspect of conducting business. As the reliance on paper shifts to electronic transactions and documents, so must the reliance on traditional trust factors shift to electronic security measures to authenticate our electronic business partners, customers and suppliers before engaging in the exchange of information, goods and services. Similarly, the need for confidentiality and confidence in the integrity of exchanged information is critical. Extending this list of security services, there may be further need to establish the non-repudiation of agreements, and to digitally certify and securely timestamp transactions.

Digital signatures support all these security services. Let us take a look at some applications in different vertical markets that can benefit from the use of digital signatures:

- **Financial services**: payment authentication for stock purchases, access control for online banking, digital notary of loans.
- **Insurance**: digitally sign quotes, authenticate online payment of premiums, version management of documents.
- **Government**: electronic ID-cards, automated and electronic response to RFPs, secure messaging with the government.
- **Industry**: digitally sign electronic contracts, linking procurement systems in an automated way, access control for business partner to online applications, establishing a web presence.

The PKI market

In the late 1990s, market analysts predicted a bright future for digital certificates. The market for PKI – the technology needed to generate certificates – would become the fastest growing segment in the IT security space. Reality was different, though. PKI projects did take off, but most of them never got beyond their pilot phase. As a consequence many PKI vendors ran into financial problems, and some even went out of business. The PKI market has not delivered on its promise because the implementation and maintenance of an in-house PKI requires highly specialized internal staff. After all, PKI is a combination of very specific technologies, infrastructures and practices.

What companies and governments want are digital certificates to secure their communications and applications. They do not necessarily want the hassle of implementing and maintaining a complex PKI infrastructure. Some companies in the IT security market have realized this, and have come up with an alternative model: the so-called outsourced PKI solution. This means that companies that want to implement digital certificates today have three choices to get these certificates:

- purchase certificates from a public CA such as GlobalSign or VeriSign;
- operate a private CA, meaning the company has to purchase and implement its own PKI;
- go for an outsourced PKI solution, offered by companies such as GlobalSign and Ubizen.

The first alternative is a good solution if, for instance, a company wants to provide its employees with digital certificates to sign confidential e-mail communications. If a company wants to deploy certificates across different applications, involving both internal and external parties, or if it wants to be a CA itself, it will have to choose between the last two of these three options. The main parameters related to the decision between these two options are time to market, size of population, application, interoperability, financial and human resources, legal framework and more.

For early implementers of PKI with huge budgets and sufficient IT and administrative capacity, deploying an infrastructure on an in-house basis was most appropriate. However, as PKI attracts increasing interest from a larger number of large and medium-sized companies and organizations, the case for outsourcing PKI becomes favourable. Outsourced PKI solutions provide a multitude of benefits for business. Although the underlying idea is to transfer the burden of implementation and management of the PKI solution to a service provider, there are undoubtedly important strategic and financial advantages in outsourcing trust as well.

Electronic identity cards are on their way

So far digital certificates have typically been used as part of projects in the private sector, that is, securing e-mail communication within a company, securing access to a specific web server, or securing a VPN connection. With the rise of electronic identity cards this will change dramatically. E-ID cards will make sure that the public at large will get digital certificates in a very user-friendly way. The certificates will simply come with each e-ID card.

In 2003 we have seen one of the first large-scale rollouts of e-ID cards in Europe, namely in Belgium. The BelPIC project will provide each Belgian citizen with an electronic identity card over a period of five years. The Belgian electronic identity card comes in an ID1 (bank card) format, displays a photo, some basic identity information, a signature of the cardholder and incorporates a microchip. The microchip on the e-ID card holds the same data as the physical card but is, in addition, equipped with two key pairs and their related digital certificates, articulated by a private PIN code. One certificate is used for secure identification, the second for electronic signing.

The e-ID card, safeguarding the traditional purposes of the former identity card, will give Belgian citizens simpler, faster and more secure access to administrative procedures. As such, over time, citizens will have access to numerous e-government services and be able to vote electronically, submit tax returns online, communicate changes of address, obtain civil records, declare household employees, and declare births or manage birth certificates. In addition, as the e-ID cards are based on referenced standards, they can also be used to access other than e-government applications requiring a certified identity. It is interesting to note that for this large-scale project the Belgian government has opted for an outsourced PKI solution (provided by subcontractors Ubizen and GlobalSign).

3.5

Biometrics

Clive Reedman and Bill Perry, Emerging Technology Services

Biometrics is the automated identification, or verification of human identity through the measurement of repeatable physiological, or behavioural traits. In general terms identification means the search of a biometric sample against a database of other samples in order to ascertain whether the donor is already contained in, or new to the database.

Verification refers to the 'one to one' comparison between a sample and another to ask the question, 'Are you who you say you are?' The majority of access control applications utilize verification techniques, rather than attempting searches of databases, which could compromise accuracy and raise costs. The one major exception to this is iris recognition, which is nearly always implemented in a 'one to many' scenario.

The benefits of biometrics

Look at it this way. Security is now usually based on either 'something you know' or 'something you have' or a combination of both. Take the example of a cashpoint card. You *have* the card and you *know* the PIN number. However, the card may be lost or stolen, or your PIN may be stolen by stealth, or simply because it is written down and kept with the card! Maybe the 'something you know' is a password, but how many of us have multiple passwords, and how many of us write them down and leave them where they can be found? How many costly calls to IT help desks are concerned with forgotten or compromised passwords? How many employees are 'clocked' in and out by friends when they are actually somewhere else, or permit their passwords to be used by others? The integrity or quality of data entered to, or extracted from, systems is often trusted implicitly. However, how can anybody using that data rely on it unless they can be sure who it was that entered it, or manipulated it? For instance is a 'signed' e-mail actually to be trusted if all that is required to sign it is a password, used to release the appropriate key(s)? Can you be sure that an unauthorized person who may have access to the required passwords at the receiving end cannot read an encrypted e-mail? What real trust do we have therefore in the data audit trail?

Traditionally, security of data and the trust in data relies on the use of 'something you know', for instance, a password, or PIN and/or 'something you have', such as a smart card. Used in combination, a reasonable level of security may be possible. However, there remain a number of risks associated with the use of the 'have' and 'know' scenarios.

```
Something you  ←——————————→  Something you
   HAVE                            KNOW
         ↘                      ↙
           →  Something you ARE ←
```

Figure 3.5.1

Biometrics adds a 'something you are' (see Figure 3.5.1). Can you leave your fingerprint, face, voice and so on at home in the morning like you can your office pass? Can your iris be stolen? There lies the prime advantage of a biometric. It is part of you and is not therefore easily compromised. Consider also the issue of 'non-repudiation'. I could claim that I had lost my cashpoint card before money was withdrawn, or that somebody had found my computer password. However, it is hard for me to claim that somebody had copied my iris pattern! (See Table 3.5.1.)

Table 3.5.1 Security methods

Method	Examples	Properties
What you know	User ID	Shared
	Password	Many passwords easy to guess
	PIN	Forgotten
What you have	Cards	Shared
	Badges	Can be duplicated
	Keys	Lost or stolen
What you have combined with what you know	Cashpoint card and PIN	Shared
		PIN compromised
Something unique to each user	Fingerprint	Not possible to share
	Face	Repudiation unlikely
	Iris	Forging difficult
	Voiceprint	Cannot be lost or stolen
	Signature (dynamic)	

How biometric systems work

All biometric systems work in much the same way. A sensor (camera, microphone and so on) captures a physical or behavioural characteristic. The 'image' is then converted to a numerical code (template) using a proprietary algorithm. The data is often then compressed for transmission within the system, which may be self contained, or spread over two continents! The extracted feature data is either then stored, or compared against other numerical codes created during the 'enrolment' process. The result of the comparison is an automated decision (see Figure 3.5.2). This may be, 'does this person have access to the building', or 'can this person be logged on to a computer network?' However, the range of applications is vast and spread throughout all areas where data integrity and security are issues. Remember though that in some applications, security is not the reason for implementing a biometric system. Occasionally it is purely to provide a measure of convenience to the end user, such as perhaps a task-oriented computer program, which normally requires a number of key presses to change 'modes'. A biometric may relieve the user of the need to remember how to navigate complex menus, or may make the use of 'hot desk' scenarios simpler, as for all intents and purposes the data network can recognize exactly who is logging into a given terminal, without the need for that person to remember passwords or carry any cards.

Although the vast majority of feature extraction and search algorithms are proprietary in nature, international standards for biometrics are beginning to emerge. These standards are mainly focused on the need to make biometric systems more interoperable across differing vendor platforms. It is unlikely and possibly unrealistic to expect vendors to give up their proprietary code in favour of global interoperability. However, the effort is now focused on how to achieve the goal of large-scale acceptance and adoption of biometrics without undue damage to the commercial base. In general, this can be achieved in a number of ways, particularly the specifying of data interchange standards that specify how images should be transferred across diverse systems. Given a good quality image of the biometric trait, such as a face, finger or iris, it becomes possible for most data to be encoded by any suitable biometric system.

The International Standards Organization (ISO) has an active program through Standards Committee 37 (SC37). To develop the standards the work was divided into six distinct working groups, and convenors were appointed. These groups are:

- WG 1 Harmonized Biometric Vocabulary (do we speak the same language?).
- WG 2 Biometric Technical Interfaces (how do we transfer data?).
- WG 3 Biometric Data Interface Formats (what form does the data need to be in?).
- WG 4 Profiles for Biometric Applications (what are we trying to achieve?).
- WG 5 Biometric Testing and Reporting (how do we ensure the system works well?).
- WG 6 Cross Jurisdictional and Societal Aspects (what are the legal and social imperatives?).

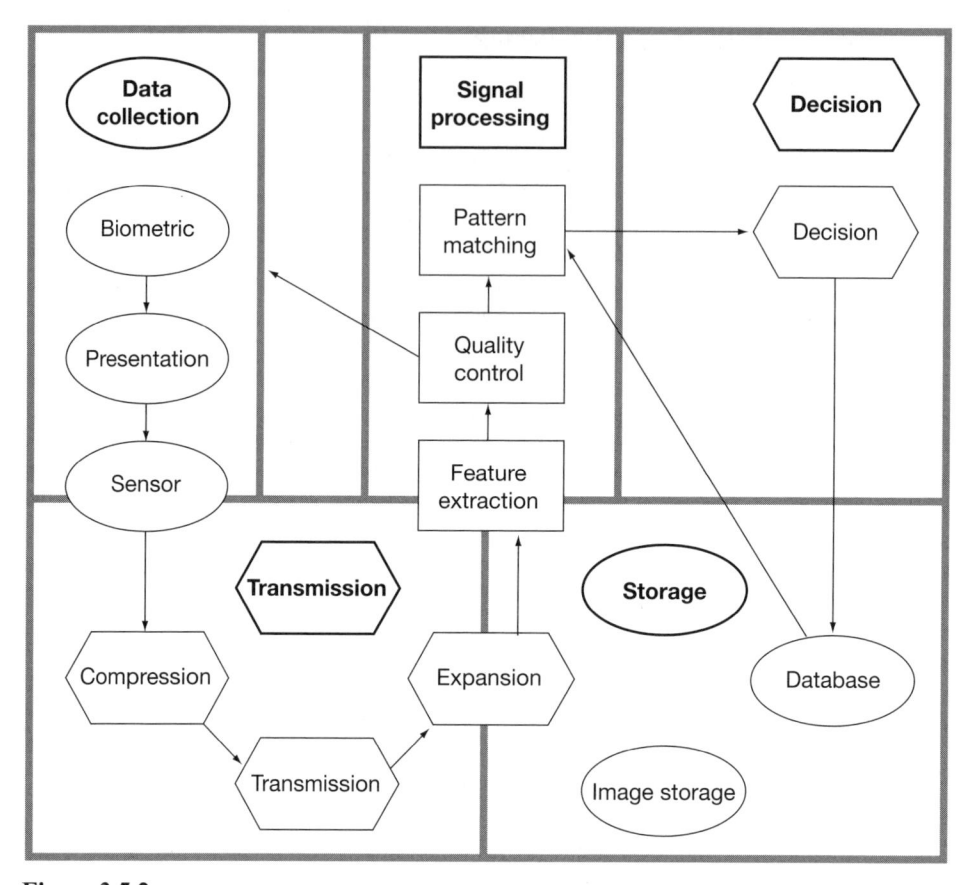

Figure 3.5.2

How biometrics is relevant to e-business

Reliable user authentication is becoming an increasingly important task in the e-business world. It is one of the cornerstones of transaction security, and linked intrinsically to confidentiality, integrity and non-repudiation. The consequences of an insecure or untrusted authentication system in a corporate or enterprise environment can be catastrophic, and may include loss of confidential information, denial of service, and data integrity being compromised.

The established techniques of user authentication, which involve the use of either passwords and user IDs (identifiers), or identification cards and PINs (personal identification numbers), suffer from several limitations. Passwords and PINs can be acquired unlawfully by direct or indirect observation. Once an attacker acquires the user ID and the password, that attacker has total access to the user's resources. In addition, there is no way to positively link the usage of the system or service to the actual user, that is, there is no 'real' protection against repudiation by the user ID owner. For example, when a user ID and password is shared with a colleague there is no way for the system to know who the actual user is, and it is consequentially extremely difficult for any organization to institute criminal charges or internal disciplinary measures. A similar scenario arises when a transaction involving a credit, debit or charge card is conducted over the internet. Even though the data being sent over the internet may be protected using secure encryption methods, current systems are not capable of assuring that the rightful owner of the card initiated the transaction.

It is also of course important to note that the source of a great number of criminal attacks on systems emanate at the administrator level, or amongst those who have an element of control of the data system above that held by the general user. Indeed, 'shop floor' data users are less able, or likely, to attack the system simply because existing security policies prevent them doing so without expending a great deal of effort in the attempt. A biometric access control system adds a level of assurance that those persons with access to the control of system configuration and security are themselves subject to another layer of security and audit. Consider how often computer rooms themselves are left relatively insecure because anybody with the appropriate card, or knowledge of a door code, could enter them.

With the emergence of multiple new services on the internet, a great deal of importance is now being placed upon the personal and commercially sensitive information transmitted over open public networks and stored on often shared commercial servers. Security techniques such as PKI are becoming more and more the order of the day. However, these security techniques only ensure that the correct, authentic digital certification is being used during the transaction. There remains the assumption that the correct person is actually using that certificate *and* that he or she has the authority to do so. Biometrics is the only technical solution that is able to closely couple the actual person to the authorized transaction, ensuring that the complete circle of authenticity, confidentiality, non-repudiation and trust is evident.

Biometrics, as a technological solution, has been slow to attract the interest of the general public and large corporate bodies alike. To a great number of people it is still viewed as 'science fiction' and not really for this world. They could not be more wrong. Biometrics not only provides the capability of filling a large hole in the transaction security world, but also offers various other solutions to common business process challenges. It should also be remembered that process efficiency always results in a cost benefit for the business. Estimates of just how much it costs individual businesses to deal with forgotten or compromised passwords vary considerably, from a few pence to many pounds. A biometric solution can alleviate this burden and subsequent cost by a considerable amount, releasing IT staff's time to perform other duties and reducing the overall costs of IT system management. Large systems integrators quote return on investment as being within months rather than years.

With the ever-increasing use of wireless technology in the office, roaming laptop and mobile phone environments and internet based, secure e-commerce brings a new challenge to secure identity authentication. As mobile e-commerce takes off, and the value of transactions increase, secure user authentication will become ever more important.

Today, anonymous transactions permeate modern life. People misappropriate the identities of other people, giving them access to that person's money and everything else. With biometrics, once you are identified by your biometric, whether it is a fingerprint or iris scan or another unique identifier, you can use it everywhere as proof of your identity. Biometrics is the key, not a password or knowledge-based system.

3.6

From 'Made in Hollywood' to 'Appearing in your local car boot sale' – piracy and the business of digital entertainment

Simon Mehlman, Macrovision

Introduction

There's a digital dilemma facing the digital entertainment business today, and it will probably affect you either professionally or personally. Whilst we take for granted certain 'living expenses' such as food, accommodation, transport and utilities, have you ever paused to consider how much money you spend on watching television (licence fee, satellite, DVDs), CDs and electronic games? It's likely to be a significant sum of money and, in spite of growing demand, the economies of digital entertainment are undergoing a revolution caused by the revenue-depleting explosion of digital piracy.

Supply and demand – what's changing

Fuelled by rising demand and established distribution channels, the digital entertainment sector is growing rapidly. This can be seen in falling hardware costs; for example, DVD player sales have soared whilst the unit cost for the hardware has dropped, with players appearing for £20 in the 2004 UK Christmas retail market. Perversely, this hardware price fall makes some new DVD releases more expensive than their player! The fall in prices of hardware has outstripped the fall in prices of DVDs, CDs and music, clearly illustrating that in this market, 'Content is king'.

To fuel continued growth, the entertainment business needs consumers to purchase their product and is prepared to offer great deals to get more revenue. The value is clear, the costs are clear and the demand has never been higher; unfortunately the factors underpinning supply and demand are a lot less certain. This growing business with established distribution channels is now under siege from unauthorized distribution and delivery in the form of professional and casual piracy.

Modern consumerism is based on choice: the choice of buying a range of goods legitimately, acquiring them illegally or, when funds are insufficient, 'doing without'. Curiously, consumers have the capacity to embrace pirated content whilst ignoring any issues of theft that might normally be associated with acquiring goods illegally, such as through shoplifting. Many of the organizations that combat piracy refer to the prevalence of a 'copy-culture' and its broad acceptance by consumers.

Forms of piracy

Digital entertainment piracy can take many forms, and often their supply channels overlap and interact. Pirated product appears in car boot sales of counterfeit CDs and DVDs sourced from Eastern Europe or made overnight by a neighbour's child; or it can appear as amateur recordings made on a camcorder in a cinema in Asia or the United States, or as professional copies that are compressed to squeeze a 6Gb DVD movie on to a 700Mb CD and then distributed around the world using a file-sharing network. The combination of physical and online piracy at local, national and international levels has created an incredibly complex illegal distribution channel whereby consumers looking for cheaper buys are willing to condone the acquisition of what are, in effect, stolen goods.

Advances in consumer electronics (CE) technology, such as DVD recorders and hard-disk based PVRs have made complicated tasks easy; many employ the phrase 'as simple as pushing a button'. This drive to simplicity may be the single biggest advance in CE. Making a great product that requires tweaking and tuning is fine for the high value, low volume market, but to make real money requires mass market adoption and that in turn requires simplicity: fewer wires, simpler instructions, the prerequisite of a 'user-friendly' interface.

In addition to increasing access to easy to use sophisticated CE technology, digital entertainment has been stimulated by the massive uptake of domestic broadband. The

Business Software Alliance (BSA) states that worldwide, 'Today, there are 70 million broadband households. By the end of 2007 there will be an additional 100 million.'

The combination of increasing consumer demand and the means to create perfect copies simply and illegally, and then distribute them easily around the world, has seen an unprecedented explosion in consumer and professional piracy. This is not simply a case of counterfeit copies made to look like the genuine article. The dilemma facing the digital entertainment business is that it now risks competition from its own customers, who may supply a high quality copy of the original product to the market, leaving the content-owner to miss out on the revenue from thousands of transactions taking place every minute of every day; the World Wide Web never sleeps.

The rapid evolution of file-sharing peer-to-peer (P2P) networks has provided unparalleled ease of access to illegally distributed electronic files such as song tracks and movies. Increasing broadband speeds now also allow for complete 'disk-images' of 4 gigabytes and upwards to be transferred and downloaded with the same ease as 700Mb compressed formats were in 2003. One P2P site I visited offered a single 31Gb download that consisted of a four-DVD boxed collection.

Studies and statistics vary slightly in their findings but most concede that the scale of the problem is massive. A study undertaken by Pew Research concluded that 'at least 1.58 billion files per year are downloaded and/or swapped without payment' whilst the most recent annual piracy report by the British Phonographic Industry (BPI) stated that 1 billion song files are illegally downloaded in the UK every year.

The high profile victims of this technological abuse are the music and film industries. The World Intellectual Property Organization (WIPO) concluded that 99 per cent of music files exchanged on the web are pirated, clearly dwarfing the legitimate downloads now available from commercial sites online. The Motion Picture Association of America estimates that between 400,000 and 600,000 films are being illegally downloaded from the internet each day. The IFPI 2005 report on digital music lists an estimated 870 million tracks illegally available for download from the internet.

At the 2005 Screen International summit on European film piracy, data was presented on behalf of IPSOS UK that highlighted the financial impact of piracy upon film revenues in the UK: 30 per cent of pirate DVD purchases cannibalize cinema box-office earnings; and in the last 12 months, the number of video pirates who go to the cinema has fallen by 15 per cent whereas non-pirates attendance has fallen by only 8 per cent.

Illegal copying and distribution poses an equally significant threat to the revenues of the electronic games business and even broadcast television programmes. The Industry Trust for IP Awareness, formed in March 2004, claims, 'downloading of illegal film and television files has tripled in the last twelve months and over 1.6 million people are now estimated to be downloading illegal films and TV programmes every week' (www.piracy-isacrime.com).

Console and PC games have fared little better with seasoned hackers vying to deliver cracked versions of popular games before their street release dates. One P2P website I looked at had listed over 11,500 successful downloads for pirated games for a single console game platform.

Analogue, digital and network holes

In addition to files transferred over the internet, physical media piracy is rampant. Physical piracy of DVDs can take place in large-scale operations or at home using CE devices such as VHS and DVD recorders (which can now be found on the high street for £120). Analogue copying (via a SCART lead or phono/co-axial cable) can produce very acceptable results; this form of duplication and inherent loss of revenue to the rights' owner is referred to as 'the analogue hole'.

Digital copying or 'ripping', via a PC, allows users simply to transfer content from a physical medium, such as a DVD, to their computer's hard disk. This also allows users to condense larger films from commercial DVDs and 'burn' a copy to fit the smaller capacity blank DVD-Rs. PCs can also be used to download files from file-sharing networks that may have been ripped and uploaded by people half a world away, or next door. Digital ripping is referred to as 'the digital hole', and illegal file-sharing systems for distribution and downloading are referred to as 'the network hole'.

The latest research on ripping and downloading

Recent research has identified clear paths of interaction between the digital and network holes. In the past it was assumed that copying a single file to the internet led to immediate access by downloaders throughout the world, but it now appears that limiting the amount of data transferred on to P2P networks can also limit the ease of finding a specific track online and consequently impact the success rate of downloading it. A recent study by a Stanford professor indicated that uncontrolled CD ripping could triple the supply of unauthorized files on the P2P networks.

There have been claims that people who download from file-sharing networks are more likely to go out and buy the genuine product. This is now refuted by a 2004 research report, *Piracy on the High Cs*, compiled by University of Pennsylvania professors Rafael Rob and Joel Waldfogel. The report said the US music industry lost one fifth of a sale for each album downloaded from the internet. In their survey of music purchasing habits, the authors asked their students about the albums they bought and those they downloaded without paying. The findings supported the conclusion that music downloading negatively impacted each student's actual spending on music (declining from $126 to $100 when students downloaded music).

UK network router company, CacheLogic, has determined that the total population logged on to the major P2P networks at any one time is about 8 million sharing over 10 million Gb (10 Petabytes) of data; that is nearly 10 per cent of the number of broadband connections in the world. Jupiter Media, a well known survey and information gathering company, estimates that 75 per cent of European broadband subscribers use P2P networks every month.

How is the industry responding?

Responses to the virulent spread of piracy have been varied in their scale, approach and effectiveness. These responses can be broadly listed as:

- education;
- litigation;
- government legislation;
- legal download sites;
- technological controls.

Education

Although there have been high profile educational campaigns throughout Europe, it is very difficult to assess the real impact they have had on piracy. There are cinema campaigns, posters in the high street, and leaflets in the shops. It is, however, quite difficult to assess the effectiveness of such campaigns. Rather than informing consumers that piracy is a crime, more recent campaigns have changed in tone and begun to promote awareness of the penalties involved.

Litigation

Music trade associations such as the Recording Industry Association of America (RIAA) and the BPI have undertaken a broad range of educational initiatives, but they only really hit the headlines when they began prosecuting 'significant music downloaders'. Between September 2003 and November 2004 the RIAA filed more than 7,000 lawsuits, including more than 2,200 announced since 1 October, against alleged file traders. The lawsuits included users of the eDonkey, Limewire and Kazaa services, as well as 25 people using university internet connections to distribute music files. In October 2004 the BPI began a similar campaign targeting 'major uploaders'. At the same time, the International Federation of the Phonographic Industry (IFPI), which has over 1,450 members in 75 countries and affiliated industry associations in 48 countries, stated that a further 459 alleged file-sharers across Europe now face legal action, with France and Austria targeted for the first time.

Although very unpopular as campaigns with consumers, there is strong evidence to support the effectiveness of litigation as a deterrent. The UK Film Council's 2004 report on *Film Piracy in the UK* noted:

> In January 2004, a US survey of 1,400 internet users by the Pew Internet & American Life Project and comScore Media Metrix, a web tracking firm, found that the percentage of Americans who download music online has halved since the lawsuits began. Whereas 29 per cent of internet users surveyed in May 2003 had said they sometimes download songs to their computers, by December 2003 this figure had dropped to 14 per cent. The figures also showed that the usage of Kazaa fell 15 per cent from November 2002 to November 2003, whilst other P2P networks also experienced usage declines. The drop at BearShare was 9 per cent, while WinMX lost 25 per cent of its audience and Grokster plunged 59 per cent.

The film industry in the United States has taken up this tactic to counter online piracy. In November 2004 the Motion Picture Association of America (MPAA) announced that it would sue anyone caught swapping or downloading digital copies of films. The MPAA said the civil suits would seek damages of up to $30,000 per film.

It is worth noting that amongst those prosecuted for illegal downloading, claims that 'they did not know that what they were doing was illegal' have not been accepted by the courts. Litigation has been used successfully as a piracy deterrent in closing down some file-sharing websites that were offering unauthorized downloads of copyright protected films, music, games and software.

Legal actions against hardware pirates have recovered significant quantities of counterfeit DVDs and CDs. The sale of such goods is highly lucrative for organized crime, and the Industry Trust for IP Awareness has claimed that a kilo of counterfeit DVDs is more valuable than a kilo of cannabis. Search and seizures by local trading standards officers, the police and members of FACT (Federation Against Copyright Theft) have taken place throughout the UK, at car boot sales, unauthorized high street outlets and illegal replication (disk-copying) sites.

Government legislation

Digital piracy impacts taxation revenues and foreign investment. European governments are being increasingly called upon to address the issues, and in some areas good progress has been made. In the UK, trade associations such as the UK Film Council, the BPI and BSAC (British Screen Advisory Council) work to secure greater government support in the battle against entertainment piracy.

Macrovision, the leading developer and supplier of copy protection technologies, has also lobbied governments to secure the right to legally protect 'copy protection technologies'. Using this legislation, Macrovision works with DVD manufacturers and retailers to ensure that its technology is respected in hardware devices. Current European legislation, the 2004 Copyright Directive, also protects the video industry by making it illegal for retailers to supply 'circumvention devices' whose main purpose is to circumvent copy protection and permit unauthorized content copying.

Legal download sites

With the launch of several high profile legal download services, such as Apple's iTunes, many consumers now have a legal means of buying individual tracks, downloading them electronically, and listening to their music on their portable music devices and mobile phones.

The 2005 IFPI report on digital music notes that, in 2004, legal music sites quadrupled to over 230, the available music catalogue doubled to 1 million songs, and that around the world, paid-for music downloads increased from less than 20 million to over 200 million. Analyst Jupiter estimates that the digital music market was worth US$330 million in 2004, and is expecting it to double in value in 2005.

This is certainly a major step forward in the development of digital entertainment, and media announcements about landmark figures of legal downloads have been well received. It is still worth noting that the BPI estimated that of the 17.8 per cent of the UK population who download music, 92 per cent are doing so illegally, equating to 7.4 million people. Legal music downloads are usually protected by some form of Digital Rights Management (DRM) that provides a simple 'rights authentication' system, ensuring that purchased music downloads are not redistributed illegally. There is an increasing call for a common DRM standard to be proposed and adopted.

Legal movie downloads are just starting to appear, but catalogues and geographic access are limited. At the January 2005 Screen International European Film Piracy Summit, one of the common threads to emerge was the call for new business models to be developed to supply consumers and out-manoeuvre the pirates. For this to happen in the UK, broadband speeds need to be increased further, and a suitable DRM scheme approved and adopted.

Initial pricing for movie downloads is likely to be flexible and could vary with the terms of playability; for example a 'view once only' option for a top film might cost £4, but a three-day watching window for the same film could cost £5. Ultimately it is also possible that the P2P file-sharing networks may themselves become legitimate engines for authorized content downloads.

Technological controls

If technology delivers the means to copy illegally and distribute digital entertainment content, it can also provide a robust and effective defence against piracy, when utilized. Solutions can be applied to physical media, electronic content and even the network structure of the internet.

Copy-protection technologies evolved significantly in 2004. More emphasis is now placed on value-management and copy-control, whereby more business models can be created. This can benefit consumers by allowing more choice and increased usage rights, while at the same time rights owners can benefit from a wider range of revenue generation programs and reduced threats of piracy. Like the technologies that they are designed to counter, these solutions often have to overlap to improve their effectiveness.

Physical media protection solutions can include oxidizing dyes that limit playback time and embedded 'signatures' that mislead ripping software tools and replication hardware.

Macrovision has developed three complementary technologies for the video market that work together to 'plug' the analogue, digital and network holes referred to earlier. These solutions operate transparently to honest users; they only become visible when someone tries to use his or her video content illegally, such as ripping a protected DVD on to a PC, or copying a protected DVD to a CE DVD recorder.

To combat music piracy, U-PLAY from Macrovision is typical of the new wave of value management tools that are designed to enhance the customer experience whilst sustaining high levels of protection for the rights' owners. U-PLAY allows users to legally rip files, make copies of their CD legally and export their compressed music files to portable music devices, such as MP3 players, while respecting the Microsoft Windows Media Audio (WMA) DRM. This allows consumers to make copies of their music for playback around the house, in their cars or on their computers – it will not, however, let people transfer files to file-sharing networks for unauthorized distribution.

While a solution like U-PLAY helps combat unauthorized ripping, which is the supply side of the file-sharing networks, it cannot be used in isolation. To combat illegal file sharing on P2P networks, Macrovision has developed a complementary solution, an anti-piracy service called 'Hawkeye' that allows content owners to protect their content from being distributed and downloaded illegally. The technology behind Hawkeye is so efficient that it can start protecting files within minutes of activation and maintains very high levels of effectiveness whilst activated. Interestingly, this technology, aimed at curbing pirates, can also be used to promote legal content to fans, by pointing them to sites offering additional content or points of purchase.

What's next?

The path forward has many twists and turns. Distribution channels for entertainment are likely to change and early pricing models will reflect the need to grow a new user base. The Internet Service Providers (ISPs) that are currently competing fiercely for market share may decide that they will limit the bandwidth to P2P networks and instead promote their own new service offering legal downloads of music and videos. There are also a lot of established entertainment businesses that will seek to embrace the new technologies while defending their current markets and revenues (this is sometimes referred to as 'Tarzan economics' because of the reluctance to release one 'vine' before establishing a strong hold on the next 'vine'). Nevertheless, no matter how the landscape evolves, if digital piracy is not conquered it has the potential to leech revenues and prevent new systems from evolving or new content from being generated. For all the hits that make money in the entertainment industry, there is investment in a wider selection of potentials. Reduced revenues mean that movie studios, record labels and music publishers have less funding to seek out new talent.

Stefan Arndt, producer of the highly acclaimed film *Good Bye, Lenin*, estimated that he lost about $3 million of revenue to digital piracy. Prior to the DVD release of the movie, some 770,000 German households owned pirate copies of the film, either downloaded from the internet or purchased on pirate optical disk. This loss of revenue forced Arndt to cancel four new film projects.

3.7

Keeping on the right side of the law

Frank Coggrave, Websense

Is discovering an employee illegally downloading the latest Britney Spears song using free peer-to-peer (P2P) software just a nuisance to the IT manager? Is it just eating up network bandwidth, or is it just an unsupported application let loose on the company's IT infrastructure? To quote Peter Cook and Dudley Moore, the answer is 'Not only, but also.'

These issues are a concern to any organization, but on a more critical level, it is also illegal. Downloading pirate material not only infringes existing copyright laws but, since March 2004, it also breaches the European Directive for the Enforcement of Intellectual Property. This recently created intellectual property legislation makes the US digital media rights pale in comparison. Under this new Directive, counterfeiters and pirates will be prosecuted, facing fines and other civil penalties for breaching intellectual property rights. In the fight to crack down on this type of crime, the Directive enables copyright owners to seize users' assets and freeze their bank accounts, regardless of whether there was any financial gain.

In theory, this new law could be used by music companies and owners of intellectual property to prosecute consumers and employees who use file-sharing – or P2P – systems to illegally download music and other content. Although an amendment was included to treat consumers downloading the current number one selling single as different to that of organized gangs running large counterfeit operations, it is hardly going to do much for a company's reputation if one of its employees is accused or prosecuted under these new regulations. If the pirate music is found on the company's servers, then arguably the company could be complicit, with the finger being pointed at the IT Director.

How much of a problem is this really? Recent research suggests it's a large one. The British Phonographic Industry recently revealed that 8 million people in the UK claim to be downloading music, with 92 per cent doing so via illegal P2P software. We believe that at least 75 per cent of these downloads are taking place at work due to faster internet connections and people spending more time in the office.

So what can IT Directors do to avoid opening their systems to abuse? Should they prevent employees accessing the internet? Although this would inevitably put an immediate end to the problem, this draconian approach would do little for employee morale and could reduce workers' productivity, especially as a large number of staff need to use the internet to fulfil their job.

Even requesting employees to avoid certain websites and downloading applications from the web will not offer a completely foolproof solution. It is a fact of life that there will always be a group of users who persist in disobeying the rules, especially if they think it's 'harmless'. At the same time, companies should not be leaving themselves open to abuse. This would be the equivalent of leaving the keys in the ignition for car thieves.

P2P software is not illegal in itself. Organizations should be asking themselves if they really want to allow their employees to download these applications that pride themselves on infiltrating the network, and beating your defences. What is more, no P2P application has been delivered yet that offers a real business advantage. So why enable users to download these applications in the first place?

Ultimately, the buck stops with the IT Director, who has a fiduciary responsibility to ensure that the appropriate controls (policy, procedures, education) are implemented to mitigate the risks (and costs) associated with the use of pirated software in the enterprise. It is his or her job to ensure that employees are using the internet sensibly, according to pre-agreed company guidelines. It is not the duty of the ISPs or the file-sharing software providers to regulate how their systems are used.

Companies need to draw up clear internet access policies for employees and ensure that these are communicated effectively and enforced throughout the organization. Without this, employees will continue to use their company's internet connection for non-work reasons. That's not only a lot of wasted employee time and bandwidth; ultimately it could also have serious legal repercussions for the business.

The excuse – we couldn't stop it – does not work. Technology and processes are available from Websense, amongst others, to clamp down on this abuse and protect your hard won reputation. 'The Police' were great, but keep them off your servers, and away from your door.

4

Operational management

4.1

Flow clearing: financial supply chain management

Dr Markus Braun, Wire Card

Financial supply chain management can do more than just improve financial flow throughout the company. The uniform platform means that financial risks due to payment irregularities can be largely prevented.

Not talking about money is an old rule of etiquette. Is that why a process-based observation of financial flows has been ignored for so long? Everybody is talking about optimization processes such as supply chain management – the optimization of goods and supply flows from the supplier to the end consumer. However, the largely paper-based handling of financial processes is excluded from this discussion, and still hides significant inefficiency, leading to long process times and higher costs. If you want to do something about this, then you should take a look at financial supply chain management (FSCM). To make things clear, here is an analysis performed by Forrester as a taster: 46 per cent of a million dollars of turnover is eaten up by system costs such as wages, company administration and IT resources. Analysts predict that optimizing these financial flows could save around 60 per cent of these costs.

FSCM as a holistic system

Financial supply chain management consists of two basic components: the optimization of financial flows and risk management.

The former includes improving cash management in general, in other words, all relationships within the company that have anything to do with the cycle of money. These include not only relationships between dealers and customers, but also the different ways in which they are handled, such as points of sale (POS), call centres or self-service kiosks.

This cycle can usually be broken down into segments; for example before signing a contract, these segments include financing the transaction, securing the finance and the general credit risk. Once the goods have been transferred, the next tasks are invoicing, checking the invoice and payment. Donovan Pfaff, an assistant lecturer to Professor Dr Bernd Skiera in management and e-commerce in Frankfurt says:

> The greatest friction losses occur during the billing stage. Problems might arise when field sales staff promise a discount but do not tell the accounts department. When the invoice is issued, it is wrong, because it does not take the discount into account. A new, correct bill must be sent, meaning extra administration costs for the company.

The second and less well-known core component of FSCM is risk management. According to the Gartner Group, fraud rates in MOTO/eCommerce businesses are 12 times higher than in the offline world.

The term 'risk management' originated in banking but is increasingly used in company management. The background is this: companies are constantly faced with new, changing parameters to which they have to react with speed, focus and confidence. The factors here include internationalization of business partners and suppliers (e-business, mergers, global expansion), negative economic developments (increasing insolvency, poor payment performance) and new legal regulations (the KonTraG law on corporate monitoring and transparency or Basel II). Risk management is the evaluation of the general financial risk in commercial transactions. The crucial factor is always the quality and relevance of each piece of information and the entire stock of data.

For risk management in the context of FSCM, this means that two areas have to be evaluated: information specific to the customer and information specific to payment. In the first case, the company evaluates the customer as a risk. Is the given address plausible, and can that house number exist in the street? Also, it is customary to check the (national) postal address in connection with the first name and surname of the customer. If a customer calls himself Mickey Mouse or Donald Duck, for example, it's safe to say he doesn't exist.

Checking creditworthiness is also part of risk management. Mail order catalogue companies have known for a long time that poor payers often live in high-rise blocks in poor areas and are either in their early 20s or over 55. As well as long-established credit information services such as Experian or InFoScore, there is now a whole range of well-stocked databases listing private or business customers who fail to make their payments or delay them for lengthy periods. They also contain people who order products for a joke. The records usually contain detailed notes on the latest developments. You can find out when customers have come to the attention of companies or shops, and find out their full addresses and changes of address, often the e-mail addresses they use, the amount of unpaid bills, the tricks and methods fraudulent customers use and, of course, when customers have paid up after demands.

Payment-specific checks in risk management monitor the mode of payment. This includes methods such as the Luhn check, which uses the credit card number to read the credit card organization and check whether the two logically match. Similarly, methods such as the Bin check test the plausibility of the bank identification number and account number in electronic debiting transactions, by whether they logically match. Other checks include CVC2/CVV2, a test of the up to five-digit code printed on the signature field of the latest generation of MasterCard and VISA cards. Finally, there is the exclusion of groups of countries. The card type and the country of issue are identified from the credit card number and compared to the country where the goods are to be delivered or to the incoming IP address (with a Bin check this is the first six digits of the card number). If they do not match or if the country issuing the card is on a blacklist, the risk is often greater.

Preliminary considerations

As already mentioned, FSCM can bring considerable savings. However, the sum of the components of FSCM add up to a complicated whole, which is why many companies put off optimizing their financial structures.

The list of potential problems is long. The most important of these is integration within the company. FSCM can come up against political opposition, for example if a particular department is unwilling to reveal its information; and against organizational difficulties, when individual departments are classified in different areas of the company. Financial and technical problems also occur sometimes, for example due to the heterogeneous IT structures of the various finance and payment modules and databases required. Integrating systems from outside the company can also cause difficulties, sometimes for 'political' reasons, if a business partner is unwilling to integrate and has organizational, structural or legal misgivings. Whole books have been written on the problems of IT integration between different systems and companies.

Technical developments

However, no one need fear the complexity of these structures any more. Internet Protocol (IP) technology has helped us break this Gordian knot. IP is a recognized industry standard for communication between open systems. The transfer protocol defines the rules and conventions that control the flow of information in a communication system. The main job of IP is cross-network addressing. The protocol is not circuit-switched, but packet-switched.

Using the potential of IP, several software manufacturers have now attempted to solve the previously intractable problem of FSCM. Given the wide choice now available, what is necessary, what is practical and what is dispensable? Different companies naturally have different requirements, but experience with our customers has helped us identify a kind of shopping list that applies to all companies.

For example, the tool must be able to implement a uniform interface that can handle payments from various channels such as call centres, the internet or POS. Integration of various currencies is another essential criterion, especially for businesses with international activities. Integration of different national and international payment methods such as globally divergent electronic debiting, credit card prepayment or mobile payment must also be taken into account. Anyone interested in one of these tools should not only look at optimization of payment handling, but also at genuine FSCM. Any system under consideration should offer key concepts such as entity management, which is the mapping of organizational structures and payment flows from each retailer. Real-time statistics and flexible reporting options are also absolutely crucial.

Of course, every company must decide for itself what its FSCM tool features. But practice has shown that functions for managing charge-backs are extremely important. As well as these preconditions, there are several extra features to entice potential customers. These include management of the entire retailer cycle on a single system, as well as completely flexible pricing and invoicing. Last but not least, risk management functions such as blacklists and CVV must be available for evaluation at the click of a mouse.

These options make analysts' eyes light up with delight, because they mean FSCM is bound to become a real boom area which can help companies, especially international ones, make enormous cost savings. But not only those companies: small and medium-sized businesses are also becoming increasingly interested due to poor payment practices.

4.2

Developing a culture of security in the workplace

Peter Brudenall, Simmons & Simmons

After the events of 11 September 2001 in the United States, White House officials presented a sobering assessment of US preparedness for cyber attacks. They called for a new 'culture of security' in relation to information technology, in which everybody in and outside of the commercial world was to play a part.

The culture of security was described as a 'new way of thinking'; a voluntary rather than a regulatory change to the way information technology was used and secured. The Federal Trade Commission of the United States drew analogies to the responsibilities individuals take for their own safety in their everyday lives: 'we already take safety precautions in order to limit risks in our everyday lives. We wear our seat belts. We lock our houses when we leave. We need that kind of risk-minimizing thinking with our computers, and we all have to get involved'.[1]

The importance of operating within a culture of security is now recognized across the world. In the European Union, the European Network and Information Security Agency (ENISA) was set up in November 2003 by the Information Security Commission. At the time, Errki Liikanen, the European Information Society Commissioner, said that 'trust and security are crucial components in the Information Society and by establishing ENISA we continue the work to create the culture of security'.[2]

The risks for an employer operating outside a culture of security

Taking safety precautions to protect information systems is of particular, though clearly not exclusive, significance within the commercial world. Companies of all sizes, providing any product or service, are at risk of security breaches. If a company uses a computer at all, it is exposed. There are threats from outside and inside the business. These range from a hacker defacing the business's website, to e-mail-borne viruses, or to the employer facing liability for defamatory e-mails sent by an employee.

Defamatory e-mails are a risk because employers can be responsible for the actions of their employees where employees act in the course of their employment. This is known as vicarious liability. Consequently, offensive e-mails written in the workplace can result in claims for sex, race or disability discrimination, all of which carry unlimited compensation in employment tribunals. It is a problem that can easily arise in organizations that have heavy internal e-mail traffic, and a recent example involving a law firm led to sex and race discrimination claims. Following the resignation of his African-American secretary, a solicitor sent out an e-mail during the recruitment process for her replacement, saying, 'Can we go for a really fit busty blonde this time?'

Another case shows how far the employer's vicarious liability can extend. E-mails were sent by staff at Norwich Union regarding rumours falsely suggesting that Western Provident was in severe financial difficulties. Western Provident believed that these messages could be used by Norwich Union to obtain new business and to damage it in the marketplace. It instituted libel proceedings seeking to hold Norwich Union responsible for the actions of its employees in sending defamatory messages through its e-mail system. Immediately after issuing proceedings, Western Provident obtained a court order for the preservation and delivery of hard copies of the allegedly defamatory e-mails. Later, Western Provident obtained a further order allowing it to search Norwich Union's e-mail records. The case finally settled with Norwich Union paying Western Provident Association the sum of £450,000.

Other risks from inside the business include disgruntled employees, or possible mistakes by IT staff which enable users to access the wrong information. All of these are very real risks that an employer must consider before developing its culture of security.

The building blocks of a culture of security

There are practical steps that an employer can take to develop a culture of security within a company. A straightforward and comprehensive monitoring policy, together with a statement explaining it, staff training and management of operating systems, will help to protect an employer against some of the risks detailed above.

Monitoring communications systems

Monitoring the communications of staff is at the crux of a culture of security in the workplace. A well drafted monitoring policy can, and should, meet a number of objectives such as:

- Educating employees.

- Setting guidelines for what is, and what is not, acceptable use of the company's e-mail and internet systems. Clear guidelines should be set out which go beyond the simple ban on 'offensive material' and define in more detail which websites are not appropriate to access or what the appropriate content of e-mails should be.
- Helping to ensure misuse does not occur.
- Minimizing risks.
- The basis of a defence if misuse does occur.
- The basis upon which to discipline or dismiss employees if necessary.

Data protection

However, before drafting a monitoring policy the employer must be aware of the impact of data protection legislation on the monitoring of staff communications. The Information Commissioner's Employment Practices Data Protection Code (*Guidance on Monitoring at Work*) (the Code) highlights the relevance of the Data Protection Act 1998 (the DPA) to this area. The Code acknowledges the need for monitoring staff communications, which it describes as a 'recognised component of the employment relationship', but states that: 'this must be balanced against an employee's right to privacy in the workplace'.[3]

The DPA is based on eight fundamental principles. One of the principal concerns of an employer should be to ensure that the processing complies with the first principle of the DPA. This requires that the organization has a justification in place for the processing of employees' data. Under the DPA, processing is drafted broadly to include obtaining, recording or holding information or data, or carrying out operations on the information or data. The two likely justifications are either that the employee has consented or that the monitoring is in the legitimate interests of the company and does not prejudice the rights and freedoms of the individual.

However, as the Code points out, obtaining consent from employees is problematic. The Code says consent must be 'freely given, which may not be the case in the employment environment'.[4] The Code also points out that consent can be withdrawn at any time.[5] An employee may well have very little real choice.

Since the company is therefore likely to have to rely on the legitimate interests justification, the Code advocates that the company undertakes an 'impact assessment' before monitoring takes place to assess whether the adverse impact of monitoring can be justified by the benefit to the employer and others. If an impact assessment is carried out and the criteria under the Code are held to show that the monitoring is justifiable, then monitoring can be carried out without the consent of the worker being required.

The Regulation of Investigatory Powers Act (RIPA) is also very relevant to the monitoring of staff in a culture of security. RIPA's intended purpose is to ensure that the interception of communications is done in accordance with certain basic human rights. The activities it covers include the interception of communications and therefore any monitoring of employee e-mail or telephone conversations.

Under RIPA, the unlawful interception of data could lead to criminal and civil sanctions against the employer. However, a communication can be lawfully intercepted if an exception applies. It can be intercepted where both the sender and the intended recipient of a communication have consented to the interception, or it can be intercepted under RIPA and the Telecommunications (Lawful Business Practice) (Interception of Communications) Regulations 2000 (the Regulations).

Under the Regulations, interception of a communication (that is, a telephone conversation or e-mail) in the course of its transmission is lawful provided that the interception is carried out for one of the lawful business practices set out in the Regulations (as listed below) and the company has made 'all reasonable efforts' to inform every person who may use the telecommunications system that the interception may take place.

Monitoring or keeping a record of communications relevant to the business are lawful business practices under the Regulations in the following circumstances:

- to establish the existence of facts (for instance, keeping records of transactions carried out);
- to ascertain compliance with regulatory or self-regulatory practices;
- to ascertain or demonstrate the standards that are or ought to be achieved by persons using the system in the course of their duties (for example, quality control or staff training);
- in the interests of national security;
- for the purpose of the prevention or detection of crime;
- for the purpose of the investigation or detection of the unauthorized use of the communications system;
- ensuring the effective operation of the system (for instance, monitoring for viruses, backing up and forwarding e-mails to their correct destination); and
- monitoring communications to determine whether they are relevant to the business.

The Code sets out certain suggestions as to what data protection features employers might want to integrate into a policy for the use of electronic communications. These include making clear the extent and type of private use that is allowed for the internet and e-mails, and setting down the purposes for which any monitoring is conducted, the extent of the monitoring and the means used.

The Code makes it clear that simply telling staff that e-mail or internet access could be monitored may not be sufficient. Employees should be left with a clear understanding of when information about them is likely to be obtained; why it is being obtained; what the information will be used for; and, if the information is to be disclosed, to whom it will be disclosed. The monitoring statement should detail this information and be updated whenever significant changes are made, such as the introduction of additional monitoring.

The monitoring statement should be integral to the general monitoring policy: all employees should know where it is to be found and should be reminded of it periodically.

Education of staff

Having a well-drafted policy is important, but clearly there will be no culture of security unless the policy is followed. It is a good idea to include employees in the decision process from an early stage when a monitoring policy is being considered. They are more likely to follow guidelines if their needs have been considered.

Employers must also not turn a blind eye to transgressions of the policy. If there is a breach of security, the employer must be consistent both in terms of the monitoring and any misuse of the company's technology systems. A fair disciplinary procedure and a right to appeal are important parts of a monitoring policy.

Employee training sessions should be held where e-mail and internet use are discussed, in addition to emphasizing the consequences for the business and its employees if misuse occurs. Regular reminders of the rules and standards may be necessary through more training sessions or e-mails to all employees. The training sessions could also stress the alternatives to using e-mail or company telephones for matters that are confidential to the employee, such as doctor appointments or family matters.

A final option to protect a business is to consider libel insurance against the risk of defamatory e-mail.

Ensuring that operating systems support the culture of security

There are further practical protective steps concerning daily contact with the outside world that an employer can take. One is encryption – of e-mails that are being sent out, of data stored on laptops and perhaps also sensitive data stored on servers. Encryption would mean that information accessed unlawfully was meaningless to anyone who obtained it. Laptops and PDAs are a particular risk without encryption because they are more easily lost or stolen. They should be secured completely. A software lock can be used which requires an ID and password to be entered before the system can be used. This allows everything to be encrypted so that if, for example, the laptop is broken into, no information can be taken.

The importance of confidentiality should be flagged up to employees. Information is key to a business, and loss or unauthorized disclosure of information to third parties can have very serious repercussions.

Where there is no express or implied contractual obligation of confidence regarding information in the hands of employees, a duty of confidence may still exist. To protect the business, employees should be asked to sign confidentiality agreements as part of their contract of employment.

Confidentiality notices on e-mails

A confidentiality notice is a useful addition to e-mails. The notice tries to say that the content of an e-mail is confidential and should be read only by the intended recipient. For obvious reasons, the message should be put at the top of the e-mail – if it lurks at the end, the notice will only be read after the message it refers to. Confidentiality notices have a certain value but it is worth remembering that there is no legal authority concerning these notices in e-mail communications. Where such notices are added to every e-mail, it is possible that the court may find that their ubiquity dilutes their importance.

E-mail disclaimers

An e-mail disclaimer is another option for an employer. This can appear beneath the message but, more so than with the confidentiality notice, should be used with caution. There are no legal authorities on e-mail disclaimers as yet. However, guidance on disclaimers generally suggests that disclaimers of the type that effectively warn a recipient not to rely on the content of an e-mail will be of no impact. Of course, in warning a recipient not to rely on the content of the e-mail, a disclaimer may also alienate its recipient if used. Certainly, e-mail disclaimers should be used carefully.

Firewalls and filters

A firewall protects information systems by only allowing access to and from the internal systems to the outside world through a single point. This is commonly known as the 'network gateway server', and data flowing through the server will be filtered for known viruses and spam. These can help to keep unwanted visitors at bay.

When using firewalls and filters it is essential that adequate security is put in place to prevent attacks from hackers. Failure to do so can result in a breach of the DPA if personal data is revealed without the consent of the person it describes. The results could be commercially devastating: if confidential data concerning a client were to be hacked from the system of a law firm, for example, and used against the client, the liability of the law firm would be massive.

Virus protection is also important for identifying the viruses on the network as soon as they appear, so in effect being a dynamic and continuous monitoring, as are browser controls to monitor the use of the internet and therefore its misuse. The controls can include the number and time of use and what is being browsed.

Physical security

A final point for an employer to bear in mind – and one that is rarely considered when talking about information technology security – is physical security. It is very important to maintain physical security because it is far easier to get into an office and take paper from a desk by just following somebody through a security barrier ('tailgating') than it is to access that business's information technology systems.

Conclusions

To develop a culture of security in the workplace, an employer should do the following.

Protect against internal risks: this can be done through the monitoring of staff communications within the parameters of data protection legislation. A monitoring statement should be drawn up and staff educated about monitoring and its impact on them. The employer should respond to all breaches of security in a consistent manner, and adhere closely to the monitoring policy.

Protect against external risks: steps should be taken on the operation of the systems. Employers should review their own business and consider implementing encryption, firewalls, filters, confidentiality notices on e-mails, e-mail disclaimers (although these should not be applied indiscriminately) and virus protection. Physical security within the office should also be an important consideration.

Notes

1. 'Creating a culture of security', remarks by Commissioner Orson Swindle, Federal Trade Commissioner, at Privacy 2002: Information, Security and New Global Realities Conference.
2. As reported by the BBC on Friday 21 November 2003. See bbc.co.uk.
3. The Code, p 19.
4. The Code, p 19.
5. The Code, p 19.

4.3

Security as standard

British Standards Institution

'Walls have ears' – this slightly surreal cautionary wartime note was one of the first warnings about confidentiality that most of the British public had ever heard. But it presaged an imperative that was soon accepted by almost every organization in every country in the world – the need for caution, thoroughness and foresight in avoiding the leak of business-critical information to enemies or competitors. In three decades the battlefront has moved from the waste bin and the pub to IT, telemetry and corporate governance.

Of course, the stakes are now so high that information security has spawned a whole industry – and a rewarding one. But different organizations have approached it in different ways, perhaps because matters of confidentiality and security are discussed only 'on a need to know basis' or perhaps because the technology of espionage and counter-espionage is so precious it is kept close to the chest; and perhaps because bosses and IT managers do not like to deal with outside authorities on matters so intimate.

Varying standards of security equipment are permissible. You get what you pay for – and, anyway, there are British standards (BS) and international standards (ISO) to cover product and service quality, aren't there? But what about best practice in the organizations that wish to be protected? How do they know they are following the right approach? Equally important, how can their suppliers and customers be reassured that their own confidential information and trading secrets are not being misused?

Establishing the standards

Towards the end of the last millennium the British Standards Institution knuckled down to establishing an information security standard. Following extensive consultation with industries and organizations all over the world, it developed BS 7799 Part 1, Information

Security Management – Code of practice for information security management, and BS 7799 Part 2, Information Security Management – Specification for information security management systems.

BS 7799 promoted protection for intellectual property, in the same way that material goods are traditionally protected. It reminded us of how important a business reputation can be to customer confidence and ultimately to profits. Among its benefits, the promotional material listed 'fewer crises' and 'less risk of litigation'.

An Audit Commission survey of 900 UK organizations revealed that half of the public sector organizations interviewed and a third of private sector companies had been affected by IT fraud or abuse. The professional world was quickly coming to the conclusion that a simple lapse in information security can damage an organization's credibility, reduce customer confidence, and ultimately damage profits.

The whole point of establishing standards is to promote the widespread standardization of working practice; so it was inevitable that such a significant business issue was recognized to be a universal problem – one demanding a worldwide standard. Thus, it was only a matter of time before the British standard BS 7799 Part 1: 1999 became the internationally recognized ISO standard ISO/IEC 17799: 2000, Code of Practice for Information Security.

In the few years between the development of the original BS 7799 and the ISO/IEC 17799 standards, there had been a sea change in BSI's philosophy: the institution recognized that standards alone could be viewed as prescriptive and restrictive – that is, if there were not the working practices in place to meet the relevant criteria, the standard would be perceived as little more than a set of rules.

The new enlightened view was that what businesses need are management systems – in short, the structure, philosophy and working methods that inherently meet the values defined by the standard. This led to the development and release of BS 7799–2: 1999 and subsequently to the release of the revised standard BS 7799 Part 2: 2002 – Information Security Management Systems: Specification with guidance for use. Part 2 of BS 7799 then becomes a basis for the organization's own information security management system (ISMS).

By emphasizing management systems, BSI was more able to help organizations to improve their efficiency from the inside out, whereas an emphasis on standards meant change from the outside in. BS 7799–2: 2002 introduces a better way of working, based on a management system that, with its inbuilt facility for constant improvement, is self-perpetuating.

Nowhere was there a greater need for consistent, focused working patterns and management practices than in the field of information security. It is a field in which care and attention have to permeate throughout the organization – from the CEO to the casual cleaner. This was a management system that could not afford to be the concern solely of the quality manager or the CEO or the IT manager – it demanded commitment from everyone in the organization.

Both the BS and ISO/IEC standards address the issues related to conventional paper-based information systems, analogue communications, digital communications and IT-based information systems. It is worth noting that the original BS standard was conceived during the hysteria of the 'dotcom bubble' – it was, rightly, perceived that the speed and prevalence of e-mail and other digital communication posed a phenomenal risk to information security. Data was travelling faster and further than ever before, and could readily be copied and compressed into ever-smaller media.

What the international standard covers

So what does the ISO/IEC 17799: 2000 document address? It provides guidelines on how the various controls that are identified in BS 7799–2: 2002 Annex A can be implemented by an organization developing an ISMS. Although it provides detailed information on these controls, it should be remembered that end users are advised to use the controls as appropriate to their business, and to identify and implement other controls that they may determine to be more suitable to their business. However, wherever possible the ISO/IEC 17799: 2000 document should be used in parallel with, and as a supporting document for, any registration or compliance statement to BS 7799–2: 2002.

An ISMS, as defined in BS 7799–2: 2002, must cover all of the following:

- **Management responsibility**: including management commitment, and resource management.
- **Management review of the ISMS**: including review input, review output and internal audits.
- **ISMS improvements** including continual improvements, corrective actions and preventative actions.
- **A security policy**: a document that demonstrates management support and commitment to the ISMS process.
- **Security organization**: a management framework to implement and sustain information security within the organization.
- **Asset clarification and control**: an inventory of assets, with responsibility assigned for maintaining security.
- **Personnel security**: job descriptions for all staff, outlining their security roles and responsibilities.
- **Physical and environmental security**: a definition of the security requirements for the premises and the people within them.
- **Communications and operations management**: a method of ensuring that communications operate within secure parameters.
- **Access control**: network management to ensure that only authorized people have access to relevant information, and to protect the supporting infrastructure.
- **Systems development and maintenance**: to ensure that IT projects and support activities are conducted securely, using data control and encryption where necessary.
- **Business continuity management**: a managed process for protecting critical business processes from major disasters or failures.
- **Compliance**: evidence of the organization's commitment to meet statutory or regulatory information security requirements, for its clients, employees and relevant authorities.

Most organizations will already have some of these in place, but few will be doing everything. BSI client managers are experienced in working with companies to evaluate their current system's merits, and in guiding them through the steps necessary to develop their management system to the point where it can be registered under the standard.

BSI have developed client service into a fine art – they can arrange training schemes to train clients' staff, they can provide written and digital training materials for self-study and they arrange regular seminars all over the country to introduce thought-provoking and informative angles on BS 7799–2: 2002 and other management systems.

Through its intimate relationship with businesses all over the world, BSI has learnt very graphically that standards – and, indeed, management systems – are not an end, but merely a means. But to what?

Benefits

The benefits are expressed as 'benefiting the bottom line' – that is, supporting the private sector objectives of efficiency and profitability – although clearly non-profit-making organizations stand to benefit in other no less valuable ways. When you consider the health, education and police services, it is obvious that BS 7799–2: 2002 could be even more relevant to the public sector.

The direct and indirect benefits of operating a management system based on BS 7799–2: 2002 include:

- improved employee motivation;
- increased efficiency;
- better use of time and resources;
- cost savings;
- increased competitiveness;
- increased customer satisfaction;
- confidence throughout the supply chain;
- fewer crises;
- less risk of litigation;
- wider market opportunities;
- increased profits.

And there are further advantages. BSI point out that once an organization's ISMS is registered to BS 7799–2: 2002, it is in a good position to integrate this system with a quality management or environmental management system, to create an integrated management system.

Conclusion

This chapter began with the slogan 'walls have ears'. It should end with the slightly more sinister message that 'knowledge is power'. Over the years, successive boardroom coups have demonstrated that information has a tangible value and a very powerful influence over the fortunes of organizations and individuals.

In today's broadband, satellite communication world, ISMSs should not need much selling. The need for them is obvious – you cannot be unaware of how much information flows to and from your desktop, your department, and your domain.

While the threats are often invisible, it is reassuring that the solution is tangible and accessible. BS 7799–2: 2002 and its supporting document ISO/IEC 17799: 2000 are logical, practical to implement and easy to sustain. Are you going to go for it? Mind who you tell, or it will be all round the building …

Converged security – why manage three when one will do?

Mark Bouldin, Telindus

Convergence is often spoken about in the context of bringing together IT networks and telephony systems; however, it is also possible to bring together other critical business systems.

Loss-prevention applications such as CCTV, intruder and access control are one such system that, historically, has evolved outside the remit of the ICT strategy. However, there are considerable costs associated with operating an additional network infrastructure for loss-prevention and video surveillance purposes. Developments in ICT now allow a more combined approach to be taken, and with economic pressures forcing businesses in all market sectors to justify spend, choosing the right surveillance solution has never been more important.

Substantial savings can be made in the order of 0.6 per cent of turnover by converging your ICT strategy with your loss-prevention methods, and with a return on the initial investment being seen in less than two years. However, ROI should not just be calculated in terms of cost: business benefits should also be taken into account.

A converged network allows for a centralized service that provides one network for all video, voice and data requirements. This brings many different benefits in respect of loss-prevention systems and allows organizations to make greater efficiencies in their operations, and thereby lower the cost of crime.

Combined with a digital video system, a converged network brings even greater benefits. Remote monitoring becomes possible, with security being carried out centrally, and event-driven CCTV monitoring of remote locations bringing improved response and cost benefits. Image retrieval is also simple with a converged network and digital video system.

A centralized service

Networked digital surveillance increases the effectiveness of security staff and systems by creating a centralized service. For example, centrally managed access control can be integrated with personnel records, which increases security and lowers costs.

It also lowers the total cost of ownership because it is deployed across multi-service networks utilizing common infrastructures, and therefore surveillance becomes effectively just another application operating over a company network. Changes are also easier and more cost-effective since the network is scalable, with additions, moves and changes being cheaper, faster and less disruptive than disparate systems, since the change only needs to be made to one centralized system.

Companies with lots of sites up until now have had only one type of alternative to guards looking after a site. The alternative uses ISDN to transmit the images to a remote location, but compared to CCTV images, ISDN images tend to be much lower quality. Although this solution is a good idea, the decision-making capability of remote operators is limited by the speed and quality of the images presented to them.

Nowadays digital networks offer a more cost-effective, higher quality solution to this problem. Utilizing the company's digital network will allow the images to be transmitted over an existing or improved IT network infrastructure. This can reduce the costs of management, as the infrastructure is used for multiple services and can also improve the image quality and update rate as the bandwidths available offer better capacity than ISDN.

Remote surveillance

Digital video surveillance makes remote manned guarding a much more viable option and can drastically reduce the cost of securing sites. Traditionally, companies that have multiple CCTV systems have had to ensure that the operators are fully trained in not only the system but also their duties in regard to the Health and Safety at Work Act and the Data Protection Act – failure to do so possibly leading to unlimited fines. Centralizing the management of these systems reduces the costs and ensures that compliance with the regulations is easy, and enables the onsite managers to concentrate on business aims and objectives.

It is possible to replace manned guards with remote manned guards, which in turn can improve the effectiveness of staff and reduce staffing costs. For example, an alarm from the surveillance unit can initiate the generation of wider communications, from e-mails, text messages over the SMS system, to the sending of video images straight to a handheld PC, even via a Wireless Local Area Network (WLAN). These can be set to trigger automatically if required, avoiding the possibility of human error and, where there is a potential threat requiring immediate attention, making a phone call direct to the local emergency services.

A digital network, as well as carrying voice and data, can have multiple points of image presentation, ie many cameras transmitted independently to many control systems. This brings increased access to video by allowing multiple points of control to be set up to view the same images and take these images to the person, not the other way round. A typical example of this is a security department that is only interested in being alerted when a breach of security has taken place, or is deemed likely to occur by parameters predefined by the system.

It also provides greater flexibility since the network is scalable, making it easier to add, or remove, both cameras and viewing stations to the system quickly and easily, causing less disruption than installing dedicated cables to a system. Allowing simplified cabling and easier connectivity reduces network complexity. It is also more resilient because it has the capability to use hot backups, which come online without disrupting service, when a current service fails. This helps to ensure that images are still available even if multiple failures occur. Additionally, a digital system has the capability to use the fibre-optic infrastructure more efficiently. Less, or sometimes no extra fibre needs to be installed, which can dramatically reduce the cost of system installation.

The M25 London orbital motorway is a perfect example of how networked surveillance can be effective. The motorway has to cope with over 700,000 drivers each day, and the emergency services are in constant need of information to allow for quicker and more effective response strategies to incidents. Using hundreds of cameras sited around the motorway, the Traffic Control offices can advise Incident Support Units (ISUs) exactly where to go and what to expect when they get there. They can zoom in on drivers parked on the hard shoulder and tell at a glance whether they need to call an ambulance or a policeman to move the vehicle on. The overall visibility of the network also means that backup and support is provided to each control office – if one control site goes out of operation, another can take over.

Image retrieval

Evidence retrieval is easy with a digital network and can considerably reduce the time spent on investigations as well as providing the capability to correlate evidence with other systems. Footage is readily available at the touch of a button without trawling through masses of unnecessary tapes, by using search criteria for a specific time or event, such as a man running across a car park wearing a green jacket.

It is also possible for footage to automatically start recording only if a predetermined event takes place, and for an alarm to be generated to alert the remote guard and initiate appropriate action. For example, if a building is empty and motion is detected from within, the guard will receive an audible alert and the monitor will automatically show images of where the motion occurred. An alert can also be sent automatically to the local police station.

All footage is automatically documented at the time of the event, eliminating the possibility of data being changed afterwards. This can make footage and associated data admissible as evidence in court.

Technical capability

All of this sounds like surveillance Nirvana, but it's important to remember that as with any network, if it doesn't transmit and support the solution correctly, the best possible performance will not be achieved and it will be unable to deliver a truly flexible solution. Without a properly designed network infrastructure that takes into consideration factors such as traffic flows, how the user wants to use the system, whether legacy equipment should be integrated, and the likely future expansion or changes to the organization, there is a very real danger that the customer will end up with an inventory of equipment that does not deliver the 'security solution' they were anticipating.

When developed and installed correctly, a good digital network solution reduces technical complexity, leaving organizations free to concentrate on what they actually want the business to achieve. As well as added flexibility, a digital network allows for simplified cabling and easier connectivity. This reduced complexity can be exemplified by the durability of the network, which makes it capable of carrying various systems such as telephone and data.

Each of the disciplines requires different levels of service from the network. Since you would expect conversations to be understood and quickly responded to, voice and telephony need relatively low bandwidth, and a near zero delay (called 'latency') transmission system. Video, such as CCTV, requires a higher bandwidth and also low latency for the control of pan and tilt cameras. Data traffic, such as e-mails, can be a mixture of both and therefore has no such dependency or effect due to latency. For example, e-mails can be large but do not normally need to be instantly transmitted and received.

Converged networks can now communicate all types of information and this means you need to understand how to deliver a well-engineered system. Considerations include, among others, the original data for computer systems and printers, telephony, access control, public address systems, the internet and CCTV. Correctly traffic engineered networks have the capability to carry digital surveillance and data traffic simultaneously with a high degree of standardization for transmission, management, user control and maintenance. Today's digital networks are very reliable and the flexible architecture allows for the easy addition of new and existing surveillance equipment. Wireless network technology further enhances these advantages, making the deployment of new cameras even easier and more cost-effective since less cabling is required, and thus more flexible to your surveillance needs.

A digital network makes the ideal surveillance solution not only because it is already there, but because of its increased resilience. It offers the added capability of multiple routes, ensuring that data re-routes around points of failure and reaches its destination, as opposed to the point-to-point analogue systems that have little or no resistance to failure. Analogue systems can fail from a single point for reasons as simple as a fuse blowing on the matrix, whereas digital networks use hot-backups, helping to ensure surveillance images are still available even if multiple failures occur.

Next steps...

The first obstacle to overcome is convincing IT managers that putting video over the network is a good idea. They call it the 'killer app'. They will argue that video is bandwidth-hungry, that it will slow the network, and that the company will grind to a halt because the e-mails can't get through. They're right if the integration of video is done incorrectly. If we are to have one system for multi-services we need to convince the IT manager to let us have some of his or her bandwidth and recognize that the budget for the IT system probably does not allow for all the video traffic. But maybe the IT manager is the wrong person to talk to! Perhaps this issue needs to be raised with the person who holds the organization's purse strings, who may be the visionary who will understand that money can be saved by having one communication system, not three!

Conclusion

By combining your loss-prevention and security requirements with your overall ICT strategy, you can create a more effective system at a lower cost, standardized and future-proofed.

4.5

Countering cybercrime: risk management

The Fraud Advisory Panel's Cybercrime Working Group

The Combined Code

In July 2003 a new version of the Combined Code was issued. The preamble states: 'This replaces and refines the earlier requirements of the Cadbury and Greenbury reports on Corporate Governance.'

C.2 Internal control: main principle

The board should maintain a sound system of internal control to safeguard shareholders' investment and the company's assets.

The Code provides that a company's board of directors should conduct a review of the effectiveness of any system of internal control on at least an annual basis. The company should take steps to establish a formal and transparent arrangement for considering how it should apply the financial reporting and internal control principles. This includes ensuring that an independent audit committee is established. One of the roles of the committee is to ensure that the company's internal financial controls, internal control and risk management systems are reviewed.

Directors of businesses must be able to identify the steps that they have taken to protect the confidentiality, integrity and availability of the organization's data assets.

Adequate procedures to deal with cybercrime are a part of the risk management system that needs to be in place and reviewed on an annual basis.

Turnbull Guidelines

Non-compliance with the Turnbull Guidelines can result in management of a company being held liable and accountable for their failure to effectively carry out risk management and adequate checks of control processes.

Provision D2 of the Turnbull Guidelines states: 'The board should maintain a sound system of internal control to safeguard shareholders' investment and the company's assets.'

Provision D.2.1 states: 'The directors should, at least annually, conduct a review of the effectiveness of the group's system of internal control and should report to all shareholders that they have done so. The review should cover all controls including financial, operational and compliance controls and risk management.'

Provision D.2.2 states: 'Companies which do not have an internal audit function should periodically review the need for one.'

The UK government will now adopt principles of internal control set out in the Turnbull Report having published its own 'Orange Book' – an adaptation of Turnbull's recommendations to the public sector.

Data protection

The Data Protection Act (DPA) requires any organization that processes data to comply with eight enforceable principles identified as 'good practice'. Personal data must be:

> Fairly and lawfully processed; processed for limited purposes; adequate, relevant and not excessive; accurate and up to date; kept for no longer than necessary; processed in accordance with data subject's rights; secure; not transferred to countries that do not provide adequate protection for data.

Anyone who stores information about another person, be it for a commercial or other purpose, has a duty to maintain that data in accordance with the principles of data protection. This means that as well as the requirement that the data stored is accurate and not stored for a period of time longer than necessary, the data must be kept secure.

This will require businesses to take steps to ensure that their computer systems and operational functions comply. The standard benchmark is BS 7799 (now adopted as ISO 17799) for businesses and organizations attempting to comply with the DPA and other IT security issues. This is a common sense standard that every business should measure itself against even if it does not apply for full accreditation.

Freedom of information

The Freedom of Information Act provides a general right of access to all types of information held by public authorities and those providing services for them. The Act came into full force in January 2005.

Liability of directors

Directors may, under the Turnbull Guidelines, find themselves in breach of duty to the company and, consequently, the shareholders, for failing to carry out the correct risk management procedures and controls in respect of cybercrime.

Directors owe the company a number of fiduciary duties due to the position they hold within the company, including a duty of good faith and duty to act with due diligence. They also owe duties of professional competence depending upon the terms of a director's service contract.

In the event that a company loses a substantial amount of money to a cybercriminal it may be unable, or find it not commercially viable, to pursue the fraudster. In that case a company may be obliged to look to the director responsible for the implementation of risk management for redress. If the director has failed to act with due care in respect of a foreseeable risk, this may result in the company seeking to establish that the director was liable for breach of duty of care and to recover damages from that director.

Liability of accessories

It is important to appreciate that the person who has committed the fraud may not be the only one against whom a remedy can be obtained. There may be other people involved in committing the crime and therefore equally accountable. For example, in the case of cyber-laundering, a firm may become liable by virtue of the principle of constructive trusteeship, depending on whether it was at any point in receipt of laundered funds.

It is as a result of the principle of liability of accessories that banks and others used as a conduit by money launderers may find themselves becoming secondary victims.

Following the Electronic Signatures Regulations 2002 it is now possible in certain circumstances to pursue an action against a certification service provider that guarantees the veracity of a digital signature, where that guarantee is reasonably relied on by a person and that reliance causes loss (Statutory Instrument 318/2002). If one of the prescribed circumstances exists and a duty of care is thereby established, the onus is upon the certification service provider to show that he or she was not negligent. It would usually be the task of the party alleging negligence to prove that the other party was negligent. Lawyers and accountants who have been involved in setting up any scheme may also be legitimate targets.

Therefore, depending on the particular nature of your business, there are multitudes of different ways in which a business can incur liability for the cybercrimes of a fraudster.

The key to avoiding liability for money laundering is to 'know your customer'. Firms should take action in support of anti-money-laundering measures in order to comply with legal requirements and protect their corporate reputation. Evidence of identity and beneficial ownership of a company should be sought, and a higher level of due diligence undertaken where there are:

- numbered or alternative accounts;
- high-risk countries involved in a transaction such as those appearing on the Financial Action Task Force's list of non-compliant jurisdictions;
- offshore jurisdictions;
- high-risk activities;
- public officials involved.

IT governance

There is a growing appreciation of and concern for the need for effective IT governance. There is a UK IT governance website (www.itgovernance.co.uk) that reflects many of the principles set out in the Turnbull Report and Combined Code. In summary it recommends that organizations should integrate their IT and business strategies, recognizing that it is important that IT managers have a fundamental input into the development of the business objectives and strategies, as IT is increasingly being seen as a critical enabler of business processes.

BS 7799

The BS 7799 or ISO 17799 standard provides the framework necessary to create a secure system drawing on the experience of a group of professional information security practitioners. This will provide a systematic approach to identifying and combating the range of risks to an organization's information assets.

Reviewing policy and procedure

Many firms will carry out financial controls, audits and assessments. The Turnbull Report places greater emphasis on the need for assessment of risk and operational controls. This means that senior management are required to review the procedures applied to risk management and control on an annual basis and decide which areas are lacking in such controls. Essentially, they will have to start carrying out an internal audit of operational risk. The business benefit of this is that it can be stated on annual accounts and could lead to greater trust by customers.

To review policy and procedure effectively in terms of operational risk management, businesses should be reviewing their internet strategy and the related risk management issues at board level. In particular, it is advisable that organizations appoint one director to oversee the area where business strategy warrants this level of supervision, attaching responsibility for operational risk in relation to cybercrime to this individual or his or her department. This has the advantage of reducing the risk of criminal and civil prosecution of directors or the business for failure to comply with current standards and regulations, and may well reduce long-term fraud losses. It may also reduce the chances that the business is rendered liable for receiving laundered or fraudulently obtained funds under the doctrine of constructive liability. However, the fight against cybercrime must be waged on all company levels. It is necessary to establish policy and procedures that apply to everybody in the business.

Cybercrime

Policy statement

A policy statement and settled working practices should be published by the board to ensure that all employees know the standard required of them and the business stance in relation to cybercrime. Such a statement needs to be explained to every employee, and should ideally be included in contracts of employment, supply and outsourcing agreements.

The policy statement should be clear about the action that the business will take in the event of an act of cybercrime being detected. The statement should clearly express the business's policy towards cybercrime and its determination to deter fraud generally. It should be made clear that the business:

- will investigate and report to its local police or other appropriate authority any suspected acts of cybercrime;
- will assist the police in their investigations and prosecution of a cybercriminal if appropriate;
- will take civil action where possible and recover assets that have been stolen or pursue a cybercriminal for damages;
- expects employees to report any incidence of cybercrime of which they are aware, and assumes that each employee, irrespective of his or her level of seniority, has a responsibility for reporting cybercrime;
- will treat internally perpetrated cybercrime as seriously as a cybercrime perpetrated by an outsider;
- has particular procedures that should be followed in the event that a cybercrime occurs.

The DTI report says that the increase in cybercrime is partly because companies give employees access to the web and their own work e-mail addresses. It may also be of merit to include guidelines and company policy statements in relation to employee internet and e-mail use in employment contracts. For example, these might highlight the danger of opening e-mails with attachments from unknown sources, list sites that are prohibited from use, or explain company policy in relation to internet and software piracy (another common form of cybercrime).

Managing the prevention, detection and prosecution of cybercrime

Cybercrime management should be dealt with throughout the organization, and the importance of employee awareness should be emphasized at all levels.

Cybercrime needs to be treated as a business risk, and an organization therefore needs to carry out a risk management assessment to ensure that the steps taken to prevent cybercrime are effective in relation to the practices peculiar to that organization. Anti-cybercrime procedures should be tailored to match the type of business in which an organization is involved. For example, an e-tailer is more likely to be concerned with establishing the identity of the individual attempting to carry out a card-not-present transaction to make an online purchase, as this type of business is more prone to the risk of identity theft and credit card fraud. The fraudster is more likely to be an outsider.

A business-to-business company trading online may be more concerned with establishing procedures and controls that reduce the risk of e-procurement fraud, and may wish to employ fraud detection methods such as data mining, or require procedures for the making of e-tenders. In the case of e-procurement fraud, the fraud is far more likely to be perpetrated by an insider, and the methods of detecting the fraud need to reflect this fact.

Risk management of the threat of cybercrime should be approached as follows:

- Identify the areas within the business that are most vulnerable to cyber-attack.
- Establish what controls they already have in place to address these risks.
- Identify any further controls that may assist in reducing the risk.
- Monitor pre-existing controls to ensure they are being implemented effectively.
- Assess the controls to account for any changes or developments made in the operation of the organization.
- Ensure that procedures and controls are workable and supported by a sufficient level of resources.
- Establish a regular review procedure.

Whistle-blowing policy

All organizations should establish a culture of cybercrime awareness, and part of doing so is to ensure that employees know that whistle-blowing is a necessary part of the fight to prevent cybercrime. Employees should have available to them a simple procedure for reporting any suspicion that cybercrime is taking place. This may include an internal e-mail address to send details to, or a hot line to enable an employee to report his or her complaint quickly, and if desired, anonymously.

It should also be made possible for the employee to report to management in different departments or management with no direct responsibility for that employee, given that the employee may fear that his or her direct manager is somehow implicated in an act of cyber-fraud. It should be made clear to employees that all reports will be treated as confidential and where they are made in good faith the employee is normally protected under the Public Interest Disclosure Act (PIDA) 1998.

This is particularly relevant to incidences of cybercrime where, as discussed earlier, a good proportion of the problem arises from the unlawful conduct of insiders and employees. The objective of PIDA is to ensure that employees can inform their employers of wrongdoing within an organization without fear of repercussions, allowing problems to be identified and resolved in as little time as possible. The repercussions referred to cover different types of detriment that an employee may suffer after having made such a disclosure, including denial of a promotion or training opportunities, or of facilities that the employee would have been offered had it not been for the disclosure.

An employee is protected by PIDA if he or she makes a qualifying disclosure of information that he or she reasonably believes (and the employee can show that he or she reasonably believes) tends to show that one of the following offences or breaches have been, are being or will be committed, irrespective of whether the employee is later shown to have been incorrect:

- a criminal offence;
- a breach of a legal obligation;
- a danger to health and safety of any person;
- environmental damage;
- intentional concealing of information that demonstrates that any of the above has occurred.

The disclosure is protected if the employee makes a qualifying disclosure either through his or her employer's internal whistle-blowing procedure, or by making the disclosure to another person whom the worker reasonably believes to be solely or mainly responsible for the relevant failure. The employee must make the disclosure in good faith.

A worker may also be protected if he or she makes a disclosure in good faith externally, though there are additional conditions that need to be complied with, depending on the circumstances and to whom the disclosure is made. For example, if the information relates to a fraud the employee might be protected in reporting to the Serious Fraud Office, or in the case of an offence relating to the environment, the Environment Agency.

Where a business does not have the resources to set up a whistle-blowing mechanism internally, it is possible to outsource the service. For serious cases of cyber-fraud it is possible to report to the National High Tech Crime Unit.

What to do when cybercrime is detected

It is necessary to maintain a procedure for dealing with any report of cyber-fraud. The procedure to be implemented will vary depending on the size of the business and the scale and seriousness of the cybercrime being investigated.

A firm may wish to appoint one person as responsible for investigating the cybercrime. This person will in turn be responsible for researching the best methods of investigating a specific type of cybercrime. They may also be given responsibility for assessing the in-house skills available for investigating cybercrime, for example whether the firm has anyone with the computer science skills to enable electronic evidence to be detected and preserved. It will also be necessary for that person to establish contacts with specialist lawyers and investigators.

Damage mitigation is another issue that must be addressed by the firm. It should be decided how it is possible to stop a particular cybercrime from happening again, and whether improved techniques of risk management are necessary. It must be considered how the firm intends to secure and gather the evidence without alerting a criminal. The firm must address the question of how it intends to deal with a suspect, and when it should contact the relevant authorities such as the National High Tech Crime Unit.

As with all frauds, it must be considered when it is appropriate to inform the public that a cybercrime has occurred, bearing in mind the damage that such an announcement can have on a business compared with the value of the crime itself.

If an organization does intend to prosecute a cybercrime it must bear in mind the following:

- speed;
- strategy;
- surprise.

Money is transferable by one e-mail, telephone call or fax. It is therefore vital not only that any investigation/analysis is conducted in utmost secrecy, but also that action is taken before the fraudster has an inkling that he or she is being investigated. At the very earliest opportunity, an analysis should be carried out to assess:

- whether there has been any fraud;
- the extent of the fraud;
- whether it is viable to try to recover the losses sustained.

To do this it may be necessary to examine the computer server logs and individuals' computers. There is a list of 'Dos and Don'ts' at the end of this chapter aimed at helping prevent vital evidence needed for civil recovery or criminal action from being destroyed.

Third party disclosure as to assets and whereabouts

The English courts provide invaluable assistance to a victim, in that in certain circumstances they grant orders that enable the victim, without notice to the fraudster, to discover:

- the extent of the fraud;
- who is responsible; and
- who was involved in the commission of the fraud and therefore could be liable as well.

The court would, for example, grant orders against third parties who have been unwittingly involved in the fraud, whether such fraud has been committed electronically or in the physical world. For instance, the court will require disclosure of relevant information by an Internet Service Provider or a bank through which money stolen from the victim has passed. Such orders for disclosure can be combined with what is called a 'gagging order' that prevents the party who is giving disclosure from notifying the fraudster. Breach of such an order will amount to contempt of court, which is punishable by prison.

Once the extent of the fraud has been assessed, decisions need to be taken on whether it is commercially sensible (and whether there is an obligation) to pursue the fraudster and if so, to what extent. No victim, however large or small, should fail to assess the significance of publicity, given the fact that it has been the victim of fraud, which is often caused by inadequate security measures or lack of judgement.

Recruitment, training and personnel policies

Insiders and employees perpetrate the majority of financial crime. Cybercrime is no different. It is therefore essential for organizations to take appropriate steps to ensure their computer and physical security is adequate. Personnel should be carefully vetted. References should be checked, including those for temporary staff. The procedure for vetting and checking should become more stringent when employees are promoted to greater positions of responsibility, and the greater the amount of personal, financial or sensitive data to which the employee is privy.

Employers should consider multi-level security, including biometrically fingerprinting employees and implementing similar security procedures of this nature to ensure that employees are only permitted access to an appropriate level according to their role or seniority. Access levels should be reviewed on a frequent basis.

Employees who leave a firm (for any reason) should immediately be removed from the security clearance lists, and any access to an organization's database should be removed. Security lists should regularly be reviewed to ensure that those who do have access should have access, and whether access is necessary to the level permitted.

Employers should consider monitoring e-mails and communications in order to prevent fraud and other forms of cybercrime, where it is warranted.

Collaboration with government agencies and professional advisory bodies

Organizations should consider collaborating with governmental and professional advisory organizations to report how they manage information security and cybercrime threats, and work with suppliers and users to coordinate information on incidents. This will assist businesses in plugging the knowledge and information gaps, assessing where risk management procedures are lacking and where a business's vulnerabilities lie.

In connection with this, organizations may find it of great assistance to collaborate with government and industry advisory bodies to produce educational materials on the nature of cybercrime, why it has posed a problem for their particular business and how they have obtained information and guidance on the subject.

Ultimately, reviewing existing and producing further guidance on basic information security requirements and good risk management practice to combat cybercrime could be used to produce a 'Superhighway Code'. This would ideally take into account BS 7799, organizations established by the Information Systems Audit and Information Control Association, and also the work of the IT Governance Institute in the United States.

The aim is to eventually raise general awareness among industry, accountancy and the legal professions of the law relating to cybercrime and its effective precaution.

Compliance

No procedure or control is effective unless it is properly implemented throughout an organization. Regular checks must be undertaken to ensure that all necessary controls are being adequately implemented by employees at all levels, short-cuts are not being used in such a way as to dilute their effectiveness, and that these controls remain effective in the light of changes in the law or in the development of the organization's business.

Dos and don'ts for computer-based information

Computer evidence or data is fundamentally different from, say, paper evidence. Just the act of turning on a computer can change a whole series of dates and times and invalidate its use in a court or tribunal. Therefore, a few basic principles need to be followed when dealing with potentially valuable computer evidence.

Do:

- fully assess the situation before taking any action;
- isolate the computer so that it cannot be tampered with;
- record where the computer is based and all who had access to it;
- consider securing all relevant logs (for example, building access logs, server logs, internet logs) and any CCTV footage at the earliest opportunity;
- call in IT security staff or external consultants as appropriate.

Then ask the relevant expert to:

- disconnect the relevant computers from your network;
- restrict remote access;
- take an 'image' copy of the computer.

Don't:

- alert any potential suspects;
- call in your own IT support staff (they often change evidence inadvertently);
- turn on the computer if it is switched off;
- turn off the computer if it is switched on;
- make a copy of the computer;
- examine electronic logs without first ensuring that they are preserved elsewhere.

4.6

Countering cybercrime

Peter Brudenall, Simmons & Simmons

Introduction

The security of information technology (IT) and management of data will be a key area of risk for business in the foreseeable future. On both sides of the Atlantic, the legal profession is paying greater attention to the liabilities that companies and individual directors face if they fail to manage adequately the security of their systems or data, or are unable to prevent their systems being used to attack third parties. The accidental release of customer data, for example, has already led to significant claims being made against major companies, leading to negative media attention and the loss of consumer revenue.

However, despite ongoing concerns about global terrorism, the denial of service (DoS) attacks against 13 of the internet's core servers during 2002, and the problems caused in 2003 by the SQL 'slammer' bug, the recent MyDoom virus, the evidence is that there is still a considerable disregard shown by businesses to the issue of IT security. Less than a third of UK businesses have a documented security policy, and only 27 per cent spend more than 1 per cent of their IT budget on information security. There is clearly a significant lack of awareness to the risks posed by an IT security breach.

Accordingly, businesses will need to substantially increase the attention paid to IT security. With perhaps the exception of financial institutions, healthcare groups and other regulated bodies, it is fair to say that most businesses spend paltry sums protecting their corporate networks. Many firms simply do not understand the cost of a security breach, and what the impact may be on reputation, customer loyalty or revenue. In any event, increasing the budget for IT security may become a requirement of conducting business in many jurisdictions. There are already signs that government regulation in this area will increase dramatically in Europe, the United States, and in the Asia-Pacific region.

As the threat from cyber-terrorism, computer viruses, malicious hacking and technology failure increases, so too will the risk that legal action will result from a failure to implement minimum standards of security.

Risks to computer systems can be anything from defacing a corporate website to sabotaging an electricity distribution system. Each of these risks is associated with business risks. If, for example, a business incurs a serious virus infection, the costs that may be incurred will relate to:

- loss of e-mail gateway;
- loss of data;
- fall in productivity and wasted staff time;
- loss of opportunities;
- costs associated with repairs and remedial action.

There may also be damage to brand or professional reputation. When a security incident occurs, the need to be able to respond quickly and effectively is vital in order to minimize what may be some significant costs. Knowing the main vulnerabilities of IT systems will be necessary in order to plan such contingency measures. A comprehensive risk assessment is therefore essential. Once identified, the necessary personnel can then put together plans to reduce the risks that are likely to have the greatest impact on the organization's assets.

Objectives of IT security

Malicious attacks on data will threaten the core elements of trust and reliability that underpin your IT business systems. Threats to confidentiality, integrity or availability of data will render data unreliable and have serious business, and possibly legal consequences.

Data confidentiality

A key objective of security is confidentiality: ensuring that information is kept away from people who should not have it. For some industries, such as health care and finance, privacy and the confidentiality of personal data is now a regulatory issue. The US, European, Canadian, and Australian governments have all legislated privacy controls to varying degrees. When an IT system is accessed by an unauthorized person, or in an unauthorized way, the confidentiality of data is put at risk. An attacker may snoop, eavesdrop or intercept communications. Software for cracking passwords or other hacker scripts is freely available, and unsuspecting people may be tricked into divulging confidential information.

Data integrity

Another key objective of security is integrity: assuring that the information stored in the computer is never contaminated or changed in a way that is not appropriate. The basic ways to maintain the integrity of data are to keep it away from those who should not have it, and to ensure that those who should have it can access it.

Data availability

A third objective of security is availability: ensuring that data stored in the computer can be accessed by those people who have the right to access it. This is a broad subject addressing things such as fault tolerance to protect against denial of service and access control to ensure that data is available to those people authorized to access it. A DoS attack, for example, targets data availability by flooding the communication link with excessive packets precluding all other traffic. Such an attack disrupts e-mail operation and website transactions. A recent example of a DoS attack was the attack that flooded all 13 of the root servers of the Internet Domain Name System (DNS).

Data non-repudiation

The technologies used for the objectives of confidentiality, integrity and availability can also be used to achieve another objective of security: non-repudiation. This allows for the formation of binding contracts without any paper being printed for written signatures. Non-repudiation has valuable goals: assuring that messages received from the person whom the message claims actually sent it and that the message has not been altered in any way in transit. This also usually provides for the ability to prevent users who send messages from denying that they were sent.

Principles for best practice

What are the 'appropriate' IT security measures that businesses should be taking? Although such measures will change over time, and it is important to stay current with what constitutes best practice, the following represents a general guide as to what is required.

Threat and vulnerability assessments should be performed regularly

Some companies have been doing threat and vulnerability assessments for years; others are yet to introduce any program to assess cyber risks. In light of the ongoing risk of terrorist attacks, and the well-documented risks to computer systems, it is clear that assessments should be as common as other types of better-known security assessments, such as theft.

Accordingly, it is suggested that organizations consider that:

- Critical infrastructure providers might now be attractive to terrorist organizations.
- Those companies that do not manage 'attractive targets' may need to prepare for business disruptions.
- They must contemplate the ways in which such an attack may occur.
- They carefully assess vulnerabilities by hiring corporate or government agencies to conduct an 'attack and penetration' of their own networks. If successful, they can convince management that their systems can, in fact, be exploited.
- They deploy network assessments, which are more thorough than an attack and penetration.

Information about threats and vulnerabilities should be shared

As systems have become more complex, securing them has become increasingly more difficult. The challenge for the security community has been to ensure that computer users are notified when vulnerabilities are found, and that fixes are implemented. Information exchange is seen as key, and is considered a central plank of the US Government's National Strategy to Secure Cyberspace. However, there is an understandable reluctance on the part of commercial entities to reveal security flaws in their own systems. Once a company has been exploited, such public exposure can cause customers and investors to lose confidence, adversely impact equity markets and create the risk that other crackers will view the organization as vulnerable, thus inviting additional attacks.

Effective security policies and procedures should be implemented

Robust security policies and procedures are the pillars upon which security is built. While it is almost certain that regulators will insist on security issues being given more prominence in light of recent terrorist activity, there are already a number of excellent industry-led international standards regarding security (for instance, ISO 9000, BS 7799) with, as indicated above, the likelihood of more being developed with the input of the major industry players. Companies should identify gaps between their own corporate standards and these industry-wide best practices, but recognize that they may need actually to go beyond what is set out in the standard. Certainly terms and conditions with service providers managing your data should specify compliance with the appropriate standard.

Computer security should be assessed and upgraded continually

Threats must continually be reassessed as the world changes, because neither technology nor security is static. Computer security and upgrades must also be assessed continually. On the technology side, some of the considerations are that new vulnerabilities may be discovered in older products, so installing patches may be required. Old products may be upgraded, and new products deployed, thus introducing new vulnerabilities into a network.

Business changes may also require computer security to be reassessed. For example:

- Outsourcing critical functions may give contractors privileged access to an organization's computer systems. Remember also that legislation may dictate certain terms to be added to contracts, particularly if personal data is being managed or transferred out of the country.
- Entering into a joint venture may cause two organizations to connect their networks.
- Offering new applications to customers (for example, online shopping or e-banking) may create links between the public at large and an organization's internal systems. So each business change affecting the information infrastructure creates a need to reassess threats, to identify new potential vulnerabilities, and to take proactive steps to minimize risks.

'Round the clock' monitoring should be deployed

Computer security experts generally agree that most computer crimes are neither detected nor reported. This is often because many computer crimes are not self-evident. When a hacker steals a computerized customer list, the original remains in place, available to the owner, and it may not be immediately apparent that anything has been taken. Employing monitoring that is as close to 24/7 as possible is becoming standard.

Security incident response plans should be developed, and coordinated with overall contingency plans

An organization's ability to detect and respond quickly to simulated attacks should also be tested. While some investigations may be conducted merely to assess damage and restore the security of the attacked system, the primary goal should be to develop the evidence necessary to assign responsibility and take legal action.

Before such testing can be done, an organization should review and document the following:

- incident management policies, procedures and plans (including staffing, tool requirements and escalation procedures);
- processes to log network activity in the event of an attack;
- evidence collection and maintenance procedures.

Cyber security incident response plans should be closely coordinated with physical contingency and disaster recovery plans, especially since future cyber attacks may be linked with physical attacks. These plans should address ownership of an incident, escalation procedures, physical and electronic evidence handling procedures, coordination with law enforcement and media relations.

Educate customers

Educating your customers is also important to minimize the risk of identity theft or the unauthorized accessing of personal data. For example, suggesting to customers that they use different passwords, avoid common passwords and then change them frequently, can contribute greatly to decreasing the chances of unauthorized transactions occurring.

Bibliography

Information Assurance Advisory Council (IAAC) (2002) *Protecting the Digital Society* IAAC, Cambridge, UK (March) [Online] www.iaac.org.uk

Lewis, J (2000) Security strategy must focus on business issue of managing risk, *InternetWeek*, 831, Manhasset; 2 October, p 41.

Witty (2001) *The Price of Information Security, Strategic Analysis Report*, Gartner Research, 8 June, Note no: R-11-6534.

4.7

Centralized security management

Zuhamy Colton, Indicii Salus

Security is vital to businesses as a risk management tool. Risks can take many forms and affect organizations in many ways – access to a restricted resource, disclosure of confidential information, modification of information in transit between sender and receiver, the sender pretending to be somebody else and so on. Gartner Group estimates that hackers attack more than 200 UK companies every day, and according to the Department of Trade and Industry, 51 percent of companies suffered a data abuse incident in 2002, with each attack costing on average £30,000. Cryptography, specifically encryption and digital signatures, can be used to reduce many of these risks. It is a powerful tool used to secure communications and ensure the confidentiality, authenticity and integrity of a message. Yet the use of cryptography introduces new problems. In order to understand the importance of centrally managed cryptographic technology, one needs to understand the different types of cryptographic keys used and the effects of managing these keys.

Cryptography uses keys (large numbers with appropriate mathematical properties), in order to secure information. There are two types of keys, symmetric and asymmetric (see Figure 4.7.1). A single symmetric key is used for both protecting a document (a procedure that involves a mathematical transformation of information into apparently meaningless gibberish, called cipher text) and recovering the original document. Symmetric keys are mainly used to ensure the confidentiality of information, and must themselves remain known only to individuals with rights to recover a protected document.

Asymmetric keys on the other hand, come in pairs (called public and private) and have the property that what one of the pair protects only the other of the pair can recover.

Therefore these keys can be used to ensure not only the confidentiality of documents but also their integrity and authenticity.

Private keys must be kept secret. Public keys can be distributed freely, but it is important that the connection between public keys and user identities is maintained, since otherwise an attacker could substitute its own public key for that of another user and trick other users into protecting documents for it instead of the intended recipient. This can have devastating effects for an organization.

A private key is used either when digitally signing a document to prove whom it came from or when retrieving protected information received from another person. The person holding the private key is the only person that can turn the e-mail/file from completely unintelligible text into a legible document.

The public key is used either when verifying the digital signature on a document or (using the recipient's public key) encrypting for the recipient, and is given to anybody who wants to send encrypted information to the user.

One key protects and recovers the message.

The public key protects the message...

... the private key recovers it.

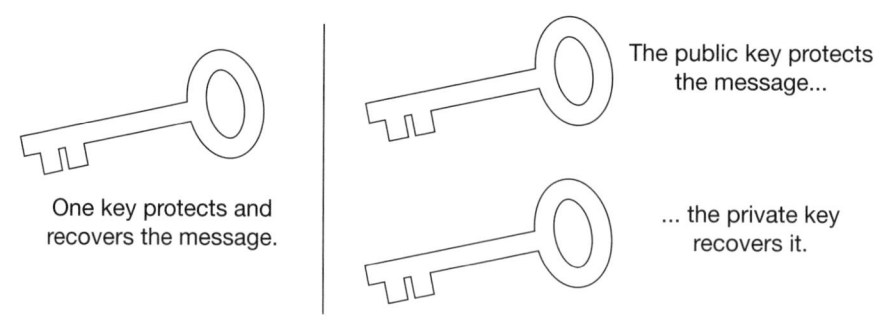

Figure 4.7.1 Symmetric and asymmetric cryptography

All keys need to be managed and protected (from both theft and substitution), which can become a costly and panic-inducing experience to organizations, especially when all conventional solutions force end users to manage their own keys. Effective key management is fundamental to the success of any crypto-based security infrastructure. Poor key management renders the security system obsolete and is an economic burden on an organization.

Client-centric versus server-centric: comparative key management functions

When most of the work involved with managing the keys is performed on the client machine by the end user, this is called a client-centric system (or device-centric); this means users store their own private keys and everyone's public keys on their devices and each of these has to be secured. In contrast, a server-centric system is where public and private keys are stored on a central server. All users access their keys via this central server, instead of having direct access to them on their devices.

These different architectures have radically different consequences and associated costs for the management of keys. In the case of a centralized system the cost is reduced in many ways: perhaps the most palpable is not having to secure the private keys on every device, only the server.

Key generation or regeneration

Good security practice dictates that keys are only used for one purpose. Users need to have separate key pairs for encryption and signing. This means each user will have several public and private key pairs. These must be generated with mathematical properties before a user can use the system.

In a client-centric system, key pairs are typically generated by performing an operation on the user's own personal device using the client-centric software. This may be done by the user, assuming the software is easy enough to use or the user has sufficient knowledge to do so, or by a system administrator performing the operation on the user's device. Either approach is time-consuming for either the user or the internal IT resources of your organization.

In a server-centric system, key pairs are generated by an administrator on the central server and are stored on that server. This step is completely invisible to ordinary users. The administrator can easily generate keys for hundreds of users without having physical access to their personal devices, therefore saving the organization time and money.

It is important that the machine where the key pairs are generated should not have been compromised, or an attacker could steal them as they are being generated. A server is a much more difficult target than an ordinary user machine, making a server-centric system safer.

Key distribution

In order for two users to communicate securely, they must have access to each other's public keys. In a client-centric system, users must either exchange public keys amongst themselves or must send their public keys to a central administrator who will then distribute a list of public keys to all users. The client-centric software may provide facilities to automate this process to some extent, but since users keep public keys (their own and other people's) on their personal devices, some user involvement in and understanding of this process is inevitably required, and once again the process is time-consuming. In a server-centric system, all public keys are held on the central server, so users can easily access them with no additional effort.

Key protection

In a client-centric system, by definition, private keys are held on the users' devices. They are usually protected with a password, but (particularly if a user has chosen a weak password) anyone who can get access to the device can copy the private key and attempt to guess the password. Devices used directly by users are often relatively easy to get access to; many employees will have physical access to other employees' devices such a laptop or PDA, which are even more easily accessed since they are routinely taken off the company premises.

In a server-centric system, the keys used for encrypting and signing are held on the central server and never leave it. Users and their personal computers never have the private keys in their physical possession, so it is impossible to steal a key by stealing a device. The worst that can happen is that an attacker is able to authenticate to the server-centric system as one of its users, which temporarily allows use of the user's keys via the server, but once the problem is discovered the administrator can immediately prevent access to the keys.

Key revocation

If an attacker acquires access to a user's private key or compromises the protection of the public key, even temporarily, other users must be notified so that they stop using the corresponding public key to communicate with the user whose key was compromised. This is a difficult, time-consuming and costly task to perform in a client-centric architecture since copies of the compromised key are distributed widely.

As mentioned in key distribution, a server-centric system holds all the keys and therefore allows the administrator to revoke the keys instantly, an important point for many organizations, particularly those with a high turnover of employees.

Disaster recovery

If a user's private key is lost or rendered unusable through a forgotten password or hardware failure, it is no longer possible to decrypt any documents encrypted for that user. This could have serious consequences for the user's employer.

In a client-centric system, private keys are held on the device, so some mechanism must be put in place to periodically take a back-up copy of keys in case something happens to the copy held on it. This represents a risk for many organizations. For instance, if a user chooses to, or is forced to, regenerate his or her keys, the new keys may not be backed up immediately and any documents encrypted using the new keys will be rendered inaccessible if the key is lost. If a user protects his or her key with a password and then forgets it, it may be impossible to recover access to the key.

In a server-centric system, all keys are on the server, so backing up the server periodically is sufficient. This is obviously much easier and less time-consuming for administrators, allowing organizations to allocate staff to other priorities of their business. Keys are stored encrypted on the server, but they are not encrypted directly using the user's password, so if a user forgets his or her password, the password can be changed to allow access to the keys without any disruption.

Ubiquitous access

Users may wish to protect or verify documents from many different devices in different physical locations. In a client-centric system, each separate device must have its own copy of the user's private keys for this to be possible. These multiple copies introduce management problems, since key regeneration and revocation require every copy to be updated. It also means that the user cannot just use any device with the relevant software to protect or verify documents, since the user's keys are not going to be present on a device. In a server-centric system, as long as users have access to the server, they can access their keys from any device in any location without having had to take any steps to place their keys on that device in advance.

Key escrow

A company has legitimate grounds for allowing certain employees to verify documents protected for other employees. For example, the personal assistant of a law firm might review the incoming e-mail of a partner, or a person might be legally required to access someone else's e-mail. In a client-centric system, users give their private keys to the person they delegate the reading rights to. This is blunt because:

- *The user does not have technical means to remove access from the reader again* (that is, the person could have copied the private key to some other place).
- *The user gives full-blown access*. In a server-centric system, the user with this privilege never actually gets direct access to the other user's private key, so there is no way he or she can take a copy of it to use in the future. Instead, access to the key is mediated via the central server.

In a server-centric approach it is possible to limit further the access to the key (for instance, allow reading only of document generated in a certain time span, only generated by a certain group of people, only e-mails but not Word documents, and so on).

Policy enforcement

A company may wish to specify various policies for the use of cryptographic software. For example, restrictions on acceptable passwords may be specified in order to avoid users choosing weak passwords.

In a client-centric system, any such policies can only be enforced if they are done so via the client software. It is certainly possible to do this, but the policies may have to be specified individually on each device, making it difficult to administer them. Also, because users have access to their own private keys, it would be possible for them to copy the keys on to a different machine, perhaps their home computer, with a copy of the client software, which does not enforce the desired policies and presents a difficulty when updating them.

In a server-centric system, the server itself can enforce policies. This provides a convenient single location from which to administer policies. Since users have no choice but to interact with the server in order to use their keys, there is no potential for accidental or deliberate policy breaches by users. In addition, any changes to policy can easily be reflected and administered without incurring the overhead of making changes to individual machines and access devices. (See Table 4.7.1.)

Conclusion

Centralized management is not only more user-friendly for an organization's user population (that is, employees, clients, suppliers and so on) but it allows organizations to have cost-effective and 'always on' security. Users are not forced to worry about whether the device they are using is secure.

Table 4.7.1 Centralized management and device-based management

Centralized management	Device-based management
Keys are stored securely on the server	Keys are stored on user machines, making theft of keys more likely
Keys are generated securely on the server	Keys are generated on the client, so a compromised client may allow an attacker to observe the process
Keys for many users can be generated easily on the server	Users' keys need to be generated on their own client devices
Keys are distributed via the server, so users do not need to be involved, thus security can be as automated as company policy dictates	Users need to exchange public keys amongst themselves or work with an administrator to share them
Key management is performed centrally by administrative staff on the secure server	Users need to manage their own keys, or administrators must visit their machines to do it for them. Client devices must be properly secured for this to be safe.
Compromised keys can be revoked and regenerated immediately	All users with a copy of a compromised key have to be informed when it is revoked and regenerated
Forgotten passwords can be reset by the administrator	Forgotten passwords make a user's keys inaccessible
Keys can be accessed from anywhere there is a network connection to the server	Keys must be copied to a client machine in advance
Keys can be backed up centrally on the server	Keys must be backed up from a distributed collection of client machines
One user can immediately be given access to another user's keys, and this access can be revoked immediately any time in the future	Giving one user access to another user's keys requires giving them physical possession of the keys, which is time-consuming. It is impossible to ensure that the second user has not kept a copy of the keys when he or she no longer has a legitimate reason to use them.
Policies on the use of the system are rigorously enforced by the server	Policies on the use of the system are enforced by client machines, making it more likely that users can subvert them
Policies can be changed and updated on the server and will automatically affect all users	Policy changes must be made on all client machines individually

The function of key management in its entirety is made simpler, resulting in better security and an overall reduction in cost due to the ease of deployment and management of the security infrastructure as a whole. From the perspective of deployment and applications, a server-centric approach not only enables better security but also it saves you time and money.

4.8

Electronic contracting

Peter Brudenall, Simmons & Simmons

Legal considerations

The core considerations are:

- the ability of parties to contract online;
- formation of online contracts;
- incorporation of an e-tailer's standard terms and conditions.

Can parties contract online?

With the exception of contracts for the sale or transfer of an interest in land, and contracts for the provision of consumer credit, most contracts can be made online and have the same basic requirements as contracting offline. There must be an accepted set of terms, and both parties must intend to enter into a legally binding contract and provide consideration.

An offer or an invitation to treat?

When information, such as a price list, is displayed on a website, is this construed as an offer or just an invitation to treat? If the prices displayed amount to an offer, and the customer's selecting and ordering the product amounts to an acceptance, then the e-tailer will be bound to sell the product at the price displayed on the website. This is unlikely to be the approach taken by the English courts. To draw an analogy with the treatment of goods displayed in a shop, the price displayed on the website is likely to be an invitation to treat and not an offer. The offer would subsequently be made when the customer selects and orders the product. The offer is then accepted by the e-tailer when it confirms the order, or on delivery of the product. This scenario may not always be the case, as the presumption that the prices on a website only constitute an invitation to treat may be rebutted by the words or conduct of the e-tailer.

Websites, therefore, should be designed so that the display of goods does not constitute an offer, and this should be reinforced by including a statement in the website's terms and conditions to the effect that the e-tailer is free to accept or reject any offer made by a customer. The significance of this analysis was clearly illustrated when a UK online retailer mistakenly advertised televisions for sale on a website at £2.99 rather than £299. The retailer would not have been bound to accept the offers made by customers for the televisions at that stage; however, an automatic e-mail confirmation was sent in response to each offer, which was arguably an acceptance forming a binding contract.

Acceptance of an offer

For acceptance to be effective it must be communicated. How should an e-tailer communicate its acceptance of an offer? The obvious way is by e-mail, although more traditional methods of communication could be used. If e-mail is used, it is unclear exactly when acceptance is communicated – is it when the 'send' button is pressed, when it leaves the e-tailer's ISP mail server, or when the customer receives it? To prevent confusion, it is best to provide details of how acceptance is deemed communicated in the terms and conditions. In commercial contracts, the provision of consideration by each party and their intention to enter into the contract will rarely be an issue.

Incorporation of the e-tailer's standard terms and conditions

An e-tailer will want the contract for sale or supply of goods or services to be governed by its own standard terms and conditions. To be binding, these terms must be incorporated into the electronic contract by bringing them to the attention of the customer before, or at the same time as, the contract is formed. If standard terms are not properly incorporated, in the event of a dispute the court will imply terms to govern the contract based on statute or a past course of dealing, which may be far less advantageous to the e-tailer.

Methods of incorporation

Just including terms and conditions on a website is not enough to incorporate them into the contract. The parties must agree to contract on the stated terms. There are three main ways in which terms and conditions may be presented to the users of a website and incorporated into the contract:

- hyperlink displayed at base of web page;
- hyperlink within sentence with wording to the effect of, 'By clicking on the "I accept" button you acknowledge that you have read and accepted the terms and conditions'; or

- click-wrap agreement: where the customer must scroll through the terms before being able to click 'I accept' and proceed with the transaction.

By analogy with earlier case law dealing with incorporation of terms into a contract, it is likely that a court would conclude that incorporation by the second or third option is valid, as the existence and content of the terms is clearly brought to the customer's attention before the contract is formed and so would be binding on the customer. The first option set out above may fail to do this. Although not indicative of the English courts' approach, US courts have confirmed the binding effect of a click-wrap agreement, while confirming that mere reference to terms and conditions as a hyperlink (such as in the first option or by use of a browse-wrap facility) would not be enough to incorporate terms and conditions, as the customer is not required to read the terms before ordering. Therefore a balance must be struck between aesthetics of a website and ensuring contractual formalities are complied with.

Reasonable terms

Not only do contractual terms need to be validly incorporated to be binding, they need to be reasonable. In the vast majority of contracts made online there will be no opportunity for the customer to negotiate the e-tailer's standard terms and conditions. As a result, the Unfair Contracts Terms Act 1977 (UCTA) will be applicable and the e-tailer will be unable to exclude or limit liability for breach of contract unless it is reasonable to do so. Whether a term is reasonable will be considered on the facts, and the case of *Watford Electronics v Sanderson CFL Limited* (2001) indicates that terms in B2B contracts are likely to be considered reasonable when the parties are commercially experienced and were aware of, or should have known about, the limitation or exclusion of liability.

As a consequence of the Unfair Terms in Consumer Contracts Regulations 1999, e-tailers entering into contracts with consumers will need to take a much more reasonable line on the limitation or exclusion of liability, as reasonableness of a particular term will be judged more harshly against the e-tailer. Plain and intelligible language should be used throughout the website.

Other considerations when contracting with consumers

E-tailers contracting with consumers via websites must ensure that they comply with the Consumer Protection (Distance Selling) Regulations 2000 (Distance Selling Regulations). Any term in the contract that is inconsistent with the Distance Selling Regulations will be void.

Distance selling checklist

Before the contract is made, the e-tailer must give the consumer certain details, including:

- e-tailer's identity, and address if payment required in advance;
- description of goods or services;

- price of goods or services, including all taxes;
- delivery costs;
- arrangements for payment, delivery and performance;
- existence of right to cancel, where the right exists;
- period for which offer price is valid;
- costs of returning goods on cancellation.

Failure to provide the above information within the required time will affect the length of the consumer's right to cancel, extending the cancellation period beyond three months after conclusion of the contract. Note that certain types of contracts, including those for the supply of food and drink, and for accommodation and transport provided at a particular time, are excluded from the scope of the Distance Selling Regulations.

Evidence of the contract

The e-tailer should ensure that it keeps a record of all online contracts entered into in a durable form to enable later enforcement of the contract, if necessary. Computer systems need to generate an audit trail to prove that the customer accepted the terms and conditions and is bound by them. It is also advisable to keep a record of previous versions of the website and past terms and conditions.

Effect of the Electronic Commerce Regulations on online contracting

If a business is trading online, it will almost certainly be affected by the Electronic Commerce (EC Directive) Regulations 2002 (E-commerce Regulations) which came into force in the United Kingdom on 21 August 2002. All e-tailers should ensure that the following minimum information, which must be easily and permanently accessible, is provided to customers, whether businesses or consumers. The easiest way to do this is by including on the website:

- The name, geographic address and e-mail address of the service provider. A Post Office box will not be an adequate geographic address, but a registered office address would. The name of the organization with which the customer is contracting must be given, and if this differs from the trading name, the reason for the difference must be explained. It is not sufficient to include a 'contact us' page alone. In addition, an e-mail and geographic address must be provided somewhere easily accessible on the site.
- If a company, the company's registration number must be stated.
- If the business is registered for VAT, the VAT number must be stated.
- If the business is a member of a trade or a profession, membership details, including any registration number, must be provided.
- Prices on the website must be clear and state whether prices are inclusive of tax and delivery costs.

These requirements are in addition to the information required by the Distance Selling Regulations, if the e-tailer is contracting with consumers.

Additional information to be given before orders are placed online

In addition to the requirements above, the E-Commerce Regulations require the following information to be given when selling online, whether to businesses or consumers:

- the technical steps that need to be followed to conclude the contract;
- whether or not the contract will be accessible in future;
- the methods used to identify and correct errors on the site before orders are placed;
- languages offered on the website;
- if the contract is not concluded by e-mail (for instance, it is concluded on the website), details of any relevant codes of conduct to which the e-tailer subscribes must be provided; and
- if the contract is not concluded by e-mail, the terms and conditions of the contract must be made available to allow a customer to store and reproduce the terms.

If the transaction is completed by e-mail the acknowledgement need not be immediate, although receipt of the offer should be confirmed as soon as possible. When dealing with other businesses, the terms and conditions can be worded to vary acknowledgement requirements.

When confirming the order, it is better to state that an order has been received and is now being processed, rather than state that the order has been accepted. This helps to avoid the problems set out above of accepting an offer for an incorrectly priced product. It is important for businesses to be aware of the regulation of contracts made online so as to take effective advantage of the commercial opportunities available by selling via the internet.

Building a relationship of trust online

The perceived risks of online contracting (including the increased risk of fraud, opportunism and the collection and misuse of personal data) lead to greater wariness on the part of potential customers. As such, the e-tailer needs to make every effort to build customer confidence. Customers will want to know that any communication they send will reach the intended recipient unchanged, and without being read by anyone else, and will look to the e-tailer to provide reassurance of this. If it is not provided, custom will be taken elsewhere. Building a relationship of trust will boost customer confidence and will give the business a competitive advantage.

There are several ways in which an e-tailer can build a relationship of trust:

- Ensure that best practice guidelines are evident and adhered to. As customers grow aware that a business has policies in place to comply with statutory guidelines, they can feel more confident as to the identity of the party they are contracting with, and that their personal data will not be misused.

- By design and regular review of a business management and organizational structure to provide a secure and trusted management framework.
- Use of electronic signatures to authenticate the origin of a message, and to confirm whether that message has been altered. Security of e-signatures can be enhanced by the use of encryption to keep messages secret, which can take the form of symmetrical or asymmetrical encryption. The Electronic Communications Act 2000 largely implements the requirements of the Electronic Signatures Directive (1999/93/EC) into UK law and provides that electronic signatures and certificates of electronic signatures are admissible in court as evidence of authenticity of the messages to which they are attached.

E-signatures can come in many forms, including typed names, scanned-in signatures, electronic representations of a handwritten signature, unique sequences of characters, digital representations of a biological aspect (such as the retina) or signatures created by cryptographic means; any of these will increase the security of a transaction.

However, technology can only assist in the creation and maintenance of trust between traders and their customers. Internal adherence to best practice will ensure that customer confidence in the business is built up and maintained, which in turn will reap commercial benefit.

Information security training

Alan Calder, IT Governance Ltd

There are two groups of people in any organization who need information security training: general (non-specialist) users of information and IT equipment (including board members and senior managers), and people with functional specialisms, including the information security specialists themselves. Each group needs a different depth and quality of training.

General information security training

Information security depends on three things: technological controls, procedural controls, and user competence. Of these, user competence is probably the most critical: you can spend a fortune on software and hardware solutions, invest ages in designing appropriate processes and procedures, only to have your entire business taken offline by someone who imports a mass-mailing Trojan through Instant Messenger, or who downloads some 'cool' freeware that comes bundled with Trojan downloaders, browser hijackers and assorted spyware.

Appropriate training for all personnel is essential, so it's not surprising that this is a requirement of BS 7799, the standard for information security. All users of the organization's information assets need to be aware of information security threats and adequately equipped to support the organization's information security policy in their work. Training should include third-party users of the organization's equipment, and all users should also get regular updates on organizational policy.

The key areas of information security that need to be covered for general users are:

- information security awareness (basic concepts, threats and controls), its importance, and the information security management system, including general controls;
- asset classification and control (including how information is classified and who should have access to what);
- responding to security events, incidents and malfunctions;
- e-mail, Instant Messenger and web access awareness and rules (this is particularly important in the context of current legislation and virus, spam and assorted malware threats);
- user access control and responsibilities (including rules about passwords), mobile computing and teleworking;
- legal compliance (data protection and privacy, computer misuse) awareness and related issues;
- business continuity awareness and procedures.

The organization also needs to have a method for regularly updating users on information security threats and counter-measures, as well as on changes to the policies, procedures and IT infrastructure.

General awareness training, staff information awareness training and staff information security briefing/updating/communication plans should be designed by the information security adviser, in conjunction with the organization's training specialists. Organizations that do not have an information security adviser should hire an external firm to provide this training, which they should be able to do cost-effectively, tailoring a standard course to reflect the specific information security posture of the client organization.

Training for staff with functional specialisms

The staff who will require user-specific training include the Chief Information Officer, the Information Security Adviser, IT and network managers, IT and help desk support staff, web masters, premises security staff, HR, recruitment and training staff, general managers, finance staff, company secretary/legal staff, internal quality assurance/system auditors, and business continuity/emergency response teams.

These staff should first be exposed to the all-staff training described above. The additional, user-specific training they require is best identified though an individual training needs analysis (TNA). Any handbook on corporate training, or a training professional, could provide appropriate support on a step that is fundamental to well-designed training delivery. The principle underlying a TNA is that, once the knowledge, skills and competence requirements of a particular role have been established clearly, and documented in the job description, the role-holder's own knowledge, skills and competence can be compared with the requirement and a gap analysis, or TNA, completed. The next step is to map out an individual learning path to meet the requirements of the TNA and close the knowledge, skills and competence gap. This individual learning path will contain a mix of self-learning, instructor-led training and experience. It should identify clearly where the training is to come from, and should set out the dates by when specific steps are to be taken, identified skills or competences acquired, and proof of acquisition generated.

While most organizations will have a TNA process for staff in generic roles, there are individuals who, for information security purposes, must have very specific knowledge, skills and competences that are in addition to those needed by the group of employees of which they may be a part. There needs to be an individual TNA for each of the people in each of the individual or specialist roles identified above. Where this is being put together for a new employee, the offer letter might make permanent employment conditional on achieving certain stages within certain time frames.

The British Computer Society is a logical starting point for investigating professional training; its website is at www.bcs.org. This site describes a range of training programmes and regimes that are applicable to information professionals, including the Information Systems Examination Board qualifications. The most important of these is the Certificate in Information Security Management Principles. This provides the foundation of knowledge necessary for individuals who have security responsibility as part of their day-to-day role, or who are likely to move into a security or security-related function. BCS claims that the certificate provides an opportunity for those already within such roles to enhance or refresh their knowledge, and in the process to gain a qualification, recognized by industry, which demonstrates the level of knowledge gained.

The qualification is said by BCS to prove that the holder has a good knowledge and basic understanding of the wide range of subject areas that make up information security management. It is possible for someone who has experience in computer support or management to attend this course and to become qualified in information security, but it is not designed for someone who has little or no practical exposure to information technology.

Candidates who have achieved the certificate, which requires a one-week study course followed by a written examination, should be able to understand:

- information security management concepts (confidentiality, integrity, availability, vulnerability, threats, risks and countermeasures, and so on);
- current legislation and regulations that impact information security management in the UK;
- current national and international standards, frameworks and organizations that facilitate the management of information security;
- the current business and technical environments in which information security management takes place (security products, malicious software ('malware'), relevant technology, and so on);
- the categorization, operation and effectiveness of a variety of safeguards.

The contact details of those organizations that are accredited to deliver training that leads to the ISEB certificate, as well as current details about examination fees and dates, are all on the BCS website. There are about 150 candidates per year for the ISEB certificate examinations and the pass rates are high.

An alternative, and increasingly widely available and highly considered, vendor-independent professional certificate is the CISSP (Certified Information System Security Professional), and examination administered by (ISC)2 – the International Information Systems Security Certification Consortium. There is a website for the certificate at www.cissps.com and there are UK training providers: a Google UK search on 'CISSP' will identify a number. The CISSP examination covers the 10 areas of the Common Body of Knowledge; substantial prior experience (or a mixture of experience and academic qualification) is required.

Those IT staff charged with systems administration should be trained appropriately, by either the software supplier or by an approved training vendor (such as those identified on the BCS website), as system administrators for the software for which they are the nominated administrator. Evidence of this training should be retained on the individual's personnel file. Those responsible for firewall, anti-virus, encryption and any other security software should have appropriate training certificates from the product vendors and should be required to keep their skills and knowledge current by attending regular refresher and update courses. These should be booked into the individual's training calendar in advance and there should be evidence that they were attended. Certainly, in any Microsoft environment, there should always be a systems administrator who has a Microsoft certificate, such as the MCSE.

Web masters need to be thoroughly trained and have their skills regularly updated. Their training needs to cover the security aspects of all the hardware and software for which they are responsible; in particular, they need to be capable of ensuring that the web servers are fully secured.

Information security staff, company secretarial/legal staff and HR/personnel staff will also need specific legal training. There are a number of particular legal issues to do with information security, and the organization needs to know how to handle them, using standard template documents wherever possible. It does not need to employ an in-house lawyer, as this can be unnecessarily expensive; external expertise can be brought in where and when necessary to deal with specific legal issues.

Staff dealing with telephone systems and network hardware and software will all need specific, supplier-certified, administration and security training that covers these products. The organization will need access to regular updates on information security issues relating to these products.

Conclusion

Effective IT training is an essential component of a secure organization; staff do, after all, make all the difference. Designing and managing an effective information security programme can be done in-house, following the principles identified in this chapter. The range of training requirements can, though, be extensive and, for many organizations, the most cost-effective strategy is to bring in an external specialist who can identify what training is needed and can then pull it together, in the context of the organization's actual information security strategy, current skills base and future skills requirements.

4.10

Outsourced solutions

Martin Saunders, Easynet

In today's corporate environment, it is common practice to allocate a diversity of business functions to external companies. The emergence of outsourcing IT is more of a recent phenomenon, fuelled by awareness of the devastating impact of viruses and their increase in number and virulence.

As a result, businesses are increasingly benefiting from outsourcing communications technology to service providers, offloading their resource-hungry technology requirements to expert organizations, and enjoying improved security coupled with more time and resource to concentrate on core business operations. A host of service providers are jostling for space in a busy market, offering the enticing proposition of management of a full portfolio of communications technology services, from telephone switchboard management, to web hosting, data back-up and e-mail management, to running an entire corporate network.

For maximum benefit and peace of mind, however, businesses need to adopt an integrated approach to their outsourcing strategy, maintaining an in-house IT function to focus on daily operations and to retain contact with the provider. This chapter will outline the options available to a business adopting an outsourcing strategy, and will identify the considerations that need to be addressed.

Research by IT services provider Synstar identified the importance of outsourcing in terms of risk management. The biggest concerns for IT managers, the survey discovered, are currently security and the economic climate. Within this survey, the most popular method for managing costs was to outsource certain aspects of IT. Selective outsourcing was viewed as the most popular way for IT departments to save money while improving performance, according to half the respondents.

Russell Flower, Director of Managed Services for Synstar, confirmed that outsourced services could help firms manage costs. 'It leaves more time for IT directors to focus strategically,' he said, adding that firms tend to outsource selectively to managed service providers rather than hand over the entire IT function to a traditional outsourcer.

Most respondents said outsourcing was an attractive option. Infrastructure maintenance and user support were the responsibilities IT managers most wanted to hand over to an external specialist. The key attraction was access to skills that were unavailable within their organization.

A diverse range of services is available to businesses looking to outsource their IT requirements but for the purpose of this chapter, these are summarized under the headings of Applications, Physical options and Network options.

Applications Organizations can benefit from outsourcing applications such as web hosting, data back-up and e-mail management. Many application service providers, or ASPs, offer the service of managing businesses' e-mail and data. Many providers also offer managed anti-virus and anti-spam services. It is the responsibility of the provider to monitor all traffic entering and leaving a business, removing entirely the burden of traffic control and monitoring from a company's in-house IT department.

Physical options that can easily be outsourced include colocation and leasing of cage and rack space. With these options, providers offer leased physical space in purpose-built data centre facilities specifically built to provide high-level security including back-up generators, fire suppression equipment, power control and cable management. Companies can hire space to house their own equipment in a fully protected environment without the expense of intensive, complex security systems. The colocation provider is responsible for the maintenance of the physical environment.

An example of such a site as this is 1bricklane®, a colocation and hosting facility owned and operated by Easynet. Providing a resilient and secure environment for organizations' IT equipment and web servers, the building has been fitted to exacting technical specifications with direct mains power from an adjacent London Electricity primary substation and back-up generators, top-level security and the latest fire detection and suppression systems. The provider offers such managed service options as 24/7 remote hands service, 24/7 device monitoring, professional tape management and managed firewall. Customer servers can also house their operating systems and some applications managed in this facility.

Providers can offer security, access, space, support, cabling, hardware and power. This means that organizations do not have to consider these issues at all.

Network options involve a service provider taking on the responsibility, to a lesser or greater degree, for the management and maintenance of an organization's network.

Firewalls enable safe connection to and from the internet. If a company runs a website, has a dial-up connection or manages a corporate network, a firewall is critical. While firewalls can be managed in-house, there are clear benefits from outsourcing the service to a specialist who will fully support and maintain the service.

MPLS (Multi Protocol Label Switching) and Internet Protocol Virtual Private Network (IPVPN) are two technologies that enable the transfer of network management from the customer, on to the provider. MPLS connects remote offices for the fast, private exchange of data across a network. Two or more geographically dispersed office locations are linked, creating a managed wide area network (WAN) that connects offices, home-workers, suppliers and field-based staff.

IPVPN is similar in functionality, but offers a higher level of service, and if it is managed by a provider offering Multi Protocol Label Switching technology, can offer users the ability to prioritize data into different classes of service (such as mission-critical account transfer information for a financial corporation, for example). Voice, video and data can be run across the same network. One of the advantages of IPVPNs is that most use IP Sec, a tunnelling protocol that ensures high levels of reliability and security while the data is travelling across a public network.

Many providers offer 24-hour network monitoring to ensure fast discovery (and repair) of outages, high availability and bandwidth at consistent quality. Companies large and small benefit from implementing an IPVPN. According to a survey by InStat/MDR, 74 per cent of firms that have existing VPNs intend to switch to services managed by providers.

Outsourcing considerations

A diversity of internal and external issues must be addressed before a company adopts a technology outsourcing strategy. Companies may choose to deploy different services to a number of different providers. While this ensures the availability of specialist skills, it can be more of a challenge to maintain communication and can be more costly than adopting a 'one provider fits all' strategy. There is also the argument that security is less of a risk when working with one provider rather than several (eggs in one basket theory and so on).

Internally, a company must have a clear objective in mind of what it is aiming to achieve from outsourcing. Whether this is a cost saving, the adoption of specialist IT skills or the redeployment of in-house IT resource, all will influence the final decision on which provider or providers to work with and indeed what to outsource.

Staff management may need reassessing, as briefings may be required in terms of the division of activity between in-house and external teams. The client's IT management team must establish expectation levels for communication in terms of weekly or monthly contact and ensure the provider has a failsafe contact strategy in place should any outages or urgent security issues arise. The client company may choose to build in checks and procedures to ensure costs are being minimized and the service provider is operating to maximum efficiency.

A range of further issues should be addressed externally, before contracting the service provider. Companies need to assess the levels of security and potential risk if placing hardware on a provider's premises. Does it have all available protection in terms of security and hazard risk? What about back-up in the event of power or network failure? If outsourcing applications, the company needs to assess where the data will be held, and look at the reliability and security of the provider's own infrastructure. How financially stable is the operation? It may well be worth assessing financial records to check the provider has a stable financial background. Once all these areas have been considered in-depth, then the decision to outsource or not can be taken.

Outsourcing technology looks set to remain a viable, cost-effective means of streamlining businesses while maintaining specialist skills and implementing secure, robust services.

Outsourcing technology in action

Case study 1

Education recruitment agency Select Education, and sister company Select Appointments, looked to outsource their network management. The companies had a requirement to connect over 30 Select Education branches and 60 Select Appointments offices to their respective head offices over a high-speed connection, enabling fast, efficient shared communication of and access to internal documents, CVs and job specifications, and other client and corporate information.

An IPVPN solution ensured the rapid and reliable exchange of data, greatly enhancing service levels. The client companies were provided with a range of optimized security solutions, a service level agreement and ISDN back-up, ensuring minimum downtime and access to business-critical applications.

The companies are reducing their costs of ownership and are freeing up in-house expertise using their provider's 24/7 monitoring service and remote hosting service, enabling them to redeploy staff at substantial savings.

David Rowe, CEO of Easynet, said: 'Working closely with Select Education, Easynet was able to offer a reliable, cost-effective solution which addressed their concerns about managing the network in-house and offered an alternative disaster recovery solution.'

Case study 2

Bravilor Bonamat specializes in the design and production of filter coffee makers for the professional and the rapidly growing market of instant beverage machines. The company has 250 employees in more than 80 countries. Noticeable growth has taken place in the last decade, placing increasing demands on its network and prompting re-evaluation of the organization's communications technology.

Provider Easynet installed its fully managed EuroVPN solution, a managed pan-European broadband service, giving each of the sales offices permanent fixed lines of communications to each other via an 'always on' internet connection. As well as safeguarding the network from attack, the managed solution reduces the total cost of ownership and avoids the prohibitive costs of in-house security expertise.

'The fact that my provider offers 24/7 service has revolutionized the way our IT team works. Their time is now free to concentrate on other critical tasks,' observed Jeroen Kok, IT Manager at Bravilor.

Case study 3

Global corporation Tchibo began trading in Germany as a mail order coffee distributor. Now Tchibo is known for much more than just coffee. Through its online store www.tchibo.co.uk, mail order and retail outlets the company provides a large variety of food and non-food products.

In 1997 the company began to develop its e-commerce strategy by opening a German online store. Security and reliability were critical, since the online shop is open 24/7. The company outsourced its server management, and has a high-speed, high-capacity data connection from its provider's data centre to the internet. Tchibo and its service provider have become close partners and agreed a cost per order model. This means Tchibo does not need to ask for faster connectivity, larger servers or bigger databases because Ision will scale the platform on demand.

The service provider now has responsibility for the availability, performance and uptime of the Tchibo online stores in Germany, Austria, Switzerland and the United Kingdom. Each year the provider adds a number of servers to the platform, in order to meet demand during the busy Christmas period without any drop in service.

4.11

Securing the mobile workforce

Andy Baines, Fujitsu Services

Today's world: new models, new threats

Many organizations are now facing commercial pressures to enable remote access to their sensitive information resources by customers, partners, outsourced service providers and a mobile workforce. Existing perimeter-based security, such as the firewall, cannot cope with these business models. Therefore, a more flexible approach to securing the enterprise is required – balancing risk with a variety of controls, some technical and some soft, including legal and business processes.

Traditional models of security placed sensitive organization assets within defined organizational boundaries and kept everything else on the outside. Known, authenticated users were allowed in, and everyone else was kept out. Today, the internet has helped to create new business models – commerce is outsourced, distributed, collaborative and interactive. Organizations have to expose internal systems to partners and customers. Concepts of organizational boundaries are blurred.

The wireless infrastructure

The need for security on any network is apparent: the prevention of eavesdropping and the desire for authentication have been the main focuses of many network administrators. However, the problems that already exist are compounded when you add wireless networking to the equation. As wireless networking becomes more popular, the flawed security of most of those networks becomes more apparent.

The security of any network is an important issue. No-one likes the idea that it may be possible that someone could be intercepting their internet traffic, reading their e-mail, ordering items with their credit cards, or sending inappropriate messages to their boss in their name. Security of wired networks is, therefore, a primary objective of system administrators.

When considering a network that incorporates a Wireless Access Point, or 'WAP', new security concerns come into play. Because wireless is 'broadcast' in nature, anyone within range of a wireless access point or card can intercept the packets being sent out without interrupting the flow of data between card and access point. For this reason, wireless network security must be somewhat more concentrated than that of wired networks.

The two main issues

There are two main issues that wireless security solutions tend to address. First, since all wireless packets are available to anyone who listens, security is needed to prevent eavesdropping. Since it is impossible physically to keep people away from the WAPs, short of erecting a fence around your building, solutions tend to rely on encryption in one form or another.

The second issue is authentication. With a wired network, a system administrator might determine who generated certain traffic based on the physical connection point that the traffic came in on. By assuming that inbound traffic from a particular connection point is always coming from a certain source, there is no need to constantly verify where the traffic is coming from. However, with wireless networking, many users can access the network at the same access point or base station making it more difficult to map who did what. It is often desirable, therefore, to allow users to identify who they are before letting them through the base station on to the rest of the network.

A growing problem

The idea of a no-wires network is becoming more appealing to home and small office users as each day passes, partly because bandwidth becomes less of an issue – wireless networks can theoretically provide speeds of up to 54 Mbps.

In terms of security, it is these *ad hoc* networks that most often provide the easiest access to outsiders. More often than not, small-network wireless users will utilize only those security features advertised on the outside of the box of the wireless products purchased. Because it is part of the 802.11 specification, a security feature known as Wired Equivalent Privacy (WEP), is available with most base stations sold today. However, WEP is by no means secure. An experienced wireless hacker has a wide variety of attacks with which to circumvent WEP. In most cases, this involves listening in on broadcasted wireless packets and breaking the encryption key. Once enough packets have been gathered the encryption key can quickly be obtained. Once that is accomplished, it is easy to join the network in question.

WEP also falls short in other areas. The use of WEP can have a significant impact on wireless network performance. Most generally available wireless hardware loses significant bandwidth (up to 40 per cent, in some tests) when encrypting traffic in hardware.

This means war...

As was mentioned earlier, wireless networking is broadcast in nature, which means that wireless transmissions can be picked up by anyone within range of a base station, whether the owner of that base station knows about them or not. Once this was realized a trend known as 'war driving' started. War driving involves scanning the airwaves for vulnerable wireless networks and attempting to gain unauthorized access.

There is a wide variety of very effective (free) software that helps the would-be attacker detect and compromise vulnerable wireless networks. This software can be run on a laptop or handheld device (a PDA for example) meaning that attacks can take place while attackers are walking around buildings or even driving by. High-gain aerials can be used to increase the range of these scanning devices up to 10 miles.

Is there a solution?

There are a number of solutions that provide additional wireless authentication and encryption controls. In particular the inherent weaknesses in WEP are addressed by using stronger encryption and better management of the keys used to encrypt data. This approach makes the 'sniffing' of wireless packets in order to decrypt keys much more difficult. Additionally, many of these packages require wireless users to authenticate (or identify themselves) before any further wireless communications can take place. These controls can deter all but the most determined attacker.

What is at risk

While attacks and attackers are certainly becoming more inventive, there is more at risk too. In the online world, an organization's virtual assets are at risk. Reputation and brand provide competitive advantage and identity in everything an organization does. Website defacement, negative publicity surrounding security breaches and carelessness with customers' personal data may not cost money, but will certainly damage reputation and lose customers.

Organizations may not even be a direct target. An attacker may just want to use bandwidth, propagate viruses around the internet or use systems to launch attacks on other targets. A fraudster may want to steal customers' identities. Organizations may not suffer directly, but they still have an ethical obligation to prevent this exploitation. Many organizations may be unaware that this is happening to them today – but even if they are prepared to take the risk they need to consider the impact of legislation.

Legislation, guidance and regulatory controls may mean that organizations have to put expensive security countermeasures in place. European e-commerce legislation and the UK's Data Protection Act make organizations responsible for the data they use to run their business.

Summary

While a mobile workforce can bring many benefits, to both employer and employee, it is vital that the risks associated with this new model are fully understood. Mobile working and the associated blurring of organizational boundaries mean that the overall level of organizational information security really does come down to weakest link in the chain. Firewalls offer a convenient metaphor for security, and it is not surprising that organizations place such a heavy burden on them to protect their business. But this metaphor is too simplistic – many vulnerabilities occur at the content layer where firewalls can do little to help. The very nature of mobile working means that the human factor plays a major part in determining overall information security levels. It is, therefore, important that users of mobile technology are educated in order that they understand the risks associated with this technology and are aware of their personal responsibilities. The very aspects that make mobile technology so attractive to the end user are also the aspects that introduce many of the security-related risks. So, in summary, the following points should be considered:

- Security policies need to reflect new ways of working.
- Policies should be driven by business requirements and use inputs from risk assessments and industry guidelines.
- Policies must be reflected (by operating procedures and design documentation) within the infrastructure.
- The risks that mobile solutions introduce must be identified and understood.
- Awareness of issues and personal responsibilities is vital.
- Exploit the security facilities available within the technology.
- Use strong authentication and encryption to protect sensitive corporate information.
- Apply the same kind of controls to mobile devices as would be applied to internal systems.
- Assess the use of emerging technologies to assist in increasing levels of security within mobile devices.

Contingency planning

Business continuity and crisis management

Dr David Smith

Around the world regulators and governments are putting great emphasis on the need for organizations to have effective business continuity management (BCM) in place. Insurance companies are setting the level of business interruption premiums according to the speed at which an organization is able to resume business. The latest pressures are coming from the credit rating agencies that need evidence of effective BCM at the time of setting ratings, and in the United Kingdom as a result of the Civil Contingencies bill which requires BCM to be established in local authorities and emergency services. It is therefore not in the interest of any organization to ignore BCM.

BCM is defined by the Business Continuity Institute (BCI) as 'an holistic management process that identifies potential impacts that threaten an organization and provides a framework for building resilience and the capability for an effective response that safeguards the interests of its key stakeholders, reputation, brand and value creating activities'.

The BCI's use of the term 'business continuity management' rather than 'business continuity planning' is deliberate because 'planning' implies there is a start and end to the process and can lead to unwanted planning bureaucracy. BCM is, by necessity, a dynamic, proactive and ongoing process. It must be kept up to date and fit for purpose to be effective.

The key objectives of an effective BCM strategy should be to:

- ensure the safety of staff;
- maximize the defence of the organization's reputation and brand image;
- minimize the impact of business continuity events (including crises) on customers/clients;
- limit/prevent impact beyond the organization;

- demonstrate effective and efficient governance to the media, markets and stakeholders;
- protect the organization's assets;
- meet insurance, legal and regulatory requirements.

However, BCM is not only about disaster recovery. It should be a business-owned and driven process that unifies a broad spectrum of management disciplines. In particular, it is not just about IT disaster recovery. Too many organizations tend to focus all their efforts on IT because of its mission-critical nature, leaving them exposed on many other fronts. (See Figure 5.1.1.)

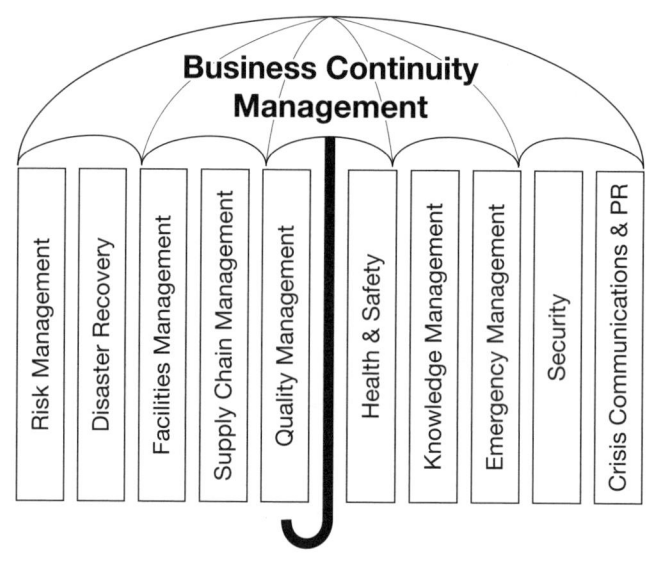

Figure 5.1.1 The unifying process

Because of its all-embracing nature, the way BCM is carried out will inevitably be dependent upon, and must reflect, the nature, scale and complexity of an organization's risk profile, risk appetite and the environment in which it operates. Inevitably, too, BCM has close links to risk management and corporate governance strategies. The importance of a holistic approach across these areas was reinforced in the UK Turnbull Report (1998).

As an organization can never be fully in control of its business environment, it is safe to assume that all organizations will face a business continuity event at some point. Although this simple reality has been etched in high-profile names such as Bhopal, Piper-Alpha, Perrier, Barings Bank, *Challenger*, *Herald of Free Enterprise*, Coca-Cola, *Exxon-Valdez*, Railtrack, the Canary Wharf bombing, Enron, Andersen, Marconi and the World Trade Center, experience also teaches that it is the less dramatic but more frequent business continuity events that can be even more problematic to deal with. Unfortunately, it seems that many public and private organizations still think, 'It will not happen to us'.

Changing the corporate culture

Ignoring business continuity issues can happen for a number of reasons, ranging from denial through disavowal to rationalization. A process of 'group think' can develop whereby an organization genuinely starts to believe its size, or some other feature, makes it immune to disaster. Or executives may firmly believe that insurance will cover them, without realizing that insurance cannot indemnify against lost market share, loss of reputation or tarnished brands.

Research shows that crisis-prone organizations tend to exhibit these tendencies seven times more often than crisis-prepared organizations. While all individuals may make use of such defence mechanisms from time-to-time, the key difference is the degree, extent and frequency with which they are used. Changing such mindsets is not easy, and blindly implementing so-called 'best practice' business continuity techniques is not the best approach. As all organizations are different, techniques that work in one organization will not necessarily work in another. Most executives tasked with addressing business continuity issues are keen to achieve quick wins, and the 'tick box' audit approach, which tries to copy successful strategies used elsewhere, is often adopted without consideration as to suitability.

Underlying the 'tick box' approach is the persuasive belief that a structure, policy, framework and plan are all that is required. While these are critical enablers, relying on structure alone tends to overlook the key issue – that it is people who actually deal with business continuity and crises.

In this context, it is worth remembering (and reminding all senior executives) that 'managerial ignorance' is no longer an acceptable legal or moral defence if a crisis is handled badly. All managers should consider the following key questions that are likely to be asked in a subsequent inquiry:

- When did you know there was a problem?
- What did you do about it?
- If you didn't do anything, why not?
- If you didn't know there was a problem, why not?
- What would you have done if you had known such a problem could exist?

Avoiding planning bureaucracy

There is no doubt that some sort of business continuity plan is essential. The plan becomes a source of reference at the time of a business continuity event or crisis, and the blueprint upon which the strategy and tactics of dealing with the event/crisis are designed. In particular, it can provide essential guidance on damage limitation in those short windows of opportunity that often occur at the beginning of a crisis. Unfortunately, reputations and trust that have been built up over decades can be destroyed within minutes unless vigorously defended at a time when the speed and scale of events can overwhelm the normal operational and management systems. A further and critical reason for having a planning process is so that the individuals who are required to implement the plan can rehearse and test what they might do in different situations. Scenario planning exercises are a very helpful technique for destruct-testing different strategies and plans.

Having said this, it is simply not possible to plan for every eventuality, and if you try to, there is a great danger of creating 'emergency' manuals that are simply too heavy to lift. A trade-off needs to be achieved between creating an effective fit-for-purpose capability and relying on untrained and untried individuals and hoping they will cope in an emergency. The spanning of the gap between the plan and those who carry it out can be achieved by either formal tuition and/or simulations. The well-known maxim that a team is only as strong as its weakest link is worth remembering here.

The exercising of plans, rehearsing of team members and testing of solutions, systems and facilities are the elements that provide and prove an effective and fit-for-purpose capability. However, simulations are not easy to devise, and because of this, many organizations do not venture beyond the development of a plan. They are, nevertheless the best way to avoid planning bureaucracy.

Using good practice guidelines: a different approach

Because of the caveats listed earlier, the BCI's *Business Continuity Management Good practice guidelines* (available on the BCI website at www.thebci.org) are not intended to be a restrictive, exhaustive or definitive process to cover every eventuality within BCM. Instead, they set out to establish the generic process, principles and terminology; describe the activities and outcomes involved; and provide evaluation techniques and criteria.

These guidelines draw together the collective experience, knowledge and expertise of many leading professional Members and Fellows of the BCI and other authoritative professional organizations. In particular, the guidelines reflect the following BCM principles:

- BCM and crisis management are an integral part of corporate governance.
- BCM activities must match, focus upon and directly support the business strategy and goals of the organization.
- BCM must provide organizational resilience to optimize product and service availability.
- As a value-based management process BCM must optimize cost efficiencies.
- BCM is a business management process that is undertaken because it adds value rather than because of governance or regulatory considerations.
- The component parts of an organization own their business risk; the management of the business risk is based upon their individual and aggregated organizational risk appetite.
- The organization and its component parts must be accountable and responsible for maintaining an effective, up-to-date and fit-for-purpose BCM competence and capability.
- All BCM strategies, plans and solutions must be business-owned and driven.
- All BCM strategies, plans and solutions must be based upon the business mission-critical activities, their dependencies and single points of failure identified by a business impact analysis.
- All business impact analysis must be conducted in respect of business products and services in an end-to-end production context.
- There must be an agreed and published organization policy, strategy, framework and exercising guidelines for BCM and crisis management.
- The organization and its component parts must implement and maintain a robust exercising, rehearsal and testing programme to ensure that the business continuity capability is effective, up to date and fit for purpose.

- The relevant legal and regulatory requirements for BCM must be clearly defined and understood before undertaking a BCM programme.
- The organization and its component parts must recognize and acknowledge that reputation, brand image; market share and shareholder value risk cannot be transferred or removed by internal sourcing and/or outsourcing.
- BCM implications must be considered at all stages of the development of new business operations, products, services and organizational infrastructure projects.
- BCM implications must be considered as an essential part of the business change management process.
- The competency of BCM practitioners should be based and benchmarked against the 10 professional competency standards of the BCI.
- All third parties including joint venture companies and service providers, upon whom an organization is critically dependent for the provision of products, services, support or data, must be required to demonstrate an effective, proven and 'fit for purpose' BCM capability.
- The standard terms and conditions of any outsourced and/or internal sourcing of products, services, support or data should reflect these good practice guidelines.

The structure and format of the guidelines is based upon the most frequently asked questions in relation to BCM, which are listed Table 5.1.1.

Table 5.1.1 The most frequently asked BCM questions

Guideline component heading	Most frequently asked question
Purpose	Why do we need to do it?
Outcomes	What will it achieve?
Components	What do we need to do it? What does it consist of (ingredients)?
Methodologies and techniques	What are the tools we need to do it? How is it done? How do we do it?
Frequency and triggers	When should it be done?
Participants	Who does it? Who should be involved?
Deliverables	What is the output?
'Good practice' evaluation criteria	How do we know if we have got it right?

The BCM lifecycle

The BCI principles and frequently asked questions have been drawn together to create the BCM lifecycle, an interactive process tool to guide the implementation of an effective BCM process. (See Figure 5.1.2.)

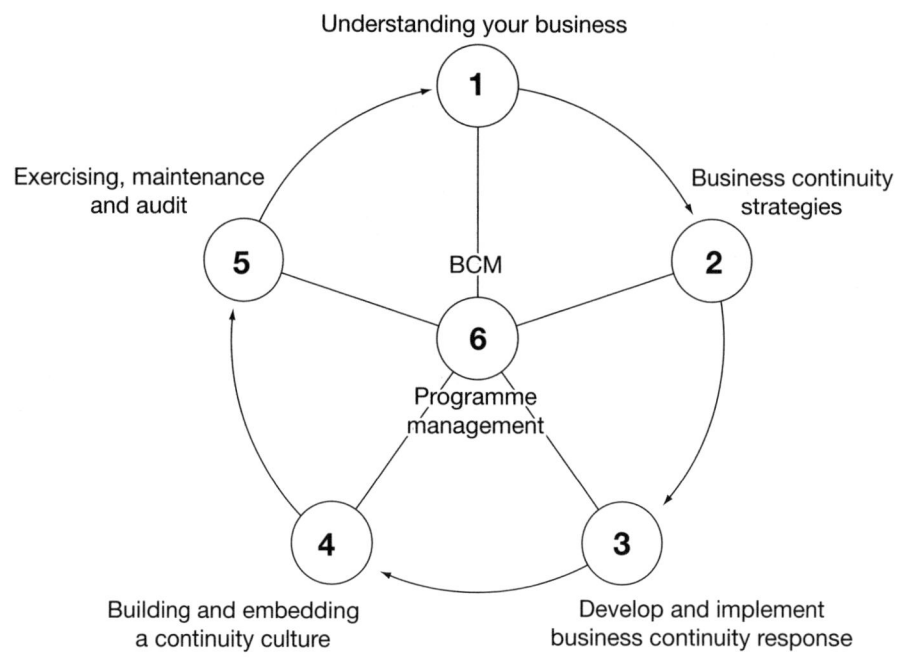

Figure 5.1.2 The BCI lifecycle

The six stages of the life cycle in more detail are set out in Table 5.1.2.

Table 5.1.2 The six stages of the BCM lifecycle

1. Understanding your business	Business impact analysis Risk assessment and control
2. BCM strategies	Organization (corporate) BCM strategy Process-level BCM strategy Resource recovery BCM strategy
3. Developing and implementing a BCM response	Plans and planning External bodies and organizations Crisis/BCM event/incident management
4. Building and embedding a BCM culture	Sourcing (intra-organization and/or outsourcing providers) Emergency response and operations Communications Public relations and the media An ongoing programme of education, awareness and training
5. Exercising, maintenance and audit	Exercising of BCM plans Rehearsal of staff, BCM teams Testing of technology and BCM systems BCM maintenance BCM audit

Table 5.1.2 *Continued*

6. The BCM programme	Board commitment and proactive participation Organization (corporate) BCM strategy BCM policy BCM framework Roles, accountability, responsibility and authority Finance Resources Assurance Audit Management information system (MIS): metrics/scorecard/benchmark Compliance: legal/regulatory issues Change management

The guidelines have been used to generate a tool for evaluating the BCM process, which takes the form of a spreadsheet current state assessment (benchmark) workbook. The workbook enables and facilitates good practice compliance evaluation, current state assessment gap analysis, assurance and benchmarking (process and performance). (See Figure 5.1.3.)

Stage	Steps			Maturity level
STAGE 1: Understanding your business	Organization strategy / Operational and business objectives	→ Critical business factors (mission-critical activities)	→ Business outputs and deliverables (services and products)	1
STAGE 2: Business continuity management strategies	Organization (corporate) BCM strategy	→ Process-level BCM strategy	→ Resource recovery BCM strategy	2
STAGE 3: Business continuity solutions and plans	Business continuity plans	→ Resource recovery solutions and plans	→ Crisis management plan	3
STAGE 4: Building and embedding a BCM culture	BCM culture and awareness programme	→ Education and culture building activities	→ BCM training programme	4
STAGE 5: Exercising, maintenance and audit of BCM	Exercising of BCM	→ Maintenance of BCM	→ Audit of BCM	5
STAGE 6: BCM programme management	BCM programme management	→ BCM policy	→ BCM assurance	6

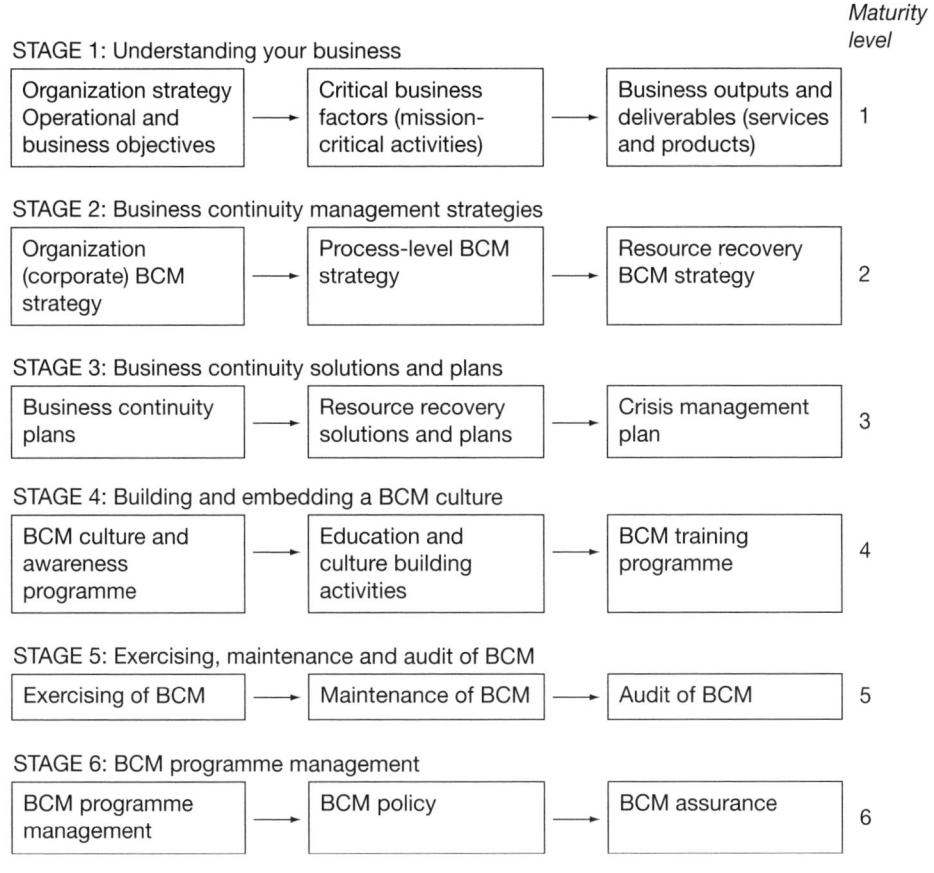

Figure 5.1.3 The BCM process

Each organization needs to assess how to apply the good practice contained within the guidelines. It must ensure that its BCM competence and capability meets the nature, scale and complexity of its business, and reflects its individual culture and operating environment.

Crisis management

The key elements of a crisis management framework are slightly different from the BCM lifecycle, and include those set out in Table 5.1.3, but the list should not be seen as restrictive or exhaustive. There are many advantages to adopting a modular approach to a crisis or business continuity situation, not least that it can be easily and quickly modified to suit local, national as well as global requirements.

Table 5.1.3 Key elements of a crisis management framework

Business risk control Monitoring Prevention Planning and preparation Crisis identification
Assessment Crisis evaluation (including an evaluation criteria)
Invocation and escalation
Management and recovery
Closure and review Formal closure Ongoing issues, eg investigation and litigation Post crisis review and report
Improvement Implementation of approved post crisis review report recommendations

However, in managing any event it is critical to recognize that a successful outcome is judged by both the technical response, and the perceived competence and capability of the management in delivering the business response. The stakeholder perception should be seen as the critical success factor, with a priority equal to, if not more urgent than, the technical solution. Consequently, the acid test is convincingly to demonstrate an effective and 'fit for purpose' business continuity and crisis management capability, and to continue business as usual. This is in contrast to the more familiar pattern of a fall and recovery of a business, which is more representative of the outdated disaster recovery and business resumption approaches.

Development of standards

Why is it so important to establish a standard for business continuity management? With BCM we are dealing with a discipline that is designed to protect an organization at the time of crisis or disaster. There must be some commonality of approach in the future, as organizations do not operate within specific sectors or in isolation. Supply chains are extensive and international. The increased use of outsource providers has placed the management of critical operations outside an organization's direct control. Insurance companies, regulators, credit rating agencies and investors require evidence that an organization is able to continue to deliver despite interruption. They are demanding that an effective BCM policy be in place. Governments need to know that their own departments and agencies can deliver their services at the time of crisis. With such pressures on organizations it is essential that a benchmark be established against which they can be measured.

The British Standards Institution (BSI), in conjunction with the Business Continuity Institute and Insight Consulting, has published a guide that clearly establishes the process, principles and terminology of BCM. The *PAS 56 Guide to Business Continuity Management* describes the activities and outcomes involved in establishing a BCM process, and provides recommendations for good practice. It provides a generic BCM framework for incident anticipation and response, and describes evaluation techniques and criteria. The *Guide* is based on the BCI's *Good Practice Guide to BCM*. The BSI Guide is the first step towards the creation of a full standard for BCM. The BSI has indicated that it wishes to proceed with this development in the next 12 months.

PAS 56 has already become an important document in establishing a uniform approach to BCM. Evidence exists of major international businesses adopting the *Guide* for their own approach to the discipline and they are beginning to measure their suppliers against it. In the United Kingdom, central government has stated that all government departments and agencies will be measured against *PAS 56* from 2005. The Singapore Standards Authority, SPRING, has developed its own BCM standard which is based on *PAS 56* and the *BCI GPG* and will start to certificate organizations against this standard during 2004. *PAS 56* is being translated into German and Japanese and the *BCI Good Practice Guide* into French.

The move towards a uniform standard for BCM is essential to ensure that there is no confusion at the time of a crisis. *PAS 56* is the foundation on which such a standard can now be built. The first stage is the creation of a British Standard (BS) but as soon as possible there must be a move towards an international (ISO) standard for use in the global village in which organizations operate.

Conclusions

An organization consists of people, and people at the top who give a cultural lead. As a consequence, business continuity and crisis management are not solely a set of tools, techniques and mechanisms to be implemented in an organization. They should reflect a more general mood, attitude and type of action taken by managers and staff.

Individual personalities play a crucial and critical role. It is the human factor that is frequently underestimated in BCM. This is of particular importance because the examination of the cause of business continuity events and crises usually identifies several warning signals that were ignored or not recognized. The key to a successful crisis and BCM capability is to adopt a holistic approach to validate each of the key building blocks of the BCM lifecycle and process.

The first task is always to identify the right people who are not bounded as individuals or within the corporate culture. It is on these criteria that the success or failure of creating an effective and fit-for-purpose BCM capability will be determined. Once the right people have been identified, they should engage in the BCM planning process, using the *BCI Good Practice Guidelines* and *PAS 56*, and training via the exercise simulations of plans, rehearsal of people/teams and testing of systems, processes, technology, structures and communications.

The organization can assist this process by appointing a BCM 'champion' at a senior level whose role is to draw together, under a matrix team approach, representatives from the various organization functions (for instance, human resources) together with key line-of-business heads to ensure a coordinated approach. The key advantage of this approach is that it builds on what already exists and has been done, thereby enabling a 'virtual capability' that provides cost efficiency. A further benefit is that it ensures buy-in throughout the organization.

In adopting this methodology and regularly exercising, rehearsing and testing, the organization maintains an effective, up-to-date and fit-for-purpose BCM and crisis management capability. When a crisis hits the organization, everyone knows what to do and a smooth invocation of the plan takes place, ensuring that the impact on mission-critical activities is minimized and reputation and brand image are not tarnished but enhanced.

References

British Standards Institute (2003) *PAS 56: A Guide to Business Continuity Management*, British Standards Institute, London

Chartered Management Institute (2002) *Business Continuity and Supply Chain Management*, Chartered Management Institute, London

Financial Services Authority (2002) *FSA Working Paper on Business Continuity Management*, Financial Services Authority, London

Pauchant, T C and Mitroff, I I (1992) *Transforming a Crisis-Prone Organization*, Jossey-Bass, San Francisco

Further reading

While the *Guidelines* are predominantly designed for the BCM practitioner, the following publications are strongly recommended as introductory reading by directors and senior managers of all organizations:

Bland, M (1998) *Communicating Out of a Crisis*, Macmillan, London
Business Continuity Institute (BCI) *Good Practice Guide to Business Continuity Management*, BCI, www.thebci.org
BCI (2002) *A Strategy for Business Survival*, BCI, Worcester
Central Computer and Telecommunications Agency (1995) *An Introduction to BCM*, HMSO, London
FSA (2001) *A Risk Focused Review of Outsourcing in the UK Retail Banking Sector*, Financial Services Authority, London
Home Office (1996) *How Resilient is Your Business to Disaster?* HMSO, London
Honour, D (2001) Heeding the lessons of 9/11, *International Journal of BCM*, **2**(1), pp 13–17
Institute of Directors (2000) *Business Continuity*, Director Publications, London
Knight, R F and Pretty, D J (2000) The impact of catastrophes on shareholder value, *Oxford Executive Research Briefings,* Templeton College, Oxford
Power, P (1999) *BCM: Preventing chaos in a crisis*, DTI, London

The following video should also be considered as introductory viewing by all managers and staff within an organization:

Business Continuity Institute (2001) *Back to Business: Planning ahead for the unexpected*, Business Continuity Institute

5.2

Dealing with the risks of peer-to-peer

Frank Coggrave, Websense

Peer-to-peer (P2P) networks may incur the wrath of the music industry, but there's danger in them for every internet-connected business.

Pirated music and films are only a small part of the risk, as P2P networks now carry significant amounts of pornography. A recent study analysed over 22 million searches on file-sharing networks, and found that 73 per cent of all movie searches were for pornography, 24 per cent of all image searches were for child pornography, and 6 per cent of all searches were for child pornography of some kind. In fact only 3 per cent of searches were for non-pornographic or non-copyrighted materials. Another study showed that 42 per cent of all searches on one of the most common file-sharing networks were for adult or child pornographic movies or images.

Then there are the viruses. Of the top 50 viruses and worms in the past six months, 19 used P2P and IM applications, quadrupling the 2003 record. And that's not counting the spyware that gets loaded onto your PCs every time someone downloads and installs one of the main P2P applications.

P2P is a problem that is going to get worse. Free file-sharing systems, like Kazaa, Morpheus and Limewire, will become more and more popular over the next few years, while legitimate music services will struggle to provide what users want. Consumers downloaded more than 5 billion audio files from unlicensed file-sharing services in 2001. Meanwhile, several US universities have reported that P2P applications routinely consume more than half of their network bandwidth. It's not surprising: at any one time, there can be 5 million users on peer-to-peer networks swapping more than 900 million files.

The file-sharing P2P networks are massive, and you'll have to expect that some of your users will find them attractive. There's a lot of material out there: more than 5 billion music files crossed the peer-to-peer networks in 2002, along with 5 million games – and around 500,000 movies a day. It's easy for a user to think, 'I'm just downloading this one song', without realizing the risks that his or her employer faces. Seemingly innocuous music tracks are not all that get downloaded, though: studies show that pornography now accounts for more than 38 per cent of all online file sharing.

In addition to music and video that are downloaded over P2P networks, you'll also find them full of pirated software, and pornographic images and films – many of which depict illegal acts. MP3 and movie files on your servers put you at risk of legal action for copyright violations, while illegal pornographic material can lead to long and complex investigations, and the possibility of criminal prosecution. All it needs is a phone call from a disgruntled employee, and you could be looking at a hefty bill from a copyright enforcement agency, or even a visit from the police. According to IDC, 'As most new computers ship with CD and DVD burners, companies may be crossing new legal boundaries as employees burn downloaded videos or music onto disks using company owned assets.'

Then there are the risks of Trojans and viruses. Downloading files from P2P networks can be risky, especially if they're copies of games or commercial software – quite apart from the fact that you're using unlicensed software that could earn you a visit from FAST, there's no way of trusting your source, and no way of knowing whether it comes with a virus or a Trojan hidden in the installation files. There are even viruses that take advantage of P2P networks, using them to pass from machine to machine. You'll also find that many P2P network clients will install spyware on your PCs.

The security risks go well beyond viruses and Trojans using P2P networks as a back channel into your systems. If they haven't been careful, your employees aren't just sharing their music and images with the world – they're also exposing confidential documents and files. It's easy enough to accidentally share every single file in a PC's 'My Documents' folder instead of just 'My Music'. While a copy of the latest number one album is coming into your network, your customer list could be on its way out, with no one knowing.

The temptation to use company resources for P2P file sharing is big. Staff will want to take advantage of your network bandwidth, downloading a movie in an hour or so over high-speed connections, rather than taking several hours at home, and that's going to affect network traffic. Not only do file-sharing applications at work have access to more bandwidth than the average home user, they also have much more in the way of storage space – and with the arrival of low-cost terabyte storage appliances there's going to be even more available. Unauthorized P2P downloads can end up using large amounts of disk space, filling your network storage with thousands of music files and movies. Although compression technologies like MP3 and DIVX do reduce file sizes, a single song will still take up 4 or 5 MB of space, and a TV programme or a movie can fill more than 300 MB.

While you may think that you've got your networks locked down, using firewalls and port-blocking, P2P applications can be tunnelling through trusted open ports, linking your PCs to a global VPN. What appears to your firewall as a persistent web connection or an FTP session could actually be someone downloading several episodes of the latest cult US TV series. As 64 per cent of companies don't monitor or control music and video downloads, you may never know just what is crossing your firewall.

If you're worried about P2P applications running over your network, here are our top four tips for dealing with the problem and keeping the threat to a minimum:

1. **Education.** Educate all of your employees and line managers so they are aware of the dangers of P2P. Ensure an acceptable usage policy is distributed to all so that there is no room for ambiguity.
2. **Report on usage.** Employee internet management software such as Websense Enterprise comes with a reporting module that can be used to run historical reports on P2P-related web access and network usage. This allows management and HR to view employee internet activity and explore data using a user-friendly reporting tool, Websense Explorer.
3. **Enforce the policy.** Websense Enterprise will also allow you to enforce a company policy to block access to P2P-related websites. It can also ensure you block P2P network traffic inside the organization, as well as blocking the execution of P2P applications on desktops – particularly important for mobile users working on laptops.
4. **Follow-up.** Make sure that your employee internet management solution is frequently and automatically updated. The internet is dynamic and forever changing, so don't choose a static solution. Websense Enterprise enables automatically updated lists of P2P-related websites, network protocols and desktop P2P applications to be detected and blocked. Furthermore, Websense has the ability to detect spyware already installed on the PC, as well as block it from sending out any data such as keystroke information.

5.3

Data recovery

Adrian Palmer, Ontrack Data Recovery

When you consider that over 90 per cent of a company's information is created electronically and less than 30 percent is ever transferred to paper, it is astonishing just how few companies actively protect their critical business information and understand the cost to their organization of its loss.

Over 31 billion e-mails are sent every day, yet a virus could destroy all the inboxes of an entire organization at the touch of a button. The corporate data of a whole company could also be erased by simple human error. To lose such valuable information could destroy any company, and for those who manage to survive, downtime would have significant financial ramifications. Yet why are organizations not taking the necessary precautions to protect their primary assets? And why do so many companies not have a comprehensive business continuity plan in place, let alone an effective data recovery programme?

Data loss can strike in many different ways, and companies must be prepared for any eventuality. After all, everyone who works on a computer will eventually experience some form of data loss, ranging from a mechanical failure, software glitch, data corruption, powerspike, virus, fire, flood, disgruntled employee, to even a simple user error.

In recent reports, Gartner analysts have said that the majority of small- to medium-sized enterprises (SMEs) have traditionally under invested in business continuity planning, and they estimate that only 35 per cent of SMEs have a comprehensive disaster recovery plan in place. Historically expensive, the cost of business continuity and disaster recovery may have discouraged SMEs from investing; however, today's market offers a broader range of solutions to meet any budget.

So what solutions exist if disaster strikes, and how do you know when it would be cheaper to call in the experts? This chapter explores how to assess the severity of data loss and gives simple advice about how to minimize any damage. It then touches on the most common incidents that require a data recovery specialist and identifies the solutions available. Awareness of the solutions, from do-it-yourself software through to in-lab recovery by engineers, will help any organization build disaster recovery into any business continuity plan.

Assessing the damage

When data is lost, it is easy to panic. However if you evaluate the severity of the damage, and know what solutions are available, a problem need not become a crisis. Data loss can come in the form of physical damage or structural damage, and both require a different approach. However, general advice in the event of either loss is:

- Never presume that data is lost for good, no matter how damaged the hard drive or magnetic band on a tape appears.
- Do not shake or remove a damaged hard drive.
- Do not attempt to dry a wet hard drive or data source by opening it, or exposing it to a heat source, such as a hairdryer.
- Do not attempt to clean the hard drive; send it immediately to a data recovery laboratory.
- Do not use utility software or maintenance tools on damaged drives or tapes.
- Do not attempt to retrieve lost data yourself – you may make a bad situation worse.

In the event of structural damage, caused by accidental file deletion, virus infection and inaccessible or unbootable partitions, free diagnostic tools exist to assess the condition of your computer system and advise whether you can repair the damage yourself. Do not worry if you cannot boot your system to Windows, as the software, which can be downloaded from specialists' websites, is self-booting, and runs even when your system cannot.

In many cases of structural damage, do-it-yourself software will be enough to restore data. However, some of the more common incidents that require a data recovery specialist include:

- **An unreliable back-up system**: without a tested, reliable back-up system, data loss of any size could prove disastrous.
- **Back-up and restore failure**: unreadable tapes, corrupt data, and improper back-up procedures compromise these processes.
- **Extensive time required for restoration of back-up process**: in many cases, this could result in significant productivity and financial losses.
- **Impractical and impossible data recreation**: data recreation or rekeying involves a number of costs including lost time, revenue, and quality that can make it an impractical, if not impossible, option.
- **Unbootable system**: even minor damage to operating system structures can keep a system from booting.
- **Mirrored or RAID system failure**: many organizations concurrently copy data into two separate storage locations. However, if that data is corrupt before it is copied, or if one (or both) of the two systems fails, the data may be destroyed or rendered inaccessible. Additionally, mirrored and RAID systems cannot protect the system from viruses, software corruption or user error.

- **Intentionally and accidentally altered or destroyed data**: data is susceptible to being deleted or destroyed by malicious viruses, security breaches, or disgruntled employees, as well as accidentally by human error.
- **Corrupted or deleted database files**: system malfunctions, power failures, and accidental or intentional deletions are some examples that may cause system-critical information to become inaccessible.

The solutions on the market

Data recovery software

Not all types of data loss require the assistance of an engineer. Powerful do-it-yourself software solutions exist that are capable of recovering and repairing lost or inaccessible data safely. Data loss caused by accidental file deletion, virus infection or software corruption can be recovered from downloaded software. This solution can restore data from most hard drives, diskettes and digital media, and works on systems that cannot boot to Windows.

There is software that is specific to e-mail recovery, inbox restoration or file system repair to name but three, and many are tailored for different sized organizations and the scale of the damage. Advanced disk diagnostics are also available to assess the health of your hard drive and identify problems that could lead to data loss, before it happens.

Remote data recovery (RDR®)

Ontrack Data Recovery is the only data recovery company in the world that offers a remote data recovery (RDR) solution. Engineers can recover certain data loss situations directly on your desktop, laptop or server (including RAID systems), via a modem or internet connection. Returning an organization to productivity in minutes/hours instead of days, this solution ends unnecessary downtime and consequently saves the inconvenience and expense involved in the removal and shipping of equipment.

For many users, the key benefit of RDR is time. A typical in-lab recovery can take about two to five days to complete. Restoring data from back-up tapes, which will never be as current as the data that was just lost, can take just as long. RDR, which is available 24 hours a day, can be completed in as little as an hour and can be performed anywhere in the world. If a drive is physically healthy, RDR can usually recover lost data. This secure solution offers the same client confidentially and security procedures implemented in labs.

In-labs, clean rooms or on-site data recovery

In more serious cases of physical damage, such as fire, flood or earthquake, recovery may take place in a lab or 'Class100 clean room'. This solution is particularly suitable for internal or mechanical failure, and can be carried out under different time scales, depending on the priority placed by the organization.

Whether it stems from security concerns or critical deadlines for the recovery of your lost data, on-site data recovery solutions also exist. Highly trained engineers will come to your location to diagnose and recover your data so that you do not need to send your systems to the labs.

What to look for in a data recovery specialist

- Do they have the expertise? Data recovery is technologically complex and requires in-depth knowledge. Look for companies that make a substantial investment in research and development, have created a significant number of proprietary tools and techniques, and have performed data recovery for a large number of clients.
- Look for a company that is a certified developer or solutions partner for Microsoft, Novell, Apple, Sun, SCO, and other major hardware and software companies. Your data recovery provider should also be able to retrieve data from every type of system (including portable and desktop PCs, Apple Mac, Unix, HP, DEC, and IBM platform servers), media (hard disks, optical disks, removable disks, flash media, multi-drive volumes and RAID systems) and tape. Also, major hard drive manufacturers should recommend a data recovery specialist.
- To protect sensitive business data, a data recovery company must have strong data security procedures in place, including proprietary protocols, data encryption, and secure facilities.

Conclusion

Until recently, data loss due to hardware and software failure, unbootable computers, viruses and human error was considered lost forever. Today however, most lost data is recoverable. Data loss can happen in the most strange circumstances and when least expected, but knowing what steps to take ensures that all is not lost. Below is a taste of some of the more bizarre situations in which Ontrack Data Recovery recovered lost data:

- An American user became so frustrated with his laptop, he shot it with a gun, before realizing there was important data saved on the computer.
- A man threw his computer out of the window, in an attempt to destroy evidence, when he found out the police were coming to seize his PC and arrest him.
- One man's laptop dropped out of his bag while he was riding his moped. The computer was then run over by a lorry before he even noticed he had lost it and needed access to the data.

However, too many companies rely on an untested back-up system as their safety net, and this too often proves to be inadequate when it really matters. Over the course of performing more than 150,000 data recoveries, Ontrack Data Recovery has identified some of the top tips to help an organization minimize data loss:

- Back up all data as often as possible, especially before 'going mobile'.
- Protect against power surges by buying an uninterruptible power supply. This avoids the risk of electrical failure leading to incorrect data being written to the disk surface, making some data inaccessible.
- Do not install software without a firm understanding of the system set-up. This is a major cause of accidental file deletion.
- Regularly test data back-up and restore capabilities. Just because you have a back-up system does not mean it will be able to restore successfully when you need it. There is also the danger that the wrong data is being backed up.

- Scan all new programmes for viruses. Awareness can be the best form of protection in data loss avoidance. Virus software should also be updated with regular virus signatures.
- Set up a thorough business continuity plan. Data disasters can happen at any time. Spending a little time thinking about the services you would need in the event of a fire, flood or simple server failure could mean valuable time and money is saved in the long run.
- Do not panic at any apparent damage and attempt to operate or repair a visibly damaged hard drive yourself. This may cause further data loss and cause more damage to the computer hardware.

5.4

Crisis or disaster management

Simon Langdon, Insight Consulting, part of Siemens Communications

The threat of disasters

During the last few years, there have been many examples of natural or man-made disasters. There have been widespread floods and droughts in Europe, the Sars virus, a petrol strike, the foot-and-mouth epidemic, major power cuts in London, the United States and Italy, the Tsunami in South East Asia and terrorist attacks around the world. Many of us have anecdotal evidence of crisis caused by extraordinary events. Recently, I have heard of the evacuation of a London mainline station because of toxic fumes coming from batteries on charge which boiled over, and an office block being evacuated because a drunken driver crashed into it and the back-up generators failing when a company suffered a power cut.

Currently, there is nervousness about the threat of terrorism – particularly in major cities. There is nothing new in this, unfortunately. The bombs that detonated on the railway in Madrid on 11 March 2004 is just another example. In 1996, suicide bombers drove a lorry into the central bank in Colombo, Sri Lanka, which exploded and set eight buildings alight, killed over 60 people and injured 1,200 more. London has suffered at the hands of the IRA. The events of 11 September 2001 were an awful escalation of terror and have done much to focus minds. As a result, many companies have been reassessing their crisis management procedures. To think the unthinkable is not so difficult now. Who would have envisaged the closure of air traffic in the United States following 9/11 or the closure of Congress as a result of the threat of anthrax contamination? Global terrorism has led to a global tension kept alive by the media. The modern media, with its worldwide reach, meant that it did not take long for us all to hear of the bombs in Madrid or the bombing of the British Consulate and the HSBC bank in Istanbul in November 2003. The response to the Tsunami disaster was overwhelming and immediate. Is it surprising that we are all increasingly aware of the threat from disasters?

Definition of crisis management

In the light of these threats or risks, how should companies deal with crisis or disasters? A definition of a crisis provides a foundation from which to work. A crisis is an abnormal situation or perception, which threatens the operation, staff, customers or reputation of an organization. Crisis management is the process by which the organization manages the wider impact of a crisis such as the business issues and media coverage.

Characteristics of disasters

To study how to respond to a disaster or crisis it is useful to consider the characteristics. Disasters are no respecters of people, buildings, companies or governments. Disasters such as a fire, flood, earthquake, airline crash or terrorist bomb are often unexpected and sudden. The timing and location may be unpredictable and the impact cannot normally be contained within boundaries. Disasters cause chaos. They have a very human impact. There may be casualties, people may be frightened, it may be difficult to think and there is a thirst for knowledge.

Making order out of chaos

Disaster or crisis management must therefore be aimed at making order out of chaos, providing a timely and effective response to ensure the safety of people, and returning the business to normal as quickly as possible. We must be prepared before the disaster – that is, now – and therefore we need a well-rehearsed plan based on good communications.

Public scrutiny following a disaster or crisis can be intense, and there are many examples of companies that have suffered a crisis or disaster without an apparent crisis management plan that have subsequently not survived. A good crisis management plan, properly implemented, will not only focus a practical response but will also do much to provide confidence to management, staff and customers that the company is able to cope.

After the Hatfield rail crash in 2002, the disruption to the railway caused by the search for hairline cracks on the line was immense. The rail industry lost almost £1 billion in three months as a result of a loss of confidence by the public, business, the media, the government and the rail industry itself. All parties felt the railway was unsafe and unreliable. The result was that eventually Railtrack went into administration and the chief executive left to seek employment elsewhere.

Risks in today's business environment

In addition to the almost traditional disasters already mentioned, there are many other types of risks in today's business environment – industrial action, fraud, espionage, human error, viruses, technical failure and the failure of suppliers, to name a few. While some of these risks can be quantified, it is difficult to predict exactly what might happen, when or where. It therefore makes good sense to develop a generic plan to ensure that there can be a focused response to any major incident, of whatever magnitude, whenever and wherever it might occur. In simple terms, if the right people are around a table, working together with a well-rehearsed and straightforward crisis management process, they will be able to cope with whatever might happen.

Geographic nature of disasters

Major incidents or disasters are often geographic in nature. In other words, they happen where they happen and the immediate effect is local from where the impact might spread rapidly. The effect is similar to a pebble being thrown into a still pond. If you imagine that where the pebble enters the water is where the incident happens, then the ripples that spread out represent the impact. September 11 was like a boulder being thrown into the pond, with the ripples being waves of impact that are still going round and round the world. It follows also that the response to a major incident must counter the impact, and that a major crisis or disaster will require a major response.

Once the geographic nature of major incidents is understood, it is easy to see why a key principle of crisis management is that responsibility must remain at the local level, where the immediate response to an incident will start. At the same time, support for the local level must be coordinated throughout the organization. As with a football team, individual skill is important but is largely ineffective if not supported by all members of the team. Communication, of course, remains the bedrock on which crisis management is built. Crisis management is all about managing the information flow, and without communication it is impossible.

Media handling

When a major incident happens there are two stories – one is how the company responds and the other is how the media reports how the company responds. The public tend to believe what they read and hear in the media. They believe the media's interpretation or perception of what has happened and so 'perception becomes reality'.

As a result of the growth of 24-hour news channels, it has become necessary to plan carefully how the media will be handled. The media's requirement is to inform the public of the facts. They will ask the simple questions following a disaster – 'What happened, how did it happen and what are you doing about it?' They will soon add 'And who is responsible?' These are all understandable questions and should be answered with facts and honesty.

The media are useful. If asked, they will include on their news bulletins contact numbers for friends and relatives to call, and they may even relay important messages. Remember that reporters are human too, they have a job to do and they like to help. Use them.

All communications with the media should be coordinated from company headquarters. Responsibility for the media at the scene, however, should be delegated to the front line. Local managers should be enlisted and trained as spokespeople in an emergency. Such a strategy positions the company to release information rapidly and effectively, anywhere and at any time, and will satisfy the demands of the media. Importantly, it will also reflect the company's ability to cope with the crisis.

The two phases of crisis management

There are two clearly defined phases in crisis management – the immediate response and the recovery. Part of the first phase, the immediate response, is identifying and confirming that there is, in fact, a crisis. This is not always as easy as it seems, as some crises appear to creep up almost unnoticed. To counter this, it is good practice to use a Crisis Impact Criteria Table that quantifies the impact of an incident against pre-determined criteria under different headings such as Operations, Staff, Reputation, Legal and Finance. The table acts simply as a tool to aid the decision on when to invoke the crisis management plan. A common adage is 'If in doubt call it out!' That is, if undecided invoke the plan and call out the crisis management team. Not to do so may mean that you are always trying to catch up rather than taking control in a timely way with positive, proactive action.

The recovery, or second phase of the response, should start almost at the same time as the immediate response and run parallel with it. It is a project in its own right that requires planning and coordination. An early start will speed the return to business as usual. As the immediate response tails off, so the recovery will become the priority.

Content of a crisis management plan

A crisis management plan should first of all identify and define the responsibilities of those managers involved in a response. Although this sounds obvious, it is often overlooked. It is important for members of the Crisis Management Team (CMT) to know not only their own responsibilities but also those of others. A list of tasks that members of the CMT should complete in order to fulfil their responsibilities should be included.

The crisis management plan should also contain the invocation procedure and list the external groups and organizations with which the company may wish to communicate at the time of a crisis. Examples include business partners, customers, suppliers, regulators and other major stakeholders. It should contain the system by which business continuity plans are invoked and coordinated, as well as the procedure for the resolution of conflicts of interest, the decision-making process and some detail about how the incident is managed 'on the ground'. An understanding of the latter assists the CMT in knowing how best to support the actions at the local level.

The plan should contain a section on communication, outlining the lines of communication within the company and responsibilities for communicating to external organizations. Contact details and a list of communication equipment to be used should be contained in an appendix.

Immediate actions on being notified of a major incident

There are many ways that one may be informed of a crisis. You could be told by a colleague, the duty manager, a neighbouring business, a passing stranger or even hear about it on the news. However the notification is made, it is important first to verify the facts. The next action is to start a log of events, to note down the time and the detail of the incident and who informed you. Then keep a note of all actions.

Once a decision to invoke has been made, it is necessary to activate the call-out system and to confirm who should attend the CMT meeting, and where and when it is to be held. It may be necessary to arrange a conference call to allow managers who are unable to attend to take part. Typically the CMT will consist of representatives of all the main departments within the company such as operations, human resources, customer services, IT, finance, marketing, facilities management and corporate communications.

It is a good practice, at this stage, to consider standing by contingency sites such as a Recovery Centre if one is available. Finally, you should consider briefing a deputy and establishing the latest status of the incident before moving to the CMT meeting.

The crisis management meeting

The first action to be taken at the CMT meeting is to appoint a scribe to take the minutes and to confirm attendance to ensure all are present. The next task is then to establish the detail of the incident and access the impact. The chairperson should obtain reports from all the members of the CMT in turn and ask them to outline their priorities. He or she should then summarize the company or corporate key issues and priorities for action. It is at this point that any conflicts of interest should be discussed between members of the CMT. The meeting should be conducted in an autocratic style – there is not time for too much democracy in a crisis. Once the priorities are agreed, decisive action is necessary in order to gain control of the situation.

It is a good idea for the CMT to have an agenda for their first meeting – not only to ensure that nothing is overlooked but also as members may be 'off balance' because of what has happened. A good way to develop the CMT meeting agenda is to hold a crisis management (table top) exercise, where a scenario is 'played' and the CMT discuss their response and raise issues as the response progresses.

Reporting

As crisis management is all about managing the information flow, there are a number of reports that can be standardized to assist in the process such as the initial Incident Report and the follow on Status Report. The Incident Report is a simple form which should describe the detail of the incident, its location and time, whether it is confirmed or unconfirmed, the impact, whether there are any injuries, what action has been taken, who has been notified and an estimate of the time to recover. The report should also include any other relevant information and list the actions that are needed. Finally, the report should indicate when the next update will be made.

A Status Report might typically contain the latest information of the response and outline other important issues such as HR, operations, the status of buildings and equipment, business impacts and details of the security of the incident site. It should contain the priorities of all the departments involved and may, when appropriate, include comment on the long-term strategic impacts, the legal and insurance implications and priorities for action. Consideration should be given to the requirement for holding a press conference.

Summary

The risk of disaster is ever present. Organizations that do not prepare contingency plans to deal effectively with them may not survive the impact that disasters bring. The aim of crisis management is to make order out of chaos, to maximize the safety of people and to return the business to normal as quickly as possible. An understanding of the characteristics of disasters will help in developing effective response procedures. The crisis management process is about managing information, and therefore the ability to communicate effectively is vital. Handling the media, by providing them with the facts of what has happened in a timely manner, must form an important part of the overall process.

A crisis management plan must be practical and simple. It is all too easy to over-plan and include ever more detail, so that the process becomes overcomplicated and the plan so thick that no one ever reads it. Even worse is to think that the plan is finished and to put in on the shelf where it will only gather dust. The plan must be a 'living document', and should be generic and sufficiently flexible to be used to respond to any crisis of whatever size, whenever or wherever it might occur.

Finally, the members of the CMT must be trained in the crisis management process and the plan must be exercised and maintained – there is little value in investing in a plan if no one knows how to implement it and it has become out of date.

5.5

Forensics

Robert Brown, DataSec

To catch a thief?

When we turn our minds to matters of e-security, our first thoughts tend to be about defences such as firewalls and intrusion detection – and rightly so. After all, there is much wisdom in the pursuit of prevention before cure. But what happens when our defences are breached? How should we respond to such an incident?

Those investigating crime have long understood the value of evidence. In its most literal sense, evidence is *'that which demonstrates that a fact is so'*.[1] By acquiring evidence we build a picture of what happened, how it came to be and, hopefully, *who* did it. The digital world is no different to the physical world in that every event leaves a trace. This *digital evidence* can be gathered and pieced together to help develop our understanding of the what, how and who of an incident. Over time, this process has come to be referred to as *computer forensics*.

The term 'forensic' is associated, by definition, with legal process. That is, the methods used to gather evidence during an investigation allow it to be deemed admissible in a court of law. Therefore, the most influential factor in the court's decision whether or not to accept evidence is the way in which it was obtained, and in particular, consideration as to whether such methods may have affected the original data or its subsequent interpretation.

Every good incident response plan will have some form of investigative foundation. An effective response relies on an understanding of what has taken place and how it occurred in order to identify the appropriate course of remedial action. But, without the appropriate precautions, the way in which such action is taken may modify or even destroy the data on which the evidence is based and, in doing so, may significantly affect the possibility of attributing accountability for the cause of the incident. By adopting some simple and logical practices when conducting an investigation it is possible to avoid compromising such evidence. The core of computer forensic best practice can be defined by three generally accepted principles:[2]

- No action taken should change the data held on a computer or other storage media that may be relied upon subsequently.
- Where original data must be accessed, the person doing so should be suitably qualified and able to explain the relevance and implications of his or her actions.
- An audit trail or other record of all processes should be created and preserved such that a third party might examine such processes and achieve the same result.

The forensic process could therefore be summarized as *preservation*, *documentation* and *justification*.

Understanding the problem

When responding to an incident, it is important to identify the circumstances in which it has occurred and the objectives of any subsequent investigation. This puts us in a position both to assess the risks that the situation may present to our business, and to form a strategy for conducting the investigation itself. In this way the type of incident will begin to define the required course of action. But what if an investigation is not expected to end in tribunal or litigation? Can we relax the standards that would normally be applied? Quite simply, what initially appears to be a simple, straightforward incident can quickly escalate into something far more serious and dangerous. For example, an investigation into a simple denial-of-service attack on an e-commerce server suddenly and unexpectedly turns out to be a platform for extortion by organized criminals. Nothing should be taken purely on face value. If we apply best practice from the outset, we avoid any possibility of compromising the investigation at a later stage, or the integrity of the evidence we may come to rely on.

We can begin to define the scope of the investigation by forming an idea of what we think has happened. This, in turn, will help to identify where we should be looking for evidence and what needs to be done in order to acquire it. Throughout the investigation it is necessary to constantly assess our understanding of what has happened and consider adapting the chosen strategy if necessary.

The methods employed in the investigation should be proportional to the seriousness of the incident. For example, it would be reasonable to consider examining the e-mail of employees suspected of sending threatening or abusive messages to colleagues or customers, but it would probably be considered unreasonable to place 24-hour surveillance on them and install a keystroke logger in their home computers!

It is vital that an investigator possesses a clear understanding of the legislation that affects the way in which an investigation is conducted. Such legislation includes, but is by no means limited to, the Human Rights Act 1998, the Regulation of Investigatory Powers Act 2000, the Business Interception Regulations 2000, the Data Protection Act 1998 and the Computer Misuse Act 1990. Familiarity with the relevant legislation allows an investigation to be conducted in such a way that it will stand up to any subsequent scrutiny. The quantity and complexity of such legislation means that it may often be appropriate to seek advice from a lawyer in order to form a legal strategy for the investigation that is to take place.

Ultimately, any investigative process will consist of both operational and strategic elements typically involving the following:

- preserving data for forensic analysis;
- forensic recovery of data;
- presentation of evidence (reports and orally);
- acting lawfully;
- working within a business (or disciplined) environment.

Preserving the evidence

The first principle of digital evidence defines the need to preserve the original data on which the investigation is based. Typically, a forensic investigator will take a low-level, or bitstream image of the media containing the data. Provided the method used complies with the first principle, the image produced can be treated as 'best evidence', which means a court of law would accept it as an accurate and true copy of the original data. An obvious benefit of this is that, now a legally acceptable copy of the data exists, it is easier to justify returning the original equipment to service, thereby minimizing business interruption.

However, it may not always be possible or practical to take a system out of service in order to capture the data it holds. In these cases we may revert to the second principle of digital evidence, which makes provision for such access and defines the restrictions and obligations with which the investigator must comply. Key to this compliance is ensuring that the way in which access may affect the data is clearly understood. The mere act of starting a computer can cause numerous modifications to be made to the data it holds. If such modifications affect the evidence that we wish to produce, we must be able to identify what changes have occurred and the effect they might have on its interpretation.

It is at this point that the importance becomes evident of maintaining an accurate and detailed record of the actions that are taken and the reasons for taking them. Such a record acts as an audit trail for the investigation. It allows an assessment of the methods used and the decisions made in order to establish the admissibility of the evidence, and brings with it compliance with the third principle of gathering digital evidence.

After the data has been acquired, it is important to maintain its evidential integrity. This can be achieved by strict control of access and by maintaining a record of its movements and the identity of those in whose custody it has been. By doing this we are creating a 'chain of custody' for the evidence with which we can demonstrate its provenance.

Building the picture

Once the data has been identified and acquired, the next phase of the investigation involves its examination and analysis. The objective is to identify evidence of what has happened with a view to establishing how the incident occurred and, if possible, who was involved. The quantity of material that can be produced by apparently trivial actions on a computer can be quite staggering. This information can present a vivid picture of the various events that have taken place in relation to an incident. The downside to such rich potential sources of evidence is that a detailed and proper analysis can be both complicated and time-consuming. There is a risk that a vital piece of evidence may be overlooked or misinterpreted. Consequently it is necessary to ensure that investigators are properly trained in forensic methodology and techniques, and possess an appropriate degree of knowledge about the systems and software they are examining.

The analysis will result in a report describing the investigation and its findings. In the main such findings will be restricted to statements of fact such as the presence of specific items of data. At times it may be appropriate for the investigator to offer an opinion on the meaning of these facts. However, such an opinion must be based on significant knowledge and experience for it to be considered reliable. An opinion should be an appropriately educated interpretation of the facts at hand and not a best guess.

If an investigation ends in legal proceedings, the investigator may be required to present his or her findings orally in court and face cross-examination as to content and reliability. This is not something to be undertaken lightly, and can be a daunting experience. Accordingly investigators should seek to gain experience of court proceedings, and preferably undertake training to act in the capacity of a professional or expert witness.

The end result of this entire process should be a clear understanding of the events associated with the incident under investigation: in other words, answers to the original questions of what, how and, perhaps most importantly, who.

By adopting a 'best practice' approach to the acquisition and examination of digital evidence we can ensure that our investigation remains forensically sound and will stand up to the most rigorous scrutiny. It is certain that as e-business becomes increasingly prevalent, so too will the attempted abuse of the systems and infrastructure that make it possible. While we do our best to prevent such abuse it is vital that we have the ability to act effectively and lawfully when it eventually happens, and ultimately bring accountability to those responsible.

Notes

1. Patterson, R F, *The University English Dictionary*, University Books
2. Association of Chief Police Officers, *Good Practice Guide for Computer Based Electronic Evidence* [Online] http://www.nhtcu.org

5.6

Forensic investigation

Clifford May, Integralis Ltd

Footsteps in the sand

The internet and the increasing drive for e-business have brought a mixture of challenges for many organizations today. Technology and the changing face of business provide new avenues of exploitation for the criminal or even employees. Investigating a potential crime or abuse of company systems has become a more complex and technology-dependent process that requires special approaches and skills to handle successfully. Computer forensics enables the systematic and careful identification of evidence in computer-related crimes and abuse cases, speeding up the investigation and ensuring accurate results. This may range from tracing the tracks of a hacker through an organization's IT systems, to tracing the originator of apparently anonymous defamatory e-mails, to recovering the evidence of fraud. As with any investigation, it is vital to know where to look to find the evidence required and, in the process, how not to destroy the very evidence you seek. This requires skill, knowledge and a lot of experience – especially as all investigations must respect the laws protecting the rights of the individual in each country and must always be handled with sensitivity.

In the internet era, investigating a crime, or even just an internal disciplinary issue, has become a complex and time-consuming challenge, especially where computers are involved. However, a properly executed computer forensic investigation can speed up the whole process and help you to 'see the wood for the trees', ensuring a good result. A forensic investigation can reveal a wealth of information about the problem, ranging from a timeline of events to the methods used by the perpetrator(s), their contacts, acquaintances, collaborators, financial health and even their character profile(s). Applications, documents, data files, e-mail systems, internet browsers and the contents of free space on computers

Your Trusted Security Partner

- Trusted by over 800 companies in the UK
- Trusted by over 3000 companies in Europe
- One of the industry's highest levels of Security trained professionals across Europe

Security is all about peace of mind. The comfort of knowing that you have made the right decision. Have the best security products available on the market with full testing before you use them. And confidence with the best full multi-language European support. Security is our business and our customers have this peace of mind and confidence. That's why we are one of the leading security systems integrators in Europe. We have highly skilled staff with an unparalleled range of expertise in every field. What's more we are the first integrator to be BS 7799 certified, CLAS and CHECK approved.

Integralis - First Choice for Security

For more information, visit
www.integralis.co.uk

Tel: +44 (0)118 930 6060
e-mail: info@integralis.com

ActivCard
AirDefense
Blue Coat Systems
bluesocket
Computer Associates CHANNEL PARTNER
CHECK POINT Software Technologies Ltd. We Secure the Internet.
CLEARSWIFT
CROSSBEAM SYSTEMS
f5
finjan software
FORTINET
IRONPORT SYSTEMS
INTERNET SECURITY SYSTEMS
McAfee
NOKIA CONNECTING PEOPLE
PACKETEER
PGP
pointsec
RSA SECURITY
SOPHOS
Top Layer
WEBSENSE

INTEGRALIS

France   Germany   Switzerland   United Kingdom   USA

can reveal a great deal of information to assist in the successful resolution of an investigation. Computers can contain a complete trail of events and actions, like 'footsteps in the sand', which can be followed by a skilled computer forensic specialist. Even attempts by the perpetrators to hide or erase their 'footsteps' are often unsuccessful and a forensic expert can frequently uncover a 'golden nugget' that breaks a case and resolves the incident conclusively.

The evidence that can be recovered in any specific investigation will vary, but usually the activities of hackers, internal fraudsters, breaches of company policy by staff and more are there to be found. With the apparent anonymity of the internet to shield their identities it has become extremely common for attackers to 'spoof' other identities to hide their tracks, leading to a trend of blackmail, extortion and harassment attempts. Organizations that rely on their e-business channels are being held to ransom in order to ensure that their systems are not disrupted by denial-of-service attacks, causing huge losses of business. Like any blackmail case, paying up leads to more demands from the attackers and does not resolve the problem. Organized crime has realized that the gains can be high and the risk small – why bother robbing a bank and risk being recognized when you can attack with anonymity from anywhere in the world?

Theft of data continues to be a significant problem for most, manifesting itself in security breaches involving competitors and staff alike, keen to gain an edge, make a killing or settle a grudge. With improved perimeter security many attackers are turning their attentions to the age-old techniques of social engineering, exploiting human relationships in order to breach security.

This can take many forms, such as fake Web sites, bogus telephone callers trying to elicit confidential information, or e-mail attachments containing Trojan code that installs itself on the recipient's computer without his or her knowledge, providing a covert channel of access for the attacker. It is common to find a variety of malicious software ('spyware') on business or home systems that have evaded technical control measures. Spyware can range from simple keystroke-logging programs to more comprehensive and intrusive software that e-mails screen captures back to the hacker, or activate Webcams and microphones. Other social engineering techniques frequently employed succeed by manipulating staff without them ever suspecting there is anything untoward. A simple request for what seems an innocuous piece of information, eg someone's mobile phone number, a line manager's name, or the name of a particular server on the network may seem harmless but the attacker can piece all the fragments together to see the bigger picture.

Computer forensic techniques have been used to solve thousands of difficult cases where evidence has been hard to determine, including fraud cases, industrial espionage, copyright issues, blackmail, sabotage, sexual and racial harassment, child pornography, and even arson and murder. Anywhere technology is involved there is always a chance that a computer, PDA, mobile phone, or anything with a computing and storage capability, may contain that vital insight into what happened.

Gathering the evidence

To be successful, the process of gathering and interpreting computer-related evidence should be carried out by someone who is trained and versed in computer forensics and evidential procedures. Many investigations of security breaches are scuppered within the first few minutes of the investigation by well-meaning but untrained personnel. Just because someone is an IT person it does not mean that he or she is the best person to investigate a potential crime or serious disciplinary issue. It is common for IT staff to destroy the very evidence they seek by failing to follow tried and tested forensic procedures for securing and examining potential evidence.

There is an array of pitfalls to be avoided when attempting to secure and investigate computer evidence. It must not be destroyed or compromised in any way, and steps must be taken to ensure that:

- the investigation process does not change anything – eg, file contents, date and time stamps;
- all steps taken can be reproduced, eg, the creation of careful notes, log files, etc (called 'preserving the chain of evidence');
- the person(s) carrying out the investigation are trained and understand the implications of their actions, such that they could provide testimony if required to do so.

Computer forensics has grown over the past 20-plus years into a discrete specialism, and whereas court and employment tribunal personnel were once largely computer illiterate, the situation is very different nowadays; a higher burden of proof and compliance with stricter guidelines are more often required. In the UK in particular, there are good guidelines on the handling of computer evidence, developed by the Association of Chief Police Officers (ACPO), which is regarded as the benchmark against which all cases involving computer evidence are measured. Failure to adhere to such guidelines leaves 'reasonable doubt', making criminal conviction in the most serious cases very difficult if not impossible. Where international boundaries are spanned, the situation can become very complex with differing standards in different countries, varying legislation, human rights and privacy issues. However, if you follow the recognized principles of computer forensic examination you will not go far wrong: they are based on practical experience and plain good sense.

A good computer forensic practitioner will plan the investigation carefully, consult with all interested parties, eg senior management, IT, HR, Facilities and Legal, take steps to establish the real facts and secure the evidence before undertaking the investigation. He or she needs to be independent enough to not jump to conclusions or follow political agendas, grudges, etc, so that a clear, unbiased analysis of the circumstances and the available evidence can be made, facilitating any legal or disciplinary action.

Gone are the days when attacks on the company IT infrastructure could be dealt with by a simple slap on the wrist or the changing of the configuration of a few technical controls. Attacks are becoming more and more sophisticated, and the potential gains to the attacker are higher than ever with less potential risk of being caught. Trends in security incidents need to be monitored and analysed, detailed investigation is required, and higher levels of proof need to be determined in order to avoid the situation worsening.

Computers hold a mine of information that can be extracted to aid an investigation of a security incident, but frequently a lack of understanding leads pressured IT staff to hastily rebuild, say, a Web server or e-commerce site without finding out precisely what happened. This leads to the reinstatement of the system with exactly the same vulnerabilities that caused the problem in the first place! Failure to secure log files and investigate the circumstances correctly will actually cause more downtime in the long run with reoccurrence of the problem. To avoid situations such as this the organization needs to ensure it has good incident management standards in place, with designated roles and responsibilities, trained staff and sound forensic procedures for every investigation. With increasing pressures on senior management to demonstrate and prove due diligence, now is the time to get a firm grip on security and the handling of security incidents within your organization.

Contributors' contact list

**BSI (British Standards Institution)
Management Systems**
389 Chiswick High Road
London W4 4AL
Tel: +44 (0) 20 8996 7038
Fax: +44 (0) 20 8996 7540

The Business Continuity Institute (BCI)
10 Southview Park
Marsack Street
Caversham RG4 5AF
Tel: +44 (0) 870 603 8783
Fax: +44 (0) 870 603 8761

Contact: Lorraine Darke
E-mail: lorraine.darke@thebci.org

CipherTrust Europe Ltd
1st Floor, Flagship House
Reading Road North
Fleet
Hampshire GU51 4WD
Tel: +44 (0) 870 990 5516
Fax: +44 (0) 870 990 5517

Contact: Claire Pitman
E-mail: cpitman@ciphertrust.com

Computacenter
Hatfield Business Park
Hatfield Avenue
Hatfield
Hertfordshire AL10 9TW
Tel: +44 (0) 1707 639 880
Fax: +44 (0) 1707 639 084

Contact: Amanda Johnston
E-mail: amanda.johnston@computacenter.com

DataSec Ltd
Allen House
Station Road
Sawbridgeworth CM21 9JX
Tel: +44 (0) 1279 313 007
Fax: +44 (0) 1279 313 130

E-mail: office@datasec.co.uk

Easynet
1 Brick Lane
London E1 6PU
Tel: +44 (0) 800 053 4004

Contact: Anne Perry
E-mail: anne.perry@uk.easynet

EMEA Nokia Enterprise Solutions
Nokia House
Summit Avenue
Farnborough
Surrey GU14 0NG
Tel: +44 (0) 1252 866 009

Contact: Jackie Hart
E-mail: jackie.hart@nokia.com

Emerging Technology Services
44 Frosty Hollow
Northampton NN4 0SY
Tel: +44 (0) 1604 660 125

Contact: Bill Perry
E-mail: bill@ets.uk.com

Fraud Advisory Panel
Chartered Accountants' Hall
PO Box 433
Moorgate Place
London EC2P 2BJ
Tel: +44 (0) 20 7920 8721

E-mail: info@fraudadvisorypanel.org
Website: www.fraudadvisorypanel.org

Fujitsu Services
Fujitsu Building
Wenlock Way
West Gorton
Manchester M12 5DR
Tel: +44 (0) 870 234 5555
Fax: +44 (0) 870 242 4445

Contact: Ian Humphries
E-mail: ian.humphries@uk.fujitsu.com

GlobalSign
Phillips Site No 5
3001 Leuven
Belgium
Tel: +32 16 287 123
Fax: +32 16 287 404

Contact: Johan Sys
E-mail: johan.sys@globalsign.net

Harrison Smith Associates
Third Floor, Diamond House
36–38 Hatton Garden
London EC1N 8EB
Tel: +44 (0) 20 7404 5444

Contact: Michael Harrison

Indicii Salus
Indicii Salus House
2 Bessborough Gardens
London SW1V 2JE
Tel: +44 (0) 20 7836 0123
Fax: +44 (0) 20 7836 0567

Contact: Vanessa Chandraskaran
E-mail: vchandraskaran@indiciisalus.com

Insight Consulting
Churchfield House
5 The Quintet
Churchfield Road
Walton-on-Thames
Surrey KT12 2TZ
Tel: +44 (0) 1932 241 000

Contact: Simon Langdon
E-mail: simon.langdon@insight.co.uk

Integralis Ltd
Theale House
Brunel Road
Theale
Reading RG7 4AQ
Tel: +44 (0) 118 930 6060
Fax: +44 (0) 118 930 2143

E-mail: info@integralis.co.uk

IT Governance Ltd
66 Silver Street
Ely
Cambridge CB7 4JB
Tel: +44 (0) 1353 659 662
Fax: +44 (0) 1353 662 667

Contact: Alan Calder
E-mail: alan@itgovernance.co.uk

Macrovision UK
14–18 Bell Street
Maidenhead
Berkshire SL6 1BR
Tel: +44 (0)1628 786100

Contact: Martin Brooker
E-mail: martin.brooker@macrovision.com

More Solutions Ltd
6 Belgic Square
Fengate
Peterborough PE1 5XF
Tel: +44 (0) 845 4589 555

Contact: Mark Rogers
E-mail: mark@more-solutions.co.uk

NetScreen Technologies
Victoria House
Cross Lanes
Guildford
Surrey GU1 1UJ
Tel: +44 (0) 8700 750 000

Website: www.netscreen.com

NTL Business
NTL House
Bartley Wood Business Park
Hook
Hampshire RG27 9UP
Tel: +44 (0) 1962 823 434
Fax: +44 (0) 1256 754 100

Contact: Paul Collins
E-mail: paul.collins2@ntl.com

Ontrack Data Recovery
The Pavilions
1 Weston Road
Kiln Lane
Epsom
Surrey KT17 1JG
Tel: +44 (0) 1372 741 999
Fax: +44 (0) 1372 741 441

Contact: Adrian Palmer
E-mail: apalmer@ontrack.com

Simmons & Simmons
City Point
1 Ropemaker Street
London EC2Y 9SS
Tel: +44 (0) 20 7825 4346
Fax: +44 (0) 20 7628 2070

Contact: Peter Brudenall
E-mail: Peter.Brudenall@simmon-simmons.com

Telindus
Hatchwood Place
Farnham Road
Odiham
Hampshire RG29 1B
Tel: +44 (0) 1256 709 200
Fax: +44 (0) 1256 740 357

Contact: Danny Williams
E-mail: dannywilliams@telindus.co.uk

TrustAssured
6th Floor Premier Place
2 ½ Devonshire Square
London EC2M 4BA
Tel: +44 (0) 20 7672 6775
Fax: +44 (0) 20 672 6799

Contact: Randle Cowcher
E-mail: trustassured@rbs.co.uk

VeriSign UK
17 Holywell Hill, Suite #6
St Albans
Hertfordsire AL1 1DT
Tel: +44 (0) 1582 621 211
Fax: +44 (0) 1582 461 107

Contact: Suheil Shahryar
E-mail: sshahryar@verisign.com

Websense
3000 Hillswood Drive
Chertsey
Surrey KT16 0RS
Tel: +44 (0) 1932 796 001
Fax: +44 (0) 1932 796 601

Contact: Rebecca Zarkos
E-mail: rzarkos@websense.com

Wick Hill Group
River Court
Albert Drive
Woking
Surrey GU21 1RP

Tel: +44 (0) 1483 227 600
Fax: +44 (0) 1483 227 700

Contact: Barry Mattacott
E-mail: barrym@wickhill.co.uk

Wire Card AG
Bretonischer Ring 4
85630 Grasbrunn
Germany
Tel: +49 8944 242 033
Fax: +49 8944 240 500

Contact: Toni Spitz
E-mail: toni.spitz@wirecard.com

WorldPay Ltd
270–289 The Science Park
Milton Road
Cambridge CB4 0WE
Tel: +44 (0) 870 742 7000
Fax: +44 (0) 870 742 7009

Contact: Simon Fletcher
E-mail: simon.fletcher@worldpay.com

Index

anomaly detection 62
anti-virus software 91
assurance management system 39
attack trends, recent 12
authentication 79, 95, 96
AVS and CVV 79

Bank of International Settlements 3
Basle 2 network 3
BCM lifecycle 189
biometrics 105
   and e-business 108
board responsibility 5
botnets 34
brand
   degradation 58
   protection 26
broadband 48
   auditing 51
   authentication and control 51
   awareness 50
   threats through 49
BS 7799 7, 145
bulk e-mail detection 61
business continuity 185
   standards 192
business e-mail; 2003 Regulations 75

camouflaged spoofed address 36

CANSPAM Act 34
card data invisibilty 79
card screening rules 37
carding 35
Central Sponsor for Information Assurance 30
certificate authority 101
Combined Code 142
communications systems, monitoring of 128
Computer Misuse Act 13
confidential information, dissemination 59
cookies 76
corporate assets, protecting 10
corporate culture, changing of 187
corporate identity theft 15
cousin address 36
crisis management 185, 192, 204
   definition 205
   meeting 208
   phases of 207
   plan 207
customer errors 37
customer trust, loss of 58
cyber extortion 14
cyber squatting 15
cybercrime, countering of 142, 145, 152
   best practice 154

data
　availability   154
　confidentiality   153
　integrity   153
　non-repudiation   154
　security   4
data protection   129, 143
Data Protection Act   4
data recovery   199
　assessing damage   200
　on-site   201
　phase   40
　remote   201
　software   201
digital entertainment   110
　government legislation   115
　ligitation   114
　　technological controls   116
digital signatures   41, 100, 102
directors' liability   144
disaster
　geographic nature   206
　management   204
　recovery   160
distance selling   165
download sites   115

Economic Resource Planning (ERP)   4
electronic contracting   163
electronic identity cards   103
electronic mail, regulations   73
e-mail
　address abuse   41
　confidentiality notices   131
　disclaimers   131
　fraud   57
employee exposure   58
encryption   78, 95, 96
enforcement   30
exploit code   34, 35

false-positives   36
financial supply chain management   123, 123
firewalls   87
　and filters   132
　flow direction   88

　nature of   89
　weak spots   90
flow clearing   123
forensics   210
　investigation   214
　preserving evidence   212
fraud risk   80
freedom of information   143

hackers   13
header analysis   61
holes, analogue, digital and network   113
hybrid attacks   33

identity theft   95
image retrieval   139
impersonation   9
incorporation, methods of   164
information security management system
   3, 6
infrastructure, building of   20
interception   9
internal control   142
internet fraud, cost of   12
internet security intelligence findings   33
internet security trends   37
ISO 17799   7
IT governance   145

key
　distribution   159
　escrow   161
　generation, regeneration   159
　strength and management   98

law, adherence to   118
layered security   65
liability, directors', accessories'   144
location data   76

management, centralized and device-based
   162
marketing   26
　challenges   28
　opportunities   29
mass-mailers   35
media handling   206

mobile internet, risks to   68
mobile workforce   178
monetization   35
multivector worms   35

netspionage and wardriving   14
network intrusion   58
 vulnerabilities   63
  core security   64
network segmentation   66

online contracting
 and Electronic Commerce Regulations   166
online payments   78
online privacy, protection of   71
 regulations   71
  2003   72, 75
outsourced solutions   173
 case studies   176

patch management   18
 testing   22
peer-to-peer networks   196
perimeter security   64
phishing   15, 23, 39, 57
 case studies   45
 prevention   40
  in enterprise networks   59
piracy   110
PKI   102
policy enforcement   161

regulatory non-compliance   59
remote surveillance   138
risk due to no security   128
risk management   27, 124, 142
 reduction   21

screening, rules for   36
security as business enabler   11
 centralized   138
 converged   137
 international   135
 management, centralized   157
 as standard   133
  BSIs   134
 in workplace   127, 132
Sender ID Framework   59
social engineering attacks   34
soft option   74
software protection   85
spam   73
spyware   82

theftware   35
third party disclosure   149
threats   8
 anticipating   9
 monitoring   21
training, information security   169
 functional specialisms   170
transaction non-repudiation   95
Trojans   92
trustworthiness   80
Turnbull
 Guidelines   143
 Report   3

ubiquitous access   160
URL filtering   61
user containment   66

virus   91
 hoaxes   93
 worms   34

web security   33
 and fraud   43
whistle blowing policy   147
wireless
 applications   67
 infrastructure   178
 protection   56
 unprotected   54
wireless (LAN) vulnerabilities   64
World Intellectual Property Organisation   112
worm wars   36

Index of advertisers

Akonix   xxvii, xxviii, xxix

Aladdin Western Europe   xv

BSI Management Systems   iii

CipherTrust   xvii

Computacenter   xix

F-Secure   xxi

Integralis   215

Macrovision   iv, 86

Simmons & Simmons   xii, xiii

Telindus   vi

Trend Micro   xxx

Utimaco Safeware   ix

VeriSign   xxiii

Wick Hill   xxv

Wire Card   x